KNOCKING ON HEAVEN'S DOORS

my spiritual journey through dreams and denominations

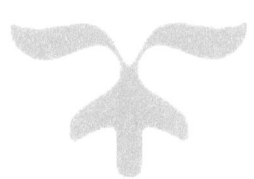

BY TRACY BLOM

Copyright © 2023 by Tracy Blom

All rights reserved. No part of this book may be used or reproduced by any means, graphic, electronic, or mechanical, including photocopying, recording, taping, or by any information storage retrieval system, without the written permission of the publisher except in the case of brief quotations embodied in critical articles and reviews.

Contents

In the Beginning 1

One Year Prior, Behind Closed Eyes 4

March 22 Journal Entry 9

Scientology: "study and handling of spirit, universes,
    and other life" 17

Southern Baptist 25

May 2, 2013: "humming sweet songs" 29

May 12, 2013, Mother's Day: Southern Baptist Church #2 35

May 19, 2013: A Dream 39

May 19, 2013: Buddhism 40

May 22, 2013: Energy Healing (not a religion, but
    good for the soul) 44

May 26, 2013: Buddhism #2 51

June 2, 2013: Greek Orthodox 56

June 3, 2013: A Dream 62

June 9, 2013: Catholic 64

June 23, 2013: Christianity 69

June 30, 2013: Christianity Part 2 74

July 7, 2013: Hinduism 80

July 9, 2013: A Visit from Mom 87

July 12, 2013: Judaism 88

July 19, 2013: A Dream 94

July 21, 2013: The Book of Mormon 96

July 25, 2013: Meeting with Pastor Amy 102

Mormon Part 2 107

August 3, 2013: Pagan 117

August 10, 2013: Spirit Guided Friends Christian Spiritualist Church 130

August 14, 2013: Dream 138

August 18, 2013: Spirit Guided Friends Christian Spiritualist Church #2 139

Dreams 145

August 25, 2013: Spirit Guided Friends #3 150

August 28, 2013: A Dream 156

September 1, 2013: Muslim 157

A Dream 160

September 6, 2013 161

September 7, 2013: Muslim #2 162

Sunday, September 8, 2013: Presbyterian 166

Reading of the Qur'an: Attempt 1 173

September 22, 2013: Center for Spiritual Living Science of Mind Church 179

Billets Class 184

September 24, 2013: A Visit from Peter 189

September 29, 2013: Sikh 191

October 2, 2013: Reflections 200

October 6, 2013: Nondenominational 203
October 12, 2013: Jehovah's Witness (JW) 209
A Dream 217
October 20, 2013: Unitarian 218
Thoughts on Einstein and Prophets 223
October 22, 2013: A Nightmare 224
October 26, 2013: Jehovah's Witness Part 2 226
Fall at the Park 232
October 27, 2013: The Grotto 233
October 30, 2013: Wiccan 1 241
November 16, 2013: A Nightmare 244
Wiccan Full Moon Ceremony 246
November 24, 2013 257
December 6, 2013: Meeting with Rabbi Zuckerman 264
December 8, 2013: Spirit Guided Friends Church 278
A Dream 286
Native American: *Wakan Tanka* and the *Tanagila* 287
Hypnosis 294
December 15, 2013: Summary of Project 297
To Those Who Are Searching 302
Epilogue 305

In the Beginning

"You need to get here now! There isn't much time." What? I yelled to the other end of the phone as I ran up the stairs and back through the rabbit hole. I had chosen to bury myself in an Alice in Wonderland–themed bar that night, drinking champagne in party dresses while playing chess in oversized chairs. Escaping the present reality of life. I stood on the street corner with sparkler and champagne still in hand as I tried to piece together the words I was hearing. The street fell silent and I could hear only my heartbeat, the fizzing of the dying firework, and the buzzing of the streetlamp overhead. Time seemed to rush by and eerily stand still all at once. This happens when you realize you are missing a moment you can't ever get back, and no matter how fast you move or think, you will never get there fast enough to be a part of it. This moment, this specific moment, created a special place in my mind I go back to every time I close my eyes. This shattering moment was the beginning of a crack upon the chalice of my subconscious, which after years, I have taken down, tried to mend, and returned to its place high up on the shelf in the back so no one can see it.

I set my glass on the pavement and removed my shoes as I sprinted barefoot down the dark alley towards my car. When I think of this now, it appears as a comic strip in streaks of yellow, shadows, and bubbled blue tears on my cheeks. I've crumpled, burned, and hid this paper away, but somehow it's become the wallpaper of my mind, in a room with music playing to the tune of my feet hitting the pavement. The entire act has become a musical. The sprinting, the baseline, the tears and heavy panting, the sad accordion, and the yelling...is just the yelling. I yelled back, hold on! Just tell her to hold on! I'm coming! The comic ends in the corners of my mind with an eerie streetlamp highlighting a dying firework, champagne flute, and the figure of a girl permanently etched in the background running after something she doesn't understand.

    I shouldn't have gone out, but decided just for one night I needed some fresh air. I had been in the house every day for the past week holding Mom's hand and taking care of her. Most nights I fell asleep holding her hand, or rubbing her back. Some nights I didn't sleep at all; I just sat there watching her sleep like she did for me so many times when I was a child. My mind rushed through every memory as my dirty foot became a concrete weight on the gas pedal. I remember the stars being so bright that night, and the road being so dark. The memories flashing through my mind were halted by flashing sirens in my rear view mirror. I was sobbing and panicked with a racing heart. There was no room for any delays right now; I had to maintain the 70 mph speed I was going if I was to make it there to see her just one last time. I'm not sure how long I held my breath for; it felt like minutes. The police car sped past me and pulled over another car just ahead of me. I exhaled as I got off the exit and went back into planning what my last words to her would be. I tore into the parking space at an angle, as I thrust the car into park. I hurled myself out the door and gave a weak effort finger roll to close it behind me. I heaved myself towards the front steps of her apartment and ran for the door. My Aunt Janet had pulled up at the exact same time, and we ran up the stairs in unison. There were no words exchanged, just a mad chaotic sprint through the apartment front door, and as if my legs saw my mom first, they quit and forced me to my knees. I held onto the bed rails of the hospice bed like cold prison bars, as my Aunt Catherine recited the end of the Lord's Prayer. I had missed it. I didn't even get to say goodbye.

I never wore that dress again, but kept it in my closet. I never watched *Alice in Wonderland* again, or played a game of chess without getting really drunk. I am no superhero, or comic-book character with special powers. I can't stop time, or go back. But I can see, and have seen, glimpses of the future embedded in my dreams. Repeated glimpses I was shown for a reason, which I dismissed, and reflect on presently…wondering, if I had just paid attention to what I was shown, would things have been different?

One Year Prior, Behind Closed Eyes

I am in a sunny golden wheat field, similar to the heavenly scene at the end of the movie *Gladiator*. Just ahead, engulfed in a ray of pure sunlight, is a beautiful white horse. As I approach the horse steadily, so not to disturb it, I feel the urge to look down to what I forgot I had been holding in my hands. In a slow-motion haze an old Polaroid camera appears in my palms, and I decide to capture the magnificence of the horse before it disappears. Each Polaroid that falls to the ground is not a picture of the horse but instead pictures of my grandpa in his happiest times. He is young, smiling, and showing me how happy he is. I decide to follow the horse further into the field, and notice when a staff is thrown into my right hand from below that I am up in the air. I turn around and look down the path I was walking on and see a bridge that is now behind me. Almost as if an invisible wall was put up, I notice that others in my family were invited to follow but couldn't get past the beginning of the bridge, for one reason or another. I keep following the horse and the wheat begins to fade away. I look around once more and notice that we are back on the ground and on familiar streets. The horse vanishes and I am left standing alone on the corner where my mom's house is. I have a feeling of overwhelming sadness like someone is there to take her.

Months pass and time slips by.

The horse appears again, only this time he is taking me for a ride in a beautiful white carriage down a busy street in downtown Cincinnati. We are going fast and I am scared, but the driver takes all the turns gracefully and I trust him. I peek out the carriage window and see other horses covered in shadows running in the opposite direction. They appear to be half-dead with their faces rotted away down to the bone. The white horse takes me to a beautiful oasis, with infinite waterfalls and lush gardens. My mom and two sisters are there as well. I have never seen so many waterfalls and then I look down and see that I have a camera in my hand again. I begin to take pictures of my mom and sisters together, but each picture becomes automatically cropped and only my mom shows up in the developed picture. She has all of her hair tied back and is not paying attention. The picture develops in black and white and becomes a beautiful picture of her. My sister Kelly takes the camera from my hands and shows me how to crop it back so we can all be in the picture. I try, but the camera keeps automatically cropping all of the photos so just my mom shows up in them. She finds a mallard duck there by the falls that she likes a lot and she seems quite happy here. I look back at the black and white picture of her, and this time her head is down; she looks sad and defeated. It is simple and pretty, but it is clear she is upset or let down.

Another month slips by and again, the horse appears.

Only this time it takes me down an unfamiliar street and stops next to a field of green grass where a play is being acted out. I am curious to see what play is showing, and it is one I have never seen before about Jesus Christ. Everyone is in white robes, as am I. I am welcomed to join the production, and play a lead part. Just before I go on, I stop to take a look in the mirror to check my outfit and notice my breast is exposed and there is a lump on it. I realize that I have to go immediately as my parking meter is running out of time. The grass turns to snow as I am running to my car. The meter reads

70 and though I keep putting money into it, it stays the same. A cop standing to the right of the meter says, "It doesn't matter how much you put in, you are going to run out of time." I begin running in the opposite direction and turn in to a restaurant where my friend's birthday celebration is taking place. We are sitting on picnic tables when someone shrieks and notices a killer out in the field nearby killing a woman. We all try to get to the dying woman, but no one can get there in time. A doctor wraps her in a red blanket and carries her away.

Winter came and the days turned a cold shade of gray. We found out that my mom had cancer not too long after the last dream I had. We took turns taking her to and from chemo and sitting with her in the room of blanketed victims. The dreams became more intense than I care to recall. Some nights I would wake up in tears screaming, and others I woke from in a state of amazement from being visited by predominant biblical figures I knew nothing of. To be honest I couldn't even tell you the story of Jesus, or Mary, or name even one of the disciples, but somehow when I would sleep, the door would be opened and they would pay me visits.

I needed to get out of the house. I felt haunted by the lingering visual of a killer in the field with the red blanket that kept surfacing in my dreams. I went to the bookstore to drown the hours of my grievous day. I found myself here often, occupying time with coffee and books I only read the covers of and put back. Most days I sat alone on the floor in the back of the bookstore staring at the wall of other people's printed success. Just as all the covers started to blur together, a red journal flew off of the shelves and nearly hit me in the head. I looked around in amazement to see if there were any other witnesses but there weren't. I picked it up, and stared at it curiously for minutes. I opened it and searched for a message but the pages were blank. I tucked it under my arm, and carefully walked it up to the register, not knowing what to do with it yet. I wasn't going to turn it in, or tell anyone else of the book's ability to fly; its secret was safe with me. That night I placed it on the pillow next to me and stared at it like it was a new lover. I wondered why this book had been heaved my way, and why it felt so right next to me on my pillow. I woke that night in a panic and eagerly searched for a pen to record the next dream.

There is a pool outside and everyone from my mom's side of the family is there congregating around it. My mom's brother shows up wearing jeans and is not dressed for the occasion. He tries to get in the pool and realizes he is not dressed appropriately and leaves. I hear that there are going to be sunny skies but the predictions are incorrect, and a storm rolls in. We move inside, to a room that looks like a bar called FB's in Cincinnati. I look to the other end of the bar and see a woman who presents herself as a member of my dad's family named Ruth. She appears a bit angelic, as if she has been on the other side for quite some time. She waves as if to comfort me. Once we are all inside a roar of thunder crashes and lightning strikes. I am standing by my Aunt Janet, who holds my hand as we watch the storm together. I have a cocktail in my other hand as I run to the back door to see what the commotion is outside. I see four black horses in the back yard where the pool once was, on the other side of a tall fence. They are upset, kicking, and whinnying. I drop to my knees and scream for my mom to come help.

Weeks later the doctor told my mother that the cancer was gone, and it "was a miracle." We all celebrated and praised her for the miraculous diagnosis. We filled the house with balloons and cake to rejoice in said miracle. My mother complained about a bit of hip pain, but she was reassured that she just had a bit of arthritis. Between the date of her last doctor visit, and the next follow-up appointment, my mother's initial cancer had spread from her breast to her hips and then to the rest of her body. By the time the doctor caught the error it was too late, and it had spread to her liver, leaving merely weeks for her to live. The doctor in the field, wrapping her in the red blanket week after week, had let us down. I had even told my mom about some of the dreams, suggesting that she get a new doctor, but by the time I realized these dreams were important, it was too late. I reflect on the precision of the dreams and the night she passed away, specifically: cocktail in my hands as I run to the back door of the bar I was in, by my Aunt Janet when the lightning struck, killer in the field, wrong predictions, mom being the only one left in the picture, the parking meter at 70 and my speed going to her house…running out of time, and of course falling to my knees when it all ended.

March 22 Journal Entry

She passed away on March 21st on a Sunday morning. I ran through the front door just in time to catch her final breath as the words, "Sweetie, hurry! She's taking her last breath!" echoed through the air. My Aunt Catherine recited the Lord's Prayer as the loss forced me to my knees. I grabbed onto the cold hospice bed rails like prison bars as I called for her over and over. She was gone, but still I called out the first word she ever taught me, "Mom." I'm glad I walked in when I did. The thought of the last minutes of struggle pains my heart. My sister recalls them being horrible, like watching someone drown and not being able to do anything about it. For reasons unknown, I snipped a piece of her hair and placed it in a cardboard jewelry box she had in her bedroom. We covered her, spoke to her, and played with the last remaining hairs on her head as we waited for the funeral home to "come get her." No one wanted to watch. We all relocated to her bedroom where we held hands and waited until the coroner had taken her away. As I lay in her vacant bed, in her spot, I listened to the puzzled cat cry. I didn't sleep that night; I just lay there in the dark staring at the wall while tightly curled in the fetal position, missing Mom.

To recall every memory would take forever, and I may have scanned through all of them that night. The night prior we had shared that bed. I held her hand all night, refilled her water every few hours, and watched her sleep. With each breath she took I wondered if it was going to be her last. I said, "Mom, is it okay if I sleep with you again tonight?" She said, "Yes, sweetie, anytime you want." I had brought her fresh orchids a week prior and couldn't help but think they would outlive her. What a horrible thought, but sadly the case.

A week prior I had cancelled my long-awaited yearly trip to Florida to stay behind with my mom. She told me to go. My heart told me to stay. That week I spent with my mom is one I will never forget. I spent every second with her. I fed her, bathed her, combed her hair, read her books, rubbed her back, and got to tell her how proud of her I was. Earlier that week I had kneeled by the couch and softly said, "Mom, I just wanted to tell you how proud of you I am and how great of a mom you are. You are such a good mom. I love you so much." As tears began to flood my eyes, I got up, hoping not to let her see them. She called me back, like any mom would, and said, "Oh, sweetie, come here, it's okay." The tears fell onto her sweatshirt as she rested on the couch with arms open for me to come in. I lay on her chest as she held me and said, "Sweetie, everyone has to die, and everyone has to live." I didn't understand what she meant by that at the time, and I didn't understand when she asked me if I could hear the beautiful music playing either. She swore it was beautiful, and often times stared over my shoulder as if she was looking at someone else. As her gaze softened just over my right shoulder she said, "I'm so scared, I don't want to die, but I'm in so much pain."

I pictured her in heaven by beautiful flowers, gardens, waterfalls, and a beach. All the things she loved so much in life. No pain, no chemo, no radiation, or daunting schedule of pills. Just peace.

I stayed calm and collected until it was time for the last people to leave the funeral parlor. I slowly walked up to the urn in the dark, candle-lit room and said, "Good night, Mom," and wept like a hurt child. I held the hands of my sisters, who greeted me at the bottom of the stairs, hit the lights, and walked out.

That night I dreamed I was in the funeral parlor again, but something was different. My mom was there but she appeared as an apparition of gray smoky static, made of ash. She was so confused and begging me to undo the cremation, and bury her. I cried, telling her that it was too late. All of it was too late to undo, and all I could do now was love her. I woke in tears. Wrote and cried on the pages, and fell back asleep.

With closed eyes I kneel by my bedside, and then feel the sensation of being lifted up, and a newfound ability to fly. I fly over water and beautiful places while looking down at pretty sea creatures that become more apparent the closer I get to the land on the other side. On the other side there is a deep river and somehow I know that there is a casket at the bottom of it. I dive down to see whose it is, but in the meantime my vehicle gets stuck down there with it. I swim out of my car, and up to the surface. There standing at the river's edge is a big black growling mean dog watching me. With another blink of an eye I change locations and find myself in a long corridor with yellow walls that is full of clothes, not all mine. There are a ton of white blouses, but I don't want to wear these. All of my friends end up wearing black, and my clothes don't fit right. My sister Jill walks down the hallway towards me, and assists me getting dressed. She fixes my skirt and places a band of dead red roses around my wrist. At the end of the corridor is my Uncle Mike again; he is dressed in a black suit and asking how my mom is. I realize that everyone is in black for a funeral. Someone says, "It is 12:10"; then I wake up.

The day of the funeral my clothes were too tight, and didn't fit me properly. I thought it would be the opposite due to the lack of food intake. I took my journal everywhere I went, as if it were a new companion I knew could only understand me. At night we flew together, and during the days I held it close to my chest. The days ran together between tear-soaked pages and reliving seeing her lifeless face on repeat in my mind. There were headaches, which seemed to last for days, and when the tears ran out I slept.

I slept in the fetal position most times, but this time I was sleeping in my bed with my head at the opposite end than it usually is.

I look up to where my headboard should be, and there kneeling over me is Mary Magdalene. I go to touch her and she starts shaking her head back and forth extremely fast. With a blink of an eye I find myself at my mom's old condo, and there on the couch is the Indian girl (the ghost my mom and I saw when we lived there). She is sitting there staring at me with a very oily face. I go out onto the back deck of the condo and a beautiful bridge expands from it out over the lake and into the distance. There are brown flowers on both sides of it, and as I walk along the bridge I notice I am up in the air again. I try to cross the bridge but can't. I look down at what was once a beach and it has turned to ice and there are penguins on it. I realize this is a sign that one world is ending and another is beginning.

I woke up and reached for more water and my journal to jot down the dream. Defeat and an achy mind pushed my eyes closed again.

I feel someone grab my hand and take hold of it. They begin to lift me up and I fight it, not wanting to leave where I am lying. The hands are warm and welcoming; there is a sort of caring touch to them. For some reason I can feel myself being pulled from my body and I panic. I start breathing hard because I can never wake up from these dreams for some reason.

My boyfriend woke me up. I lay there for a minute with eyes wide open searching for my notebook under the bed. I wrote quick notes and went back to sleep.

I dream that I am staring at a stack of pictures. Some are stuck together and in black and white. The last picture is of a handsome man that I know, but can't place how. Two smaller pictures fall out of the deck I am holding. One picture is of two images sitting on a couch; one is my boyfriend and the other I think is him, but it is not. The picture is not fully developed so I can't make out an actual person yet. The next picture is blank, but I know that it has meaning. I leave this place and join my sister for a car ride. She is upset because something is following us…a woman, with dark black hair, that resembles the Indian girl/spirit that I saw in my house growing up. We decide to drive very fast down the single-lane road, and there in the distance facing us is the Indian girl. She starts sprinting towards us, faster than humanly possible. When we clash with her we both feel her spirit go through our bodies and tingling electricity all through our hands. I try to shake my hands and get the energy off of me, but can't do it.

I wandered around the house like a zombie thumbing through cards and vases of flowers. There had to have been twenty different vases scattered throughout the house, making me realize the two-week life span of most of them. Death was all around me, in different cards, jars, and fragrances. I began wearing my blankets like a cape over top of repeated pajamas. I remember how I used to do the same thing as a kid. Running around the house like a superhero announcing to my parents and all of their guests that I was "Naked Wonder." It made me giggle thinking about how mortified my parents had to have been when they had dinner guests over and I came galloping through the house in nothing but a blanket cape announcing to them all that I was there to save the day. I heard a rustle at the front door and opened it a crack to see the world outside. Someone had left a fresh pot of chicken noodle soup for me. I scampered outside while dodging the sun and grabbed the food like a mouse coming out of its hole only to drag the cheese back in. I sat in my blanket cape and ate the first real meal I had had in days. It was nice, comforting, and somehow made me tired.

I am delighted and in awe that I am with my mom again. She looks young and beautiful. She has on a long gown with blue sapphire jewelry. She is taking my sisters and me to an amusement park. We arrive at the front gate to the park and are greeted by a man taking tickets. It is so cold and we want to go inside where it is warm. I want to give my mom my blanket but she doesn't need it. My mom goes in first, and on the other side of the iron turnstile it is warm, sunny, and beautiful. My sisters and I, still on the other side, look up at the sky in amazement at the snow pouring down. My mom stands on the other side of the gates and waves. We are not allowed through but she was. Then the gatekeeper says, "It's 12:10."

I am seeing a commonality of 12:10 in my dreams involving my mother's passing, and though I know nothing of its contents, I go to the internet to research all biblical 12:10 listings. Of the many that I dissected and mauled over, one in particular stood out: Genesis 12:10–20. As pastor Keith R. Krell comments, "In these verses, we will learn that any man or woman, regardless of his or her spirituality, is capable of faltering in the faith. Nevertheless, we will also find hope that God loves to restore people to Himself" (https://bible.org/seriespage/faith-fear-genesis-1210-134).

I was not raised with a religion, and now, without a mother, and longing to connect with wherever she is now, I find myself, here, searching. I know these basic beliefs thus far: be nice to people, don't lie, never feel like you're better than anyone else or anything else…even trees are alive, respect your world, reproduce positivity, and help others. I am inspired by Genesis 12:10 and want to connect with God, and restore where I have lost him, or never had him at all. I feel like if I can do that, I will be closer to wherever my mom is.

Here is where I fall short of other religions, or any in general. I view the Bible like a game of telephone. If the message gets altered when we pass it around a circle of twenty, how altered does it become over 3500 years and through different hands, countries, beliefs, tablets, and cultures? I want to believe there once was a man that could multiply two fish to five thousand and part a sea with his hands, but the realist in me thinks this was just a story made up to help teach people to be good, decent, and believe in a higher being, so that they wouldn't be bad people. Maybe the stories were explained in parables so that people of all ages and viewpoints could comprehend the lessons left behind, or maybe back then people couldn't come right out and say what they really meant, out of fear of being flogged or crucified for having a differing viewpoint.

I have had such trouble finding what "religion" I fit because I don't believe in the literal scripture, but I believe in God, Heaven, and a Higher Being, which leaves the question: "What am I? Am I anything?" Such a need for a label is another thing, but it would be nice to know if my limited beliefs and dreams involving the other side fall in line with any other religions out there. At this point in my journey I would label myself as a "religious virgin." So, I am doing a six-month study, not based on any books or prior research, but purely on experience of different churches and religions to find out if I have a religion at all. I want to find a connection back to where my mom is, and if it is through religion, I am determined to find out how. Maybe, there are others out there just like me, and I just haven't found them yet, or they haven't found me.

I plan on visiting every religious denomination within a six-month period and writing about each one. I figure since I have not deciphered a true religion (not the brand of jeans), and I was raised between Christian and nothing at all, that I could surely make an educated choice of what "I am" on my own.

Scientology: "study and handling of spirit, universes, and other life"

For reasons unknown, I was a little scared coming to this church, which was not a church, but a center with programs. I had predetermined thoughts of what this would be like; all include aliens, Tom Cruise, hypnosis, and men in white lab coats.

(I put on a CD of NASA Voyager [sounds from space] while writing post visit.)

I arrived at the Center for Scientology in Portland, Oregon, and noticed a sandwich board outside advertising "free personality tests, 7th floor." I felt embarrassed walking in for some reason, and didn't want anyone to see me. I lowered my chin and assumed hair-over-face disguise as I entered. I walked into an office setting with a cheerful group of three teen boys behind a small front desk wearing white unironed button-up shirts and off-center ill-fitting ties. To my left, there were five other young boys, all seated in a row of folding chairs with blank stares watching the end of a Scientology DVD. Because I missed this viewing I was led to a separate room to watch it on my own. I brought my journal for note taking. I noticed halfway through the four-hour video they expected me to watch on a Saturday afternoon that someone had been watching me through a glass window the entire time. I stayed for two hours. The first hour was spent in solitude watching the DVD, and the second hour with a consultant of some kind.

The video started with an overview of the founder. Each section of the DVD led you back to a link of a book written by the founder for sale in the lobby. The movie opened up with his accomplishments and highlights – that he was an author (science fiction), served in the Army, inventor, and also helped wounded and sick soldiers get better. The focus of the founder was studying the mind and curing people of depression, illness, etc., based on finding where the pain was coming from, and then eliminating it. The video depicted a focus on mental healing, and showed wounded soldiers walking out of hospitals on crutches after his treatments. The concept of treating mental illnesses based on pinpointing pain sounded normal, and made sense; that is why people go to therapists. The concept of all of the physical pain being a "mental block" seemed odd. Clearly if someone was shot, there is a physical problem and not a mental block that can be healed with some therapy.

The next section of the video explained that we are not connected to our bodies, and that we are souls just occupying a vessel, thus introducing the main concept of Scientology, Dianetics. Dianetics stems from Greek origin: *dia*, meaning "through," and *nous*, meaning mind. They explained it simply as what the mind is doing to the soul. Dianetics views three parts of your mind: the analytical, reactive, and somatic. The video said that there is a time track on which all of your life experiences are recorded. Scientologists believe that we store our negative thoughts and feelings in the reactive part of our mind, and through their "programs" these can be removed. They teach that once these things have been removed from your mind, you can live healthy, happy, free lives. Personally the thought of something being "removed from my mind" sounded scary, and I pictured probes and again, white lab coats. I wondered how long my face had been in the "what the fuck!?" position and recalled one of my mom's favorite phrases: "If you make that face long enough it's going to get stuck like that!"

The DVD then relates back to eight dynamics that all lead to connecting with a higher being. This helps people to understand life by placing it in compartments. The layers include:

1. Self: need for individuality
2. Sex dynamic, which they name creativity
3. Group Survival: need for belonging
4. Species: urge to exist as mankind
5. Life forms/animal dynamic: urge towards existence of animal kingdom, grass, trees, flowers, anything alive
6. Universe (matter, energy, space, time); MEST is the acronym they use
7. Spirits: anything spiritual with or without identity
8. Infinity: supreme being, God dynamic (only found if complete in all seven other areas)

This made me think that the main point was if you have a "pain point" prohibiting you from completing each dynamic, you will not find God, or whatever it is they believe in (to be determined). After this section the video circles back to introduce yet another book that is available for me to purchase afterwards in the lobby.

The DVD does mention the basic fundamentals they believe in, which I also agree with (on some level).

- Be true to your own decency.

- Love others even when we shouldn't (this could be misinterpreted, especially by me: See Catholic).
- Learn to love.
- Never desire revenge.
- Happiness is a road to greatness and strength.
- There is no destruction, just creating, and recreating. Example: the demolition of a house should not be viewed as destroying but instead creating something else, even if it is a pile of wood/rubbish. (I think this example will eventually lead to the point of them saying they are not destroying your memories but rebuilding something better.)

I am about an hour into the DVD when the topic of "cleansing" comes about. Cleansing of people reminded me of two things, one being the Holocaust, and other more positive, juice cleanses and detoxification. There are things, machines, in all of the Scientology centers called E-meters. These meters, along with a 200-question personality test, help pinpoint where your pain stems from. You could just simply ask me and I would say, my mom passed away, and most men cheat on me. Done. Nonetheless, this process is supposed to pinpoint where your pain is lying in your reactive mind so that an auditor can help remove it. The sound of an auditor of my mind sounded crazy and I repeated the face from before. Once the auditor finds your pain spots, then he or she can help direct you to the correct program to fix it.

This part in the DVD mentions that they do not use hypnotism. I think that is a weird fact to put in the DVD in the first place, and I do not eat the food that is brought in the room for me. I also think the cheese squares they brought in would pair well with wine, and the sound of a cleanse seems off-putting. This is the moment when the owner of the pair of eyes from the window behind me entered the room and stopped the DVD. He offered to have me speak with a person who could directly answer questions for me. I was led to another room full of blueprints on walls and plans for another center. There was a book with a list of centers all over the world on the table (excluding Germany). I believed they did this so that I would think that this religion is a worldwide great thing that I shouldn't be scared of. I wondered if that look was still on my face from earlier. A short man entered the room and sat down by me. He had several other video clips saved on his phone that he was extremely eager to show me, which I found more generic than corporate sales training.

I started right in on the questions I had on the "programs."

What is the first step? The first step involves a 30-day cleanse in their facilities. This involves detoxing, treadmill running, visits to the two saunas on site, and consuming oils and vitamins supplied.

I asked what the oils and vitamins are and did not get an answer.

After the detox is finished you are then to fill out the personality test and complete the E-meter and audit process. I was told, "For every problem there is a program. If you have marital problems, we have a program. If you have trouble holding a job, we have a program."

I asked for clarification on the premise of being separate from your body, and was told with great confidence there *are* past lives and our souls are not connected to our bodies. "If you get your appendix removed does your personality change?" They related this example to the soul staying independent from your body. Also, this led to the conversation of removing the negative thoughts that have been harbored in the part of the mind that holds them. At this point I was offered water and declined, as I was growing skeptical of the last hypnotism mention. Better safe than sorry. To the point of souls being separate from the body, I didn't think this was odd at all. A part of me believes in past lives and reincarnation, but the thought of removing negative thoughts seemed like brainwashing or something similar. I do think that if you are healthy and working out a lot, and cleansing your body with vitamins and nutrition, you are more likely to be in a better mood. I was just having a hard time picturing a program being able to fix every problem out there. All people are different, and one program cannot be the same for every single problem.

The man I was speaking with asked me what I do for a living and also offered me a job as an auditor. I told him I was just interested in information about the religion at this time and wouldn't be able to help others if I didn't even know, or believe in, what they stood for. He reiterated that for every problem there is a course. This was more of a self-help program, I thought, and not a church. I asked if there were church services and there were not, but there are large centers for studying and help. I also learned that these programs are not free. I was unaware of this, but learned that if I signed the pledge to their religion (an actual waiver placed in front of me pledging my religion) and took a job with them, then my courses would all be free. I wondered if these auditing sessions were recorded, and more so how much of it was kept confidential. If the auditors could be any schmuck off the street slapping a cookie-cutter Band-Aid on problems, who's to say that those costly sessions aren't being recorded to be used for whatever purpose they wish. I zoned out for a second picturing me baring all to an "auditor" about old college stories, and later having a blackmail issue locking me into the church for good.

I decided I had been here for far too long and felt pressured to either sign a document or begin a personality test. I declined both, and decided to take home a DVD (not free) for more education. I wanted to know when the aliens come in! This was always my thought – that their leader was an alien with a name. I had not gotten to that part of the DVD yet.

The first words out of my mouth as I left the clinic at a fast pace were "holy fuck," and I went to the nearest bar for a patty melt and glass of wine. Obviously the detox program would not work well for me. Not to say that I don't do juice cleanses on my own and am extremely healthy and in great shape (not to brag), but I just felt that a mandated cleansing program was not for me. I balance mentally and physically with yoga, hiking, and other physical activities. I still felt flustered from the pressure of joining and the thought of having my thoughts removed, and more so, that someone thinks he or she can heal by removing my thoughts. I am all for the power of positive thinking and taking care of your body, but I would never want a single memory of my mother erased, even the painful images of her passing away. The painful parts of my life are what helped shape me into the strong, independent woman I am today, and I would never want to lose that piece of me.

Note: There is no 12:10 in a Scientology book, or maybe there is but I didn't buy it in the lobby. However, there is a rap song written by Tom Cruise's ex on 12/10/12 speaking out against Scientology. Maybe, consult DVD or book, all available for purchase.

Later that night: 1:00 a.m. I had never clasped my hands as tight while praying as I did tonight. I found myself praying to the same God I do most nights, and saying I'm sorry for mocking others' ways today, I'm just trying to find a better way to You. I don't know if the God I went to find out about today is even the same as you because I didn't get through the DVD. But after today, I think You and I feel as comfortable as house slippers, and I don't really know if there is a better way. Maybe I've just taken you and me for granted until today. I feel like I am talking to Mom at dinnertime, simply discussing the oddities of the day; she is just laughing and passes the rolls.

Southern Baptist

Last night I didn't sleep well.

I have dream after dream where I am following a person in a white cloak through an outdoor, yet semi-enclosed, church garden. The person takes me to a frozen lake where there is trouble. I find a phone and call for help and a black man answers, he knows my name before I speak, and that I am calling for help. I feel something is wrong and I don't know if he is good or bad, or if I can trust him at all.

The next day I woke up early and prepared my outfit for my visit to the Southern Baptist church. I went with a conservative, yet Southern looking Sunday dress. That should fit. I thought about getting a solid maroon pant suit but I don't care for the uncomfortableness of having on the same outfit as others. As I drove down the street I approached a massive, very modern church with a parking lot packed full of Mercedes and other luxury vehicles. I pulled in and quickly realized I was at the wrong church. I looked at the puzzled faces of people pulling in watching me pull back out and rolled the window down and said politely, "whoops, wrong church." Just down the street was the right church with a much simpler parking lot. The people filing in were smiling, laughing, and in casual clothes.

The pastor was standing outside shaking everyone's hands that passed through the doors, and kindly greeting everyone by first name. There was also a man next to him spinning a basketball like a Harlem Globetrotter on one finger. He said, "You have to do this or you can't come in." I said, well I guess I'm out! We both laughed as he introduced himself and said he was glad to see a new face come through the doors. The church was quaint with old furnishings, and stale blue carpet. For the most part, everyone was extremely friendly. People turned around to shake my hand and introduced themselves to me with big smiles. The pastor took time to show me where the bathrooms were and then gave me a pen with the church name and address on it. He said, "This is so you remember where you're at." How fitting of a statement. I used this pen, and the paper he gave me to take down notes instead of my journal. The blank page that came with the itinerary for the sermon had these three sections: Date, Scripture, and Personal Application.

The service opened with twenty-five minutes of singing to a projector screen. My mom's church used to do this same thing and I always hated it. I don't know who incorporated this into church services, but I think it's some sort of way to try to modernize religion. They had a drummer and pianist to make up some sort of band on stage. Everyone in the audience knew the words, which led me to believe the same songs are repeated for the first twenty-five minutes of every service, or everyone is good at following along. Hmmm, maybe the screens are for following along. Mystery solved.

I couldn't help but giggle at the words "I'm in the molder's hands, hold me, fill me, walk beside me." Did anyone else think this is sexual? The service began with an example coming from Matthew 17:1, where they mention Elijah coming first. I thought this was also sexual, then really tried to listen for any important details of the story that might make it not sexual. Maybe the person that wrote the Bible was a nasty pervert, and wrote in ways that only other perverts would understand. Probably not.

The pastor opened up the service and asked that everyone take out their Bibles. There weren't any around, and I didn't bring one. Most people had their own, or knew the scripture by heart. Today's lesson was about the "mountain top experience." A lot of the stories in the Bible depict significant interactions between Jesus and his disciples taking place on a mountaintop. I wonder how high the mountains were back then, and can't imagine hiking to the top of a mountain every time I want to have an important conversation. That is just one reason why I think that the mountain could be figurative and not an actual mountain, or possibly a place associated with higher understanding. The mountain nonetheless is certainly a predominant place in the Bible, where Moses encountered the burning bush and Jesus led apostles and had his most intimate moments with his father.

In today's particular scripture Jesus leads two apostles to the mountain top. Here, they see his face become consumed by a glowing light and his clothes shine so white that they radiate, and then they realize he is in the light of the Lord. When the apostles return back down from the mountain they too have glowing faces and are enlightened. The pastor linked this to metamorphosis, where one starts as one thing and when enlightened is able to transform into something more beautiful.

I think that this transformation is what I am trying to achieve or find, though I do not know yet what it is I want to turn into, or even what I am today. The experience the pastor spoke of is called the Mountain Top Experience. I promptly thought of my urge to climb mountains here in Portland and the incredible feeling I get when I reach the top. It's this feeling of peace, serenity, accomplishment, and rejuvenation. He noted that we can't search for this experience;

it is only when we spend time in prayer and in the light that we can become transformed, and achieve this "metamorphosis."

I'm glad today was educational and made me reflect on myself and the actual point of this journey. I was able to tie in the lesson of the day with where I am on my religious "salvation" or metamorphosis. I began to question if I will change or if I will find my mountain top moment at all? Surfacing other questions: What needs to change? How will I know when it does? Maybe I'll choose the wrong religion, and when I get to heaven God will look at me and say "wrong religion, asshole."

I don't really fully understand how this church differs from the Christian churches I had been to when I went with my mom when she was sick. I know they use the same Bible and the same verses. Maybe each religion interprets the same book different ways? From what I have seen so far Baptists are not any different from other Christians, except they tend to mention John the Baptist more. I know nothing of him except that he was beheaded. Sorry, readers that know the entire Bible. Next Sunday I am going into a different part of town to a different Southern Baptist church. I don't want to fully base my encounters off of one church alone.

May 2, 2013: "humming sweet songs"

I had another weird dream last night.

I am on a plane and there is a music video being shot, except there aren't any instruments, just a person trying to make music, and record it. There are tons of people all featured in the video, so I try to get in it. All of the shots of me turn out to be black-and-white still frames of my mom holding up signs with her hands that I can't make out. I can't tell if they are signs I didn't know or if she is waving. She is young, smiling, and happy. After the song completes there are two copies of the song made. I love the song, but it is so sad it makes me want to cry. I can't have a copy of it yet, but I will have it someday.

I wake up with the song from *Dangerous Minds* in my head, just the one line, "even my mama thinks that my mind is gone." Weird, I know.

Later that day, I flew home to Cincinnati for my Grandma's 80th birthday party. I took my seat on the plane with full intentions of having a few glasses of wine and reading a bit, but what to my wondering eyes did appear but a Hindu woman sitting next to me. I assumed she was a certain way, or believed certain things based on her appearance. I pondered if it would be completely distasteful to ask an airplane stranger about her religion, something I had zero knowledge on. I noticed a MIT college ring on her hand so I figure she had to be pretty intelligent and could bring insight in one way or another. We had been in the air but a few minutes when I looked at her kindly and said, "I don't mean to be invasive, but can I ask you a question? Are you religious?" She thought for a second and said, "Yes, I'm Hindu." As I silently high-fived myself for being correct, I blurted out another question, "What's your favorite part about it?"

The woman next to me had been through the same ups and downs as I have, well...in terms of believing, questioning if this religion "fits," and deciphering and grasping all of the concepts. She said when she was young she wondered if there was an actual God, but not like the God in our Bibles. I think this "higher being" she speaks of is generally the same concept for all religions I have experienced so far. Is it an alien super-being like in Scientology? No. Is it something we all yearn to understand and ultimately become one with? Absolutely. She explained, in Hinduism there are four ways to get to the same means. The first is karma (doing good). If you put out good things you will get good things back in the next life. Basically, the better of a person you are the closer you become to enlightenment and securing a better life next time.

The second way to reach enlightenment is through Solitude. She said this is the preferred method for a lot of the Yogis, which was weird to me because I practice yoga once a week and never really connected back to the actual meaning, which is "to reconnect." She said a lot of people practice yoga in Hinduism and mold the practice so they can reconnect both spiritually and mentally in their own unique ways. I told her I take yoga once a week and my instructor's class is quite physical, but I find it funny that I can focus on just my breath and all of a sudden I forget I've been standing on one leg for a few minutes. My instructor always says, "Balance is in the mind, not the body." I agree. It's only when I start to think about other things or how I should be struggling I get off balance and fall. My seatmate said that a lot of their meditations focus on breathing and if you can clear your mind for at least five minutes you can allow for both peace and balance. It seemed like she was still trying to figure these practices out herself. We didn't touch on the other two ways to reach enlightenment, but she mentioned that reasoning is one of the other ways.

She said that you can practice whatever method suits you best to achieve enlightenment. As she continued on I looked out the window, and realized that here, high above the clouds and literally looking out to the mountain top, I was having my first Mountain Top Experience. It was like a light bulb flicked on and revealed this moment of clarity when I realized I was exactly where I was supposed to be at this moment in time. Something so simple as sitting next to a person of a different faith helped me to learn about her culture and connect the dots about myself and what I am really trying to achieve with this project.

I asked her if she was raised with religion or if it was just something she discovered. She spoke so highly of her parents and said that her dad reads the holy book and meditates every day. Her parents didn't force her to practice a certain way, or attend any ceremonies. Instead, they told her when she was ready she could join them in their trips to the temples and readings of the Krishna. She said her childhood was great, and they lived on the fourth story of a beautiful terrace in Delhi. In the daytime elephants and hummingbirds wandered about the gardens, and at night the mockingbirds would post up on the balconies and sing. She then asked me about my mom. I didn't know if she would think I was crazy or not, but I decided to tell her about last night's dream. I explained that I thought it was as if there was a sad song with no music playing and my mom was right there with me on the plane showing me a sign. She then told me that her name, in Hindu, actually translates to the word "song or humming." There I was, learning about a new religion, speaking about my mom, on the plane with "the song."

We discussed reincarnation, and I mentioned that my mom loved hummingbirds. She used to overload her hummingbird feeder with so much sugar that the birds couldn't resist swarming to her feeder. My mom always said it was kind of like hummingbird crack! When times are tough or I have had a bad day I often see a hummingbird. The Song's thoughts were that spirits remain untouched by the impurities of the mind, and karma determines what we will be in the next life. The soul starts one place then goes into another body based on its previous life's karma. She said it is very possible for souls to manifest in the animals they liked after they pass. So in short, yes, that could be a manifestation of my mom. She asked me if my mom liked to sing. I said, yes, she actually had a very pretty voice but was always embarrassed of it. She said that, maybe, the hummingbird represents finally being free and happy and able to sing the songs she always wanted to sing, or in my case communicate important things, and voice my thoughts for the world to hear. The doctrine that the soul repeatedly dies and is reborn is called *samsara* (Sanskrit for migration). I find a weird coincidence that the act of migration is also brought up in the Bible when Jesus dies on the cross. The exodus or migration is what he was planning when he was on the mountain for the very last time in Matthew 17.

She did mention there are different layers you have to master through higher understanding in order to move on to the next layer. I would like to study this hands-on, among the actual culture in order to understand it further. I do think that all three religions I've experienced so far have the following foundations in common:

- We are a part of something bigger, that we all strive to understand further.
- Hindu and Scientology both have levels you master in order to achieve the highest level of spirituality.
- The soul is separate from the body and negative thoughts and actions act against us becoming One with God.

Different religions explain it in different ways. The Baptists view us as "children of God," all going back to the Father in Heaven after we are forgiven for our sins. Scientology believes we all return to the Thetan, or the higher being once we pass on. I would like to experience Hinduism more in order to give an educated comparison, but I think they envision all of their Gods collectively as One, and the Gods represent strengths and characteristics embodied in God.

- Each religion I've experienced so far believes you are rewarded (in one way or another) for living with goodwill.
- Scientology and Hinduism both seem to view the soul as separate from the body. The soul remains pure and when life is over you return back to the form of purity…well, based on karma or how many programs you have completed in Scientology.

I refrained completely from asking her about cows and how they came to be sacred. I was also wearing a brown leather corset, which she seemed not to care about. She said I shouldn't rush this experience and should really consider submerging myself in the cultures themselves to get a full understanding. Oh, and back to the original question: "what is your favorite part about it?" She said, "It is the ability to reach higher understanding and peace in so many wonderful ways." Maybe I will find something wonderful in each of the religions I encounter, and achieve my own higher understanding in the end.

May 12, 2013, Mother's Day: Southern Baptist Church #2

Mother's Day is always hard for me. Out here in Portland, I have no family to be with and no grave site to visit. Only a day of reflecting on memories past and holding pictures, wishing I still had my mother to hug. Attending church today is hard. I don't know if I will be in tears most of the time, and looked at like a stranger, or if I will make it through an entire sermon with dry eyes.

As I walked into the church I was greeted by two smiling gentlemen wearing impeccable black and white suits with white gloves. The formality and demeanor reminded me of royalty, or boarding the *Titanic*. One man handed me a Mother's Day service pamphlet and kindly showed me through the door. At the end of each pew was a stack of fans. I didn't take one since I'm normally cold all of the time. The church was beautiful and had high vaulted wooden ceilings. There was a choir in the front of the room composed of about fifty or more women in their Sunday best, all adorned with sparkling smiles and Easter-colored dress suits. I looked around and noticed a lot of big Kentucky Derby–style hats, and people all hugging and shaking hands around me. There was a baptism going on as I took my seat, and then the pastor asked if we all remembered where we were in our lives when we made our commitment to God? If we were thankful for all of the doors that were opened to us that we couldn't even see? With that, the choir began. It was the most angelic, billowing, blessed sound I have ever heard in my life. The immediate sound of the choir brought me to tears, and I noticed I was not alone. There were tissue boxes under each pew and I now know why. I can't describe in enough words the majesty that came from the front of the room, but it was incredible.

The energy in the room was genuine, caring, and loving. The pastor was seated at the piano playing and singing intensely alongside the choir as the people in the pews all rose up their hands, clapped, and sang praise. I clapped along and grabbed for more tissues when they sang a song for all the mothers in the room. I knew mine was with me, just not like she used to be.

I miss the moments where I would go to church with my mom and hold her hand and rub her back as we sat together. I do know that if she was still alive I wouldn't have moved out here to Portland alone, and I wouldn't be right here at this moment. I would still be in Cincinnati taking care of her, sure not to leave her side.

We all took our seats as the pastor moved to the front of the room again. Today's sermon was taken from Corinthians 12:20:31. He had been doing thirty days of Corinthians; apparently I had already missed 12:10 but know its scripture: 'So I take pleasure in weaknesses, insults, catastrophes, persecutions, and in pressures, because of Christ. For when I am weak, then I am strong."

Today's topic was around spiritual gifts. The pastor stressed that we all possess spiritual gifts and our role is to identify them, and then develop them. Once we know what our spiritual gift is we can use it to serve faithfully through the strength God has supplied us. He compared all of us as individuals to the individual parts of the body. We all have special functions and roles, even though some don't seem as important or visible as others. We are all a part of something bigger, and being faithful every day is more important than we realize. He said there have been doors and windows all opened and closed for us for specific reasons, and for this, God has placed each and every one of us in the exact place we need to be in at this point in our lives. Even if we don't realize it right now.

The pastor gave the example of how our bodies function all of the time without us really paying attention to how each individual part contributes. Most people just expect their body to function all of the time, but if just one of its parts didn't operate faithfully, we would know it. Some of the parts go unseen and don't get the honor and glory they deserve, and some don't desire or need that at all. I had a feeling he was not talking about body parts now, and more so that each of us plays a significant role as a part of the bigger picture. He ended this portion of the service by saying, "Once we acknowledge our gifts and do the role that we were set out to do, the body can grow."

There were a few mentionable aspects of the service that led me to believe that Baptists are very conservative people. When discussing the parts of the body the minister said that some parts are not meant to be seen, and we women need to cover our bodies more. He said there are some men, even in the church, that are recovering sex addicts and instead of helping them get better we are making the problem worse by dressing the way we do. He also said that beauty is fleeting and we should want to be valued by our minds, not our bodies. I agree with that, but if I want to wear high heels and a nice dress it is because I like how I look in it, not because I am seeking the attention of a man or trying to drive him back into a sexual relapse. Also, in regards to the parts of the body that don't need to be covered up, like the face, he stressed that we should not be wearing makeup because that is not how God intended us to look. If we have money for cosmetics we should have money to give the church. I do understand and value his conservative notions, but I also value my freedom, of both speech and expression, whether it is something I write or something I wear. I also think that God probably doesn't care how we look, and refer back to the old "don't judge a book by its cover" phrase.

The service was two hours long and flew by. I took diligent notes, clapped, praised, and walked away reflecting on the message of the day. If we don't recognize our gifts, and the purpose of them, they will either be lost or abused. He compared this to buying food and leaving it in the refrigerator to spoil, when others could have benefited from it, but instead it becomes wasted. I know that this book is something I am supposed to write, and the message it brings me and others needs to be heard. I don't know the reasons, but I know I am exactly where I am supposed to be in my life.

I have been doing research on ways in which I can travel to India and study other religions abroad. The price of both travel and paying my monthly bills is starting to add up. I figure that without some sort of investor, or act of God, I will not get to do this, at least not for a while. After church today I had a call with an angel investor that I met on LinkedIn. I sat in the church parking lot hopeful that he would be thrilled to give me money to fulfill my dream. The point of this being a dream is reiterated when he said the odds of me finding an angel investor are like winning the lottery, and most of the time angel investors turn out to be a friend or family member that truly believes in the project. I am not letting this blip on the radar slow me down or change my path. If anything, this will make me work harder to find a way to make this happen.

May 19, 2013: A Dream

I had a dream last night that I was on a beautiful sun-kissed beach.

The water skims just over the sand to reflect miles and miles of sparkling shells. There is a long white scroll with a story I can't understand spread for miles down the beach. I keep trying to turn it over and the wind keeps blowing it back so I can't read it. There are white geese there, or swans, not sure. I am looking for my camera to capture the beauty but I didn't have it this time, instead, I think, I will have to just remember this in the moment. My mom is there too, and she is upset about something related to money. My grandma is also there on the other side of a wall, and she is saving my family from something.

May 19, 2013: Buddhism

This morning I went to my first Buddhist temple. I have seen beautiful pictures of temples in books, but never in person. My boyfriend, who hasn't been to a church in about six years, joined me. We were greeted by a nice smiling man who welcomed us and asked us to sign the guest book. There was a mix of people of all cultures seated in pews inside the temple. I felt comfortable somehow knowing that I was going to be seated on a pew, and reminded myself how stupid this comfort zone of mine has become. How is it that a pew would be any better or "safer" than sitting on a nice floor pillow anyway? I was happy that at least I realized the limited boundaries of my comfort zone as I took my seat.

This particular temple was founded in 1903, and is the oldest Buddhist organization in Oregon. Golden lamps, white candles, scrolls, red silk tablecloths, and flowers accented the magnificent yet humble temple. The smell of fresh burning incense filled the air as people filed down the aisle towards the *koro* (giant incense burner) in the front of the room. Each person bowed when they got to the end of the aisle, and took a small piece of incense and placed it horizontally in the burner, bowed again, and returned to their seats. I was unaware, but the burning of incense is a general custom in Buddhism. They burn it for three main reasons: 1) According to some sutras, the smell of incense is one of the ornaments in the Pure Land. So they offer incense to praise the virtue of Amida Buddha. 2) By using the incense, we purify our bodies. 3) By smelling the incense, we become calm so that we can listen more effectively to the Right Teachings of the Buddha.

This particular Buddhist temple practices Jodo Shinshu, a sect in the Pure Land stream of Mahayana Buddhism. Shin was founded by Shinran Shonin (1173–1263 CE) in Japan during the Kamakura period. Today, Shin is the largest Buddhist sect in Japan, with ten schools and approximately 25 million adherents. Their head temple is Nishi Hongwanji in Kyoto, Japan, but they also have an American location in Berkeley, California. I felt a bit uneducated coming into this temple. Going into most churches I typically know the general beliefs, and at least the general language. I went to their website and briefly read a few facts that helped me understand a bit about how they originated and what they believe. This center began as a community to service the religious and spiritual needs of Japanese immigrants, and as time went on it became more diverse. This particular sect is also referred to as "blue collar Buddhism" in the sense that they are non-monastic, and their open doors and minds have welcomed people of all backgrounds, ethnicities, and religious upbringings. There is a lot I don't know about Buddhism, but what *I think* I know is that enlightenment is strived for, and Buddha is worshiped and followed. I am not sure about what book, if any, they read from, what their thoughts on life/death/heaven/hell are, and the history of the religion.

The songs they sang were all in Japanese, but had English subtitles at the bottom of the pages. At first I was thrown off by the Japanese singing and thought, "How am I going to get anything out of this when I can't understand them?" Then I began to read along and decipher meaning for myself. All of the verses were deeply moving to me, and focused on the light within us and spreading the light to the world through kindness and goodwill. The concept of light coming in and replacing all of the dark parts of the mind makes me think back to yesterday's yoga session, when the teacher softly placed her hand on my back and said, "now breathe in, and imagine inhaling sparkling light that is filling all of your body, replacing all of the darkness and pain." Envisioning inner light, reconnecting with the world, and self-healing through the light is a very soothing concept to me.

The scripture for today also highlighted that Buddhism doesn't force us to believe a certain word or written story. Contrary to other religions that enforce believing in the word of God or in the written Bible, Buddhism suggests that we think for ourselves and deduce our own meanings while always reflecting on ourselves, amidst our feelings of regret and joy.

The focus of today's lesson was living for the day and not putting off things that we think we can do another time, because another time may never come. The leader of the temple, also known as an abbot, began with a story about a boy who had lost his mother, and was to be ordained the next day. The boy realized how fleeting life is, and insisted that he become ordained at once. After losing his mother he realized that tomorrow is never promised to anyone and he should be grateful for the people in his life and what he presently had. We were reminded throughout the story that a lot of people are ungrateful for the things they have, and possess a mindset of "I deserve this salary, or I deserve this thing" because they are self-righteous instead of thankful.

The abbot mentioned that with Mother's Day being last weekend, he was reflecting more and more on the relationship he had with his mother, and things he could have done for her, or things he should have said to her. The things we cannot change we can instead turn into a lesson. He said, for those who still have mothers around they should be thankful for them, and pass on gratitude to the rest of the family. For those who do not have mothers anymore in their lives, like me, there is a nurturing presence in spirituality. He said that many of the great founders of this practice had lost parents early on in life and then turned to spirituality. There is something comforting and warming in the light that many people have found after losing the physical light that was once "mother."

After he concluded the service there were a few moments of silence taken for self-reflection. I don't know if there were soft bells playing or not, but I thought there were. In my moments of reflection I closed my eyes with hands to heart center and let peace set in. I opened my mind and then had a vision of a tree. The tree was made of light, and kept growing bigger and bigger until it was too big to capture in my sight. I opened my eyes as I inhaled one last breath, and then bowed my head in gratitude. My boyfriend did the same.

May 22, 2013: Energy Healing (not a religion, but good for the soul)

Tonight after work I went to a Reiki master. I have never been to one before and noticed the odd coincidence that all in the course of three weeks three different people (a yoga instructor, a stranger in a coffee shop, and the Reiki master) told me I need to remove some "blockage." I read a bit about energy healing and decided that this would be a good way for me to remove this "blockage."

I met her at a group meeting for the Oregon Surfriders Association, which is a group of people that get together once a month to discuss helping the environment, clean water, and of course surfing. After the last meeting we started talking about what she does, and she invited me to come down and check out one of her sessions. Of all the people in the room I felt especially inclined to talk to her. She was bright eyed and petite and had a hummingbird (of all things) tattooed on her neck. After talking with her for about twenty minutes about energy healing and having "blockage" removed, I decided to set up an appointment.

The weather was typical for a Wednesday night in Portland, or any day for that matter. I grabbed my hooded jacket to shield me from the rain and headed downtown to her clinic, which focuses on different aspects of natural healing. I could smell cedarwood and vanilla candles as I walked down the long hallway towards the clinic. Soft yellow walls gave off a calming vibe as I made myself comfortable in a simple wooden chair in the waiting area. I was guided back to her office by her small Collie, which lay on the ground next to the blanketed massage table for the entirety of the session. The lights were dim and the music was very peaceful. She explained that she knows people come into these things with preconceived notions and expect to get certain things out of the experience, and she was just there to help me accomplish these goals. I really wanted to remove any negative energy and see if there were any messages from my mom.

At first I was restless lying there on the table, then after a matter of time I had images start appearing in my mind. This is kind of like recalling the face of a person that you know, and going over all the features of their face in your mind, except these images were ones I have never seen before. I felt surges of warmth throughout the session on my feet, crown of my head, and on my back between my shoulder blades. She said this was normal since there was energy moving and things leaving me that no longer served me.

As I shut my eyes I could feel the shadow of her hands over my eyelids. My mind raced as I thought of all the weird things she would pick up from me, or how my mom would come forward and say "tell her she masturbates too much" or something. I slowly started controlling my breathing and settling into a state of calmness and relaxation. During this time I had a lot of images pop into my mind. The first, of my mother in her final days on Earth. I pictured her lying on the couch with my head on her chest sobbing. Directly after this vision I pictured letting go of a purple balloon in a field against a sky filled with sunlight. Next, there was an image of large wings and I was sitting on the back of a bird looking down over the city below. I remembered thinking that I wish I could fly like this forever, what a magnificent view. After that I saw the Reiki master's shadow on the wall in front of me but it looked like Jesus. I thought to myself how stupid of me to think for a second that she was Jesus. I had some images come to me that I had never seen before; a woman stepped forward in old black witch-looking shoes. She was either a giant or I was incredibly tiny. I was so small I could only see the bottoms of the shoes and nothing else. There was an image of a woman in an old period dress getting her head pushed into a horse trough full of water, and then nothing. I am not sure how long the nothing feeling lasted, but it was nice. Throughout the session I felt like I was being rocked back and forth on a boat in the sea, and then slowly lifted up higher and higher on a cloud. I felt as if I was floating and had little Chinese lanterns tied to all of my limbs lifting me away from the world. Then suddenly I saw a ball of light crash into my chest and then she told me that the session was over.

After a few minutes she came back into the room with a cup of water and sat down to discuss her visions with me. She asked if I had trouble breathing or had sinus problems. I told her that actually I had been having trouble breathing recently and had to go to the hospital about a week ago. She said that during the session a motherly woman stepped forward and was telling her that I have allergies and that is what the tightness was in my chest, and it would pass. She also said the woman told her that I have been through a lot and have a heavy heart right now. She believes that was my mom. She also acknowledged that I often talk out loud to her when I'm alone and she can hear me. That made me smile, and almost cry.

She said that a very odd thing happened during the session, and it normally doesn't happen that often, actually hardly ever. She saw large, sparkling, light pink wings appear from my back. I made a shocked face, and sat in silence as she continued to share her opinions of this. At this time in our world there are a lot of things changing. This period of time is crucial and there are people who have spiritual gifts and sensitivities, and these people have been called up to do special things in the world, and answer their calling. She said that she seldom sees wings on people and that this is something special. This makes me think that maybe when I saw the wings of the bird that she was actually seeing wings on me.

She said she would be there to help me through my sensitivities and suggested that I obtain some stones to ward off negative entities. I was concerned about this, and she said that during the session about twelve spirits left my body, two of which had been there a long time, and those eventually left too. "Imagine walking down a dark alleyway and seeing one house with a light on, where do you think people are going to go?" After discussing this further she added that I was that light, that beacon, that these spirits gravitate to, and if I am not grounded, that they can attach to me. She said that when a part of something else moves in, a part of me moves out, and this is not good. I asked where the two spirits went, and she said that "one left with Jesus, and one left with an Angel." I smiled and said that I actually saw a shadow of her during my session and thought it looked like Jesus. She said that during that point in the session Jesus actually appeared at my feet and mirrored where she was standing, smiled at her, and then took the one soul. I liked how she said it so casually, like "oh yeah, Jesus showed up" as if it was some party and she just remembered that he came by for a bit. I was instructed that through meditation and picturing myself being grounded I can prevent some of these spirits from attaching again. This makes me wonder if not all angels are good? If Jesus took one, and an angel took the other, why did they go to different places? She did say that one was of a child-like figure, and the other was a dark shadow person. I wonder if this child is the Indian girl that my mom and I saw when we lived in the haunted house. That would explain why I feel like every house I move into is haunted.

Finally, she said that she saw a spirit animal! Mine is a polar bear. She printed out a section of a book she had about spirit animals and what they mean. The polar bear actually represents strength when you are embarking on a spiritual journey and working between the spirit world and ours. It also represents not expending a lot of energy into things that are not going to produce positive outcomes. She told me to go home and drink plenty of water, because just like a physical massage there are a lot of elements of my body that were moved and I need to hydrate and cleanse. She also advised that I take sea salt and cleanse either in the bath or shower to get the remaining energy off.

Lastly, she asked about my heritage and mentioned that there was a black man and also a woman speaking in a different language that appeared to her. I wasn't sure about that, but I have had a black man in a lot of recent dreams. He appears as a shiny faced youthful man, in old servant-like clothing. Often times he hands me water that he has placed in cups that rest on his shoulders, and part of me feels like he loves me. I didn't tell her this, but I also had a dream where I saw him die:

We are in Greece by the Parthenon, and my family (none of which I recognize) is having a family dinner. The sun is shining in on the rustic stone table and I can see the sand blowing outside in the breeze. As we sit down to eat, the peaceful music that is playing comes to a halt. I panic and look for him, and run hastily towards the balcony outside. I see him standing on a chair with a rope around his neck. My family did this to him. He looks at me and I can hear him thinking, "this is going to hurt," and despite my efforts I am unable to save him.

I kept this dream to myself, as it was disturbing for me to think about. She told me that maybe I should look into my heritage and find out where my roots lie.

Also, she suggested that I decrease my stress level and really examine the energy I am putting into my day-to-day career and try focusing more on what I love, which is writing. She also said I may have crazy dreams tonight, and as I get older more and more things will open up for me.

I left there around 7 p.m. in the pouring rain with no umbrella. I walked lightly with a large smile on my face and thought, I don't need an umbrella, I have wings.

The next day I felt like I had a Band-Aid ripped from inside my chest. Apparently this is normal since things were pulled out of me. I also picked up a few stones to wear: smoky quartz, hematite, and an ivory- colored amber ring. These stones all have different symbolic meanings that line up with my spirit at the moment. The smoky quartz represents healing, being grounded, and transmuting negative energies. It also opens paths for perception and endurance. The hematite represents positive effects on the bloodstream. It increases resistance to stress, energizes, draws out negativity, grounds you, and encourages you to reach for your dreams. The ivory colored amber ring was not a recommendation of hers, but I really liked the ring. Amber is recognized for restorative healing, protection, and enabling the body to let go in order to generate fresh pathways. It is said that amber sparks a fire within you to help humankind.

The next day she called me and told me that she had a dream about me last night and asked how I slept. I told her I slept incredibly well and had a dream that my house was extremely clean, shining, and sparkling. I wish. I am a little achy today and my chest hurts a bit, but all in all my energy is high and I feel like I am lighter in a way. She said her dream about me confirmed my light and gifts and she could feel my chest aching. She told me that it literally looked like a slit in my chest with spirit after spirit popping out like a jackknife. No wonder my chest hurts today. She said that once all was removed there was an opening from above and I was blasted with a beacon of pure white light. We discussed some odd occurrences lately and she reassured me that there are no coincidences and that everything happens for a reason. I also decided that I am not going to focus on the publishing of this book, but instead the passion of what I am experiencing. If one day it gets published then maybe it can help others to embark on journeys of their own to become enlightened.

May 26, 2013: Buddhism #2

I don't think Buddhism is a religion you can just attend one or two services and fully understand. Not the kind of religious institution you attend once a week and politely let your neighbor out of the parking lot but then call them a choice word two minutes later. I think this religion requires education and practice and then shapes you into a better way of experiencing life. This "emptiness" that they keep speaking of would normally be viewed as a bad thing by most people. I am wondering why it is looked upon so profoundly here. Today I went to another Buddhist temple in Portland. Today is also the first time I attended a place of worship and didn't think about my mom, or try to connect the dots of the service to my personal tragedies. This time, it was much different.

The temple I went to today focuses on Zen Buddhism, and required more of my morning than the other churches I have attended. I arrived at 8:30 a.m. for seated meditation. I have never meditated before and to try this for an hour is extremely hard. I walked slowly into the dark temple and removed my shoes. I was quietly greeted by a smiling woman in a long robe. She asked what had brought me there that day and I replied that I was on a spiritual journey and trying to reconnect, or connect with something. Her smile grew, and she said she would help guide me through the morning services and for me to watch others and pick up on the rituals as we go.

She guided me into the semi-dark room where others were seated peacefully on cushions on the floor in rows. Behind the cushions was another row of wooden chairs for those who didn't want to kneel. Everyone seemed so still and peaceful, and a few had silk bags next to them that contained what looked like small wooden scrolls. There was another service going on upstairs and the sound of chants echoed through the walls like a heavenly choir in the dark. I could smell the incense but didn't know where it was coming from. I sat in the back row in an old simple wooden chair that looked like one of the kitchen-table chairs from my childhood home.

I didn't know quite how to start. Slow the breath? Concentrate on clearing my mind? Then I thought isn't the thought of clearing my mind a thought in itself? After about ten minutes of restless thinking I began to picture my breath flowing in and out of my body, slowing down and turning into golden light. The light filled my lungs, spilled down my spine, and flooded towards my fingertips: cleaning out all thoughts, darkness, and doubt. I imagined the light coming from the sun, bright above, shimmering across my face. My wooden chair slightly sinking into small grains of sand on the beach with just the sound of subtle waves and soft breeze. The ocean brushing just over the tops of my feet, and then…somebody coughed. Then someone got up to pee. Then the sound of what I thought was someone doing dishes. Every time I closed my eyes another sound: this time a choir of stomachs. Did no one eat today?? Then as if my stomach was replying back to all the others, it roared out the longest, loudest grumble I have ever heard come from my body. Then I cracked. Laughing during meditation is a big no-no, I imagine. So I collected myself from my prison of laughter and inhaled again. This time I envisioned being back on the island but on my yoga mat, lying down, sunning my entire body. Here, it was peaceful and warm with nothing but ripples of water whispering, "shhhh, be still and relax"; then a bell rang, and another, and another. An abbot chimed in that we could now stand or do walking meditation, the idea being that if we can achieve Zen moments while seated, we should be able to do the same thing standing, and eventually in our everyday lives.

I remained seated. As a first timer I didn't feel I was anywhere near that state of mind, especially given my recent giggle. I bet the standers don't giggle. After the standing portion was completed we all lined up and slowly walked upstairs. The smell of incense became more predominant as we entered the main temple. Everyone bowed as they reached the top of the stairs and moved to seating cushions in the main room. The woman who greeted me came back again and guided me to a different chair. She said, just watch the others and they will help you. This chair she put me in was like a meditation cushion with training wheels. No one else was seated in this type of chair, not even the mentally handicapped kid that I just noticed. It was much more comfortable than the wooden chair from downstairs though.

I noticed while all of the noise was going on downstairs that the people who looked like meditation masters placed these scroll-looking weights on the tops of their heads. I have no idea what these were. My new meditation highchair was pretty nice. I felt like I was seated on a cloud facing a magnificent yellow stained glass window that had been infused with pure blue rain. The sun shone through the window as I shut my eyes. I envisioned sitting up on a cloud with sunshine pure as gold on my face. I was sitting in a swing that was hanging down from a blossoming cherry tree. It looked like it was snowing, but it was just a soft cloud of white petals flowing down from the tree. The sunlight sparkled on the light pink wings springing from my back that were soaking in purest glory, and then the handicapped boy in the front of the room shouted, "OH YEAH!" I wanted to laugh but didn't. Instead, I took another deep breath and put my hands to heart in prayer. There was about a thirty-second period of just nothing. Right before that moment of nothingness I pictured the purple balloon again floating up out of my hands toward the sky. I bet everyone else in the room had a complete hour of nothingness. Is this the emptiness they talk about?

I pictured a flower. The flower is alive, breathing, flourishing, withstanding elements, connected to the ground and affecting all other living things no matter how minute. Still and quiet, alive and silent. Stillness is what I wish I could achieve. As I sat there, a buzzing bee among still flowers, I thought about how much practice this transformation will take.

The next hour consisted of chants, bows, more chants, more bows, and finally tea and cookies downstairs. I thought that tea and cookies would conclude the three-hour morning but it was just the intermission. We all filed back into the main room and took our seats facing the abbot in the front of the temple. Once everyone was comfortable and still, he began with a lesson from a sutra that meant garden. How appropriate.

The story was about a king who wanted to create a magnificent net that covered the entire sky. Each lattice of the net contained beautiful gemstones. Each gem was cut, polished, and different in unique ways. The king went to the mountain top (here it is again!) to string up his ornate web and it covered the sky and the entire universe. When he stepped back to admire his work he realized that one gem held the reflection of another gem within it. Then he realized all of the gems resembled the others, and within one gem was the reflection of millions. Like a house of mirrors, he looked into the largest one and saw the infinite beauty of every stone within the web. If one gem was removed it would affect everything else in the universe; even the smallest of stones made a difference. So, he realized everything in this world is connected and must be held in the highest regard no matter the size, shape, or role it plays. The way we treat others sends an infinite ripple across the universe, and shapes the world we live in.

This story also reminds me a bit of the message that was conveyed by the minister at the second Southern Baptist church, in the way that we are all connected and every person plays a significant part within the functioning whole. With that I thought about the lives that could be touched by sharing my experiences with others. Even if my words would help one person in the world I would be happy. Though I know my journey is unique to me, maybe I can inspire someone else. Then for once, my mom's last words to me made sense, "Everyone has to die, and everyone has to live." I believe that when she was removed from the lattice, something shifted in the universe, and redirected light to reflect within me, and in turn shoot out to all the others within the web. We are all connected, and the loss of her light has in turn shone through me and out in so many other directions.

I feel at home with the Buddhist practice, and almost wish I had saved it for last so I could continue going to church here and not devote time to all of the others on Sundays to follow. I am a little confused at night when I find myself praying. Last night I started my prayers as I was taught and said, "Thank you lord Jesus for..." Then I changed and said, "I mean, thank you God? Or Buddha? Or Lord? I'm not sure. Anyways, thank you for the lessons of today."

June 2, 2013: Greek Orthodox

I wondered what made Greek Orthodox any different than other Orthodox churches. The word Orthodox itself is Greek, and means "right/correct belief." Anyhow, I decided to visit the Greek version of its Greek beliefs.

As I pulled into the parking lot I was overtaken by the angelic sound of chants echoing from the sky above. I looked for speakers on the street lamps or some sort of choir but found nothing. I thought maybe it was coming from within the heavy golden doors of the cathedral but it resonated from the other direction. I was very tempted to follow the glorious hymns and knock on the door of its producers at the sanctuary across the street, where I saw men in white robes and turbans heading inside. Instead, I avoided the urge to impulsively walk into whatever place sounded so enchanting and carry on the plan of the morning.

I pushed through the heavy gold doors and entered into a dim candle-lit room where two long tables covered in white sand stood to my right and left. Thin white candle sticks were placed sporadically throughout the sand, and around the perimeter of the table stood a row of red glass votives. The overall room was fairly lit and gave way to the opportunity to look around at others for what to do in this particular room.

There were ornate old-looking paintings standing upright on easels that people stood in line to kiss before walking into the main church. I thought of all the germs and opted out of this ritual (also because I didn't know the meaning). As I slowly walked into the main cathedral I was left in awe from the radiant beauty filling the room. Red plush carpet flooded the aisles between what looked like shiny hand-carved wooden pews. The walls to my left and right were ripples of pink stained glass that looked like feathers stacked one upon the other up to the ceiling. At the tops of each window was the symbol of the trinity and between each pane of pink-hued glass were depictions of Jesus, angels, disciples, mountains, white horses, and the Last Supper. There were symbols in Greek that I didn't understand encased in all of the windows as well.

In the front of the room stood a magnificent hand-carved wooden archway that stretched the width of the nave. There were polished and dusted gold carvings lacing around and throughout the statuettes and paintings within the woodwork and old brass lamps that hung down from thick gold-linked chains that illuminated the tops of the wooden arch in a reddish glow from the red glass within. In the center of it all was a beautiful chandelier that hung down. It had candles in tiers all the way around it, red stained glass, and gold trim that made it glow like a hanging golden anchor grounding everyone's attention. Through the wooden arch was an area I could barely get a glimpse of, but from what I could see it looked like a palace. I could see gold staffs and bells, candles and paintings, and a table with a silk cloth covering it. All of the altar boys walked from behind me in a line, cloaked in yellow silk robes. Some had candles; others had gold staffs with flat circular ornaments on the top that looked like someone took a doily, dipped it in gold, and left it to dry atop a staff.

The service started in Greek song, none of which I understood. I looked around and saw others reaching for books in front of them for guidance. I looked at a few people nearby to find what page we were on and to my dismay all three were on different pages. I wondered if everyone was as lost as I was. I finally found the right page when the priest stopped and said a few words in English. After a lot of Greek hymns the priest did a burning of incense ceremony. I was delighted that there was incense incorporated into this service, and eager to see what the meaning was. I was not delighted that it smelled like Axe body spray mixed with a funeral home. The Buddhist incense is much more pleasant. I read the English subtitles that described this ceremony and actually after this is completed everyone in the congregation is supposed to experience pure emptiness in order to let the light of God in. This concept is a familiar one, though in the Buddhist practice incense was used just to help calm, not to allow for the emptiness…that came from within.

I looked around and thought of all the people coming to worship today. Coming to worship *their* God every Sunday, and then thought of all the other churches doing the same exact thing. How is it that people can't for a second just question if someone else may be right? What if the Qur'an is the right book, or the Torah, or maybe even a book that never made it into circulation because it was destroyed by someone seeking power? What if…there really is just one God? One God overseeing all of the universe, and we…the people, have made a mess of it all. Dividing the One up into books, and waging wars against each other based on our own interpretations? What if, huh?

What if I find a piece of each religion I agree with? I am fearful that the further I go into this journey, the more I will find more and more parts of different sects that I adhere to, and will be left with nothing more than a patched-together quilt of stitched beliefs. I am scared I will be led right back to the beginning of the maze. No religion, just tidbits of interpretations I semi-agree with. Like a Franken-religion. At the end of this, if I find a sincere connection with God, feel enlightened, and that I have helped others in some other way, I will be completely happy. I wonder, if I find this connection and relationship with God in this way, will I not have the same "salvation" that has been promised to every other religion?

The priest stated that today's service would end with the memorial closing in honor of two people that had passed. It appeared to be two children, one only four and the other six. The memorial closing is also for those who have died in their way with God and want to find him again.

The main service was only about fifteen minutes long. The rest was two hours of Greek hymns, most of which repeated the common theme of "Jesus died for our sins, lead me to salvation and have mercy on my soul." I have also never done as many "father, son, holy spirit" chest motions as I did today. I should have counted but I bet it was about twenty. I also took communion. I figured since I was baptized at fifteen, and even though I was called the wrong name in my baptism, I think it still counted. I read in the English side notes that at one time it was Greek custom to kiss your neighbor in church; then it was abused and turned inappropriate. Judas was named as the person to blame. They mention that we should not act like Judas, and not kiss our brothers. This also reminds me that vagueness can lead to misinterpretation.

For reasons unknown I kissed the priest's hand after he gave me my communion. I didn't know what to do when I got up to him in the first place, since it had been a good fifteen years since I had done this. So I just opened my mouth and let the priest insert a little spoonful of mushed wine bread into my mouth. I then thought of all the germs I had just come into contact with and swallowed it quickly with a gross face.

After communion came the service (in English). The priest came forth in his green and white silk robe and looked out to the full room of silent onlookers. There was a beautiful hum from the choir above in the balcony. Then he began.

The lesson was about a woman in Samaria who had come to a well to draw water. Jesus sat beside it and asked the woman if she would give him some water. He was a Jew and she was offended he would even speak to her. He told her if she knew the gift of God and who he was she would give him a drink, and if she would only ask him he would give her living water. She countered and said, "You have nothing to draw water with, and the well here is so deep." She questioned him as a person, and he replied, "Everyone who drinks of this water will thirst again, but whoever drinks of the water that I shall give him will never thirst, and the water I give him will become in him a spring of water welling up to eternal life."

To me, this is a figurative story telling us that if we don't believe in God we will not be fulfilled in life, but if we do, we will have an everlasting source within us that will keep us quenched both in this life and the next.

At the end of the story she believes who he is, and helps spread the word of the Lord to others. The priest concluded by saying that in any journey where we are trying to become closer with God, we must understand that this is a life process, and not a quick change. This is a living, breathing, experience that must be kept alive. Only by acknowledging the presence of coldness, darkness, and dryness do we find the need for warmth and light. Only when we acknowledge coldness and darkness inside of us can we have the power to clear it away and allow for "nothingness." Once the dark is removed, only then can God come in. He reiterated that in order to be like the Samaritan and accept new things and change, we must be willing to turn our world upside-down. Only when we are willing to accept this metamorphosis can we allow for salvation to enter our lives. I thought about yoga for a second, and the anxiety around the handstand. I used to fear the handstand and the uncomfortable balancing act it inflicted, but after I had tried it a few times I learned that it is healthy to turn our worlds upside down and gain new perspective on a daily basis. Getting out of our comfort zone, trying new things, and getting the blood flowing again is certainly something we all should get used to doing.

After the service I reflected on the lessons of the day as I perused the aisles of the grocery store. From behind came a voice: "Ma'am, do you need help finding something?" I realized I had been aimlessly staring at the toilet paper for who knows how long and laughed. I said, "No, I'm fine, I just need toilet paper but I'm taking my good old time getting there!" She smiled and said back, "As long as you know where you're going you'll get there!"

June 3, 2013: A Dream

I had a dream last night that was frightening. It started as a dream and continued when I awoke.

In my dream I am an angel that was captured for experimentation. There is an old man and he is trying to clip my wings, perform studies, and force me to reproduce. I am flying, most of the dream, through a dome-shaped mile-high cathedral. At the top of the cathedral were French windows encircling the dome. I am able to hide in a cocoon for a bit until I am discovered, and then the old man begins hunting me down to trap me. I finally realize my powers to both freeze time and become invisible, and it allows me to outsmart him and fly to the top of the dome. I push out the French doors and grab the hand of a handsome winged male with blond curly hair and icy blue eyes. He usually appears in dreams from above, and watches me to make sure I am safe. He goes by the name of David. He had come down to save me. We both become invisible as we rub our hands together. As we fly away I realize a third entity is attached to me that is not invisible, and everyone had seen where I had gone. This was not the scary part.

When I awoke I looked out my large bedroom window to the tree tops. Outside, the sun was an hour from awaking and the sky was a light shade of blue and shadows. Then I saw a dark shadowy figure out in the trees. I blinked and the shadow jumped to another branch. I blinked again and it jumped to another branch. I thought it was a bat, but it kept growing bigger. I blinked again and it expanded throughout the sky and turned the color of blood. I fumbled for my glasses to make sure I was seeing what I was seeing. I put them on and saw the sky outside was completely red. I blinked again, and it was gone.

This scared me so much. I thought, was this some sign telling me to stop treating my journey like an experiment, or was something bad coming?

June 9, 2013: Catholic

I left the Catholic Church in tears (insert inappropriate priest joke here). As I sat through the service I had an overwhelming feeling of failure come over me. Failure in my journey and the harsh realization that I may never find a religion that fits me. I sat there staring up at the wax Jesus hanging from the cross bleeding, thinking about how I understand the messages the Bible teaches, but simply do not agree with some of the ideas that each religion preaches. How is it that I can sit there and not agree, but want so badly to? A curtain of sadness draped over me as I bowed my head in defeat, and then realized that no one religion so far has made me feel like I will ever get to "Him" in the correct way. Is there a correct way? Is it even a Him? Why can't I just believe in the teachings of the Bible and apply the lessons of the words to my daily life? Why is it that if I don't believe someone actually parted a sea or Jesus placed a hand on a casket and resurrected a dead child that I am wrong? It is baffling that a church would make its followers say aloud that they are only faithful to this church, this religion, and it is the only way. It is baffling that they do it.

I kneeled as I prayed today, and though I didn't know their prayers I respectfully conducted the same mannerisms and followed along. I felt like Bambi trying to walk for the first time as I positioned my folded hands several different ways, sliding them up and down the pew awkwardly as I prayed. I didn't know which way was right. Then I stopped for a second and thought that there is no right way to fold your hands or bow your head. What matters is what you are drawing from the words spoken, what you will do to incorporate them into your life, and that your prayers are your own. Not everyone has the same things they are praying for so why is it that we should all repeat the same prayer in unison? I looked up at the wax Jesus as if he would blink and respond to me and say something like, "this is just so they all feel better for the sins they are committing daily." I want to be a part of a religion that doesn't focus week after week on repenting for sins, but instead gives new ideas and ways of thinking that enhance our perspective on the world and quality of life. A religion that shows us ways to respect the world we live in, and helps us to understand that the little things we do all affect the world as a bigger picture. A religion that teaches us **not** that sinning is okay as long as we ask for forgiveness weekly, but instead encourages us to live wholesome lives. I want this to be a living breathing thing that builds my character, not something I turn to for repenting and forget about until next Sunday. It would be wonderful to find a religion that encompasses the Buddhist principles, but also incorporates the teachings of Jesus and the Bible. If only Jesus were a Buddhist and created a new hybrid religion for people like myself.

I didn't take communion today. It was mentioned a few times that if you were not baptized a Catholic that you are not to take part in the communion. I got to thinking as I sat back and watched everyone go up to ingest the body and blood of Christ. In most of the churches I have gone to thus far that have offered communion, the message before the breaking of the bread is the same, in every religion. In the Bible it states that before Jesus was crucified he had his Last Supper with his disciples. Here he explained to them that they were to drink the wine as a symbol of his blood, and eat the bread as a symbol of his body. This act was to demonstrate to them that he was dying for mankind, and that each time this ceremony was performed again, it was to be honored and remembered what he did for us. The daily bread in my opinion is the reflections of the teachings, and daily thanks that we give in his honor. Both are symbolic of the actual lessons left behind. I sat there and thought, is this not the same Bible that I worship (though I admit I haven't read much yet), and the same God that I follow? If I was baptized Christian or Catholic, why am I not to partake in a ceremony that has just as much meaning to me as it does everyone else in the room? Surely the Last Supper in Christianity is the same Last Supper in Catholicism. I looked again at all the people sipping from the same cup and was a little less bothered that I didn't get to partake in this week's communion.

After the communion the priest began today's lesson from Luke 7:11–17, and it was titled in the pamphlet: "A great prophet has arisen among us!" The story was about a mother who had lost her only child. The funeral was taking place and the woman, also a widow, was weeping. Jesus saw the woman and felt compassion for her and said "do not weep" and he placed a hand on the casket and said "young man, I say to you arise," and the dead man sat up and began to speak, and Jesus gave him back to his mother. I looked at the wax Jesus again with questioning eyes and thought, now, wait a second, are you saying that you actually brought a corpse back from the dead and healed all of the dormant rotting body parts, or are you quite possibly saying that you are able to breathe life back into things that once were dead? In my interpretation I see this scripture as saying that people who have died in their ways with God, or have pain, suffering, and hardships can find relief and compassion if they trust in God. I don't think he actually brought a cold dead corpse back from the dead and healed all of his embalmed decaying organs, but instead told this story to teach people that if you are wounded and hopeless, there is hope if you just trust in the Lord and his guidance.

I thought that after this was read aloud the priest would somehow relate this to us in our everyday world and explain how to apply this story, but he didn't. There was just a silence and everyone turned to a page that I couldn't even read aloud because I didn't agree with it. I don't think that all people are the same, and I don't think that everyone should agree that Catholicism is the only true religion and way to salvation. I actually stopped speaking mid-sentence and thought, "There's no way I am going to continue reading this out loud."

I thought back to the Buddhist church a few times during the service, like I was on a date with a new guy but still thinking about the true love of my life. I wondered what wonderful life lessons I was missing out on while sitting here biting my tongue. I suppose this in itself is a lesson that needed to be learned. I also thought about my mom today, and how she used to take me to church with her when she was sick. Most of the time I went with her I didn't even listen to the service, but instead held her hand and rubbed her back as she absorbed her own meaning of the service. I would do anything to go back to that moment and sit with her one more time, in any church.

I find it interesting that I went to the Church of St. Michael the Archangel. Michael is said to be the leader of the army that defeated Satan. Michael also was the angel of healing. In some readings he is the angel of death. In paintings and books he is often depicted weighing souls on a scale when they die, and if the bad outweighs the good he lets the heavier side take over. In other readings he is the angelic model for the virtues of the spiritual warrior, with the conflict against evil viewed as the battle within. Right now, I feel like I embody a lot of that conflict, and maybe today Michael was present and just helping me to sort it all out.

June 23, 2013: Christianity

I took a Sunday off of church to move into my new home. Now that I am all moved in, I am both extremely worn out and poor. I spent the first few minutes of church not focusing on the surroundings, but thinking of how I was going to buy any food or coffee that day for myself. I spent the last few dollars in my bank account bringing a soy latte to my boyfriend at work and now have less than a dollar to my name. I wondered how I got to be this poor, and now sitting here in a completely packed church began to come back to Earth and focus on where I was at, not how I got here. The church itself looked like a castle from the outside with billowing igloo-shaped gray bricks stacked high above the monstrous trees. It was enchanting from the outside, and looked like it would have served a king at one point in history. Now, it serves as a Christian church filled with a bookstore, food bank, community center, and chapel. It was nice that they had a full coffee bar set up to greet me when I walked in the door. I walked into the chapel and was really taken back by how many people filled the church. Not a pew was left vacant; even the balcony above was filled. There were people in jeans, dresses, and all sorts of outfits. Drinks were welcome (as well as every crying baby in the city).

The service started with a band onstage, go figure, and everyone was singing and clapping along. After twenty minutes or so of music and rejoicing, the priest took the stage. He made a few announcements and welcomed a new member who was to be the new elder to the church. I didn't know what this was, but apparently it is someone that serves as a leader within the church, and is divinely appointed. After the divine torch passing I waited for the priest to come back up and begin the service, but he didn't. Instead, a movie began playing on the large projector screen in the front of the church. A man that was not present in the service appeared, looking somewhat like Vincent D'Onofrio from *Law and Order*. Confused, I looked around to make sure I wasn't missing where the live person was standing, but he wasn't there. This was a podcast. I was in a church, watching a podcast.

The podcast's focus was around what makes a church a church. He disqualified Bible study groups, praise by yourself, and praise in God-made places like nature; he said these were not churches. You needed to belong to a church, and worship among the family of God. This seemed odd coming from the person that was not present in the church at this moment and could have been doing the podcast from his basement for all I knew. He did mention that there are other ways of worshiping God in several other parts of the world, and just because they are not doing the same exact thing as we are, that the principles remain the same. That is something I completely agree with. I feel that if people are worshiping God in any way, in any country, and it is out of love, then it should be accepted by all religions and not scrutinized.

He then focused on the lesson of the day that came from Acts 2:14–47. All of the modern Christians took out their "Virtual Bibles" and followed along. I gave a smug cringe and picked up the old-fashioned normal Bible from the pew in front of me. He said that in tough times when we may be struggling to pay our bills and afford things, that at least we don't have to pay for our sins. Thinking of it like that made me feel like an asshole for making such a big deal about how I would afford the day's coffee. He consumed the entire hour and a half with an acronym, "Jesus Church," that he applied to different parts of Acts. Amongst all of the acronyms the podcast priest spent the hour on, I pulled this part of the lesson out that spoke to me:

> With many other words he warned them; and he pleaded with them, Save yourselves from this corrupt generation…They sold property and possessions to give to anyone who had need. Every day they continued to meet together in the temple courts. They broke bread in their homes and ate together with glad and sincere hearts, praising God and enjoying the favor of all the people. And the Lord added to their number daily those who were being saved.

Among the examples given of a corrupted generation, one in particular stood out. There are things I have done in my past that may not have been so great, primarily stealing. I used to steal a lot. I used to steal things for profit, for fun, and for sport. Though I was only a teenager, it was still wrong. I only stopped because I didn't want to get caught like others I had seen. The priest said that there are certain things in this world that are wrong, and one is stealing. When things are not yours they are not to be taken, and if you have taken from others and you truly feel repentance for it, God will forgive you. With this lesson comes change. Only if you take this forgiveness and change your way of life, and change the way you act going forward, you will find salvation. At this very moment I glanced down toward my feet and saw something sparkling.

The priest continued on and gave an example of Christmas time, and how some people get more satisfaction and glory by watching the reaction of those that receive gifts than getting gifts themselves. I thought about how happy my mom was one year when she unwrapped the $500 red winter coat I got for her. I had stolen that coat. Though she didn't know it, it brought me such joy to watch her unwrap it. Now that I have a job, and a sustainable income, well not really, I have less than a dollar to my name, I still vowed that I would never take what was not rightfully mine ever again. I looked down again, and saw that right next to my foot was a sparkling item – a diamond. I thought, you've got to be kidding me, this has to be a test or a fluke of some kind!! This is the kind of thing that happens in movies or Bible stories to teach lessons. Years later kids will read this and be like, oh I bet that didn't really happen and this is just a story to teach us a lesson, but yes, this did happen. I picked it up and studied it, rubbing over the sides and looking into its depth of prisms. I watched as the offertory basket skimmed the aisles and thought about just putting it in the basket and not saying a word. The headlines would read, "Mystery Angel Puts $30K Diamond in Offering Basket at Church, Saves Day" Then, somewhat like Gollum, I put it back in my palm and held it tight.

I sat there for a moment and thought about how this was not mine to take, and though it may pay off my debt and furnish my new home, it may be a treasured loss to someone else. I brushed the cartoon devil off of my shoulder and set it atop the Bible next to me as I got up to take communion. I was happy that I was able to take communion today, and just as I dipped my bread square into the grape juice there was yet another mentally handicapped boy yelling out, "OH YEAH!" I laughed and shoved the square in my mouth. I thought this couldn't possibly be the same boy from the Buddhist temple, somehow following me around and cheering me along? Part of me really liked it. It was as if someone was just showing up when I have these moments to remind me "HEY, YOU, good job. You're finally getting it!"

As I left the service I dropped the diamond into the lost and found and said to the priest in a snarky tone, "It's probably fake anyway." He looked a bit confused about what I had just dropped into the basket, smiled back, and said thank you.

June 30, 2013: Christianity Part 2

There's a church over on the other side of town with extremely steep steps that I used to walk past every day on my way to work. Normally, there are homeless people seeking refuge in the doorway at the top of the steps, and I never bothered to go near it. When I looked this church up online I didn't know it was this same church that I had passed a dozen times before. I had always wanted to go inside, and never did. I walked up the steps and into the beautiful church. Simple piano music filled the air as I took my seat on the cushioned pew that looked like old curtains that used to hang in my grandma's house. The robin's egg blue ceilings were outlined with gold accents and had chandeliers hanging down from them. Sunshine streamed through the stained glass windows that depicted Jesus being graced by light on his face. Other windows displayed doves, candles, crosses, and scenes from the Bible. All scenes were pleasant. There were two Kelly green banners that hung on the sides of the nave. At the base of each banner was a picture of a white fish. As I moved my eyes up the banner I noticed the transformation the fish was making. It grew wings with each drawing, and by the time my eyes reached the top of the banner the fish had turned into a beautiful white dove. It looked like the posters for evolution where the fish crawls out of water and then walks away a lizard. This is also weird to me since the Bible does not talk about evolution, and instead stresses that God created all things. Regardless, it was interesting to me, and also made me reflect on the changes I have made personally thus far. Right now I suppose I'm somewhere between fish and tadpole. There was also a table set in the middle of the room with clay chalices and bread placed upon it, and off to the right stood a wooden rack adorned with multiple crocheted blankets.

    The service began with a young girl and her guitar singing a few songs. Everyone sang along with her. Her voice sounded like Norah Jones and was so simple and beautiful. There were no bands, no projectors, no podcasts: just a single girl and a hymnal. After she sang, the female minister came forward and welcomed everyone to join in for another song. I thought, oh here we go again with more music to occupy the first half hour of the service. Though, this particular song struck a nerve with me. This is the song that was once one of my mom's favorite songs. She had even given me the CD of it, and I still keep it hidden away in my car. I never cared for the "Bible beater" songs that were on it, but since she liked it so much I kept it. After she passed away I listened to it one more time, and cried for hours. The words of it were so uplifting for her. The words of this song ("Here I Am Lord," by James Kilbane) in particular said "Here I am Lord, Is it I Lord? I have heard you calling in the night, I will go Lord, if you lead me." My mom started liking this song when she realized the cancer wasn't going away, and that it had spread. I always considered it her coping/acceptance song. She would play it and sing along, and when it would play in church she would raise her palms towards the sky as if to signal that she was okay with being taken. I grew contempt for the song, and almost began to hate it. It made my stomach turn, and the thought of her going away made my sinuses surge salt into my eyes. I never listened to the rest of the song until today. It isn't all about being taken to the lord, or being taken away. It is about opening up to God and allowing him to lead you and walk within his light. I wanted to cry, not out of sadness but out of happiness. I had found new meaning in something that once made me so sad and bitter.

Today was a special day for three high school graduates and active members of the church who were being awarded grants from the church. These kids were exceptional people. All three kids were 4.0 AP level scholars, one was a valedictorian, one was a deacon, and one had taken the next year to help develop new software down in San Francisco he had created. All of them were given a part in leading the service today. The first boy was given the opportunity to lead the service and share a lesson. He was passed down a long sash that the pastor's brother had once given to her when she began her journey as a minister. His lesson was about a blind man who heard Jesus was coming through his town. He heard a commotion and began to call out for Jesus. The crowd grew silent and someone in the crowd helped the blind man walk through the crowd and make his way up to Jesus. Jesus said to the man that he would give him a gift because he had the courage to call out for him even though he couldn't see him. He asked to be given back the ability to see, and with that, Jesus gave him back his sight. The preaching student said that it is important to gather from this lesson that even though we cannot see God, we need to have faith to call out for him and ask for guidance, because he is there all of the time.

He also told a story about how he was at a store one time and a woman in front of him in line had left her change behind. Though it was only a dime and a few quarters, he thought he should give it back to her. By the time he spotted her she was at a different exit than he was headed to, and he let her leave without giving it back. He said he still thinks about that moment all of the time. He goes to church every Sunday and calls himself a Christian, but if he doesn't act as a Christian then the point is defeated. This really resonated with me since I have been searching for a religion that I can grow with, and carry into my day to day life. I never envisioned that ever coming to fruition in any other religion besides Buddhism, until today when the boy with the shaky voice got up and spoke. He concluded his lesson by saying that he was going on to serve God and teach others not just to be Christian, but to be practicing Christians.

The next student led the children's service. All of the kids came forth and sat happily in their Sunday dresses and bow ties. She asked all of the kids, "How many of you like candy?" All raised their hands. She asked, "How many of you like jelly beans?" and all raised their hands. She then said, "How many of you think that if you shut your eyes and hold out your hands that your favorite jelly bean would appear in your hands?" All hands remained down. She told them all to close their eyes and think about the story of the blind man that had just been told. That man couldn't see Jesus, but he put his hands out and reached for him. She placed a bag of jelly beans in each of their hands and said, "Now open your eyes and know that miracles do happen, and even when it is dark we need to trust that someone is there listening." All of the kids skipped back to their parents with jelly beans in hand.

Next a woman came forward to speak about each graduate. She revealed the symbolism of the crocheted cloaks that hung in the front of the room, and presented each student with one of their own. These were hand made by a church knitting group offering protection, warmth, love, and safe keepings on this journey from here to wherever they may go. She said each wrap, each thread, represents a ripple of love they hope that each one will continue to share with whomever they meet.

The pastor got back up and stood at the table. As she broke the bread she said that those who open their bodies and hearts like Jesus did will be forever filled with his love and light. She addressed the congregation and said, "Now, who is welcome at God's table?" In unison, everyone said, "Everyone." All were welcomed forward to take part in the communion. They even had gluten-free body of Christ, which I liked. I noticed that instead of going back to their seats, everyone lined up around the room and started forming a circle. All joined hand in hand until all that remained in the center of the church was the empty table and pews. The singing billowed through the church and echoed throughout. I had never seen anything like it, except on the Grinch when all the Whos in Whoville did the same exact thing around their Christmas tree. After the song concluded the woman to my right kept hold of my hand. She introduced herself and said she had never seen me there before. I told her it was my first time there, and then, for the first time I opened up to a stranger about my project. I told her I wasn't raised with religion and since my mother had passed on I was trying to find my way to God again. She was delighted and said it was nice to meet another writer. She guided me right to the minister and introduced me. Her name was Amy. She asked me how I had found my way to their church and where I had come from. I think it was a letdown when I said, "I just Googled Christian churches in Portland and yours popped up." She was still delighted I had made it and asked me if she could take me out for coffee sometime to talk. We exchanged information, and then she thanked me again for coming in.

I left there with a feeling I had only felt a few times before. I was full of such glee and peacefulness. This is the exact feeling I have every time I wake from a dream about my mother. The sun was shining, and I reflected on the last words of the service, "Thank you for bringing us here today, and for the inspiration and gifts you have given us."

I went to the park and lay in the shade of a redwood tree. Inspired, I began to write, hoping to share my gifts and continue on the ripple of the day's lessons.

July 7, 2013: Hinduism

It's hard to write after experiences like today. I feel so moved by my visit to the Hindu temple that I don't quite know where to start. I picked a temple at random from the internet and for some reason decided to arrive forty-five minutes early with hopes to snap a few pictures on my own. As I pulled down the pine tree–lined path towards the white marble temple I saw a white man standing at the top of the steps directing other white people inside. I checked my phone again to make sure the picture of the temple matched the one in front of me, confirmed the match, and then decided to park my car. As I walked up he said, "Oh you're just in time, they just started the tour. Remove your shoes and head on in." Inside the echoing temple stood a monk leading a group of twenty or so college students, explaining the various shrines one by one. I quickly walked to the front of the temple where the tour was, and joined the end of the line-up.

The leader was a small bald man with a radiant smile and dark rimmed glasses. The monk, or Guru, not sure yet…was cloaked in a burnt orange robe and silk scarf. He smiled and giggled as he made a few jokes to lighten the intense mood. Everyone seemed anxious, curious, uptight, and a bit intimidated. He began explaining the different shrines and statues that were situated around the temple. Each statue was built of white marble, except for one, which was a rich black rock said to be made from the tallest mountain in the Himalayas. The Gods depicted around the temple included Buddha, Krishna, Hanuman (monkey), Ganesha (elephant), Shiva, mother goddess, God of Death, and Ram. While explaining to the class the different meanings that each God or Goddess bestows he asked the class, "Does anyone know the God of Hinduism?" Different answers surfaced, repeating the different Gods he had just mentioned, and he responded, "There is just One. All of the Gods here represent different aspects of one whole. There is one God, one love, one light." He pointed to the opposite corner from where we stood and said, "Does anyone recognize that God?" It was a marble statue of Mary carrying the baby Jesus. The founder of this temple, at one time, went on a search for God as well, and realized that despite the different denominations behind the Gods that are worshiped worldwide, they all embody an aspect of "God" and therefore received a shrine in the temple he built. Though the Bible was not preached from, quoted, or mentioned (besides a cute joke about preaching from the Bible on the fifth Sunday of the month if we wanted to come back for that), he did recognize that Jesus is also a deity and holds a place in this temple.

I was really comforted in knowing that I was in a place that embodied Jesus, meditation, and enlightenment, and tied them together in a way that I seemed to follow. All of the statues were magnificent and cloaked in gold, silk, flowers, jewels, and weapons. That threw me off for a second. I immediately thought that weapons must represent war, or some sort of slaying they were famous for. The Guru said that these weapons are not for slaying others, but for slaying the enemies within us. We all have negative aspects that need to be put to rest before we can see God clearly: greed, pride, envy, etc. I noticed that every statue had one hand raised as if to say "stop." Most people thought this was to symbolize stopping what we were doing and worshiping, but the palm is actually a sign of peace. Next he pointed out that all of the eyes on the statues were disproportionate compared to the size of the statues themselves. The eyes are all much larger than they would be on a normal person – the reason being that we can't look for God, he/she is looking for us. The goal is to get to a point where you can see God and he/she can see you too. He said that we will never be higher than God, and the larger eyes also represent the ability to be the all-seeing of the entire universe.

We moved on to another statue of a monkey that was holding a mountain in one hand, and dancing with a smile on its face. The story goes that the monkey was very powerful and quick, and was sent into town to grab medicine from a part of the mountain. Along the way, the forgetful monkey forgot what part of the mountain he was to grab so he grabbed the entire mountain and toted it back to the city to save everyone. The monkey God, or Hanuman, is one of the most powerful Gods and represents great power and the ability to save through great strength.

The tour ended and it was time to go to the second building for the next part of the worship, which involved meditation and chants. We slipped our shoes on for a brief period of time and walked through the rose garden towards the wooden building just down the path. We were instructed by the Guru to remain quiet, observe the chants, find our own meaning within the experience, and to enjoy our time.

We filed in and sat on the floor Indian style atop thin quilted blankets that lined the floor. There were several other Hindus of all ages that sat throughout the sanctuary. They brought forth apples and bananas and set them at the foot of the shrine in the front of the room. The shrine in this room was beautiful, and had smaller statues of the Gods among it. There was orange silk draped throughout the shrine, and two black and white pictures of men framed on the floor.

In the center was a large white marble statue of the mother goddess with a tiger beneath her red silk robe. She held a dagger in one hand, and what looked like a shake weight in the other. She also held a trident, and held another hand up in peace. To the right of the statue was a small stand that looked like wooden sticks holding up a white conch shell. After we all settled in, the Guru told us to all shut our eyes, slow our breath, and feel the air coming in our bodies and slowing down. Feeling all parts of our bodies connecting with the breath, the feet, hands, eyes, and chest...all just letting go. "Do not try to control your breath. If you picture a small twig entering the river, it may not like the way in which the river is flowing so it tries to stop it, but it cannot, it is just a small twig and will never be able to control the direction of the water. Be like me!" he said, "just let go, and be carried away, and you will go...somewhere...because when we meditate and let go, things will happen." I realized how much worry I had been carrying with me lately, constantly worrying about money, my job, and bills. Even sitting there trying to relax I was so tense that my feet were stiff against the wood floors. So, like the twig, I let go, and imagined being a simple lotus flower placed on the water reaching for the light and being carried wherever it was I was meant to go.

Chanting began softly and slowly at the end of the meditation. When the room fell silent we all opened our eyes. The Guru said that there is no Sunday service, and connecting with God and meditating is something that should be done daily. Though the temple is open all of the time, it is best if everyone that is practicing Hinduism has a shrine of their own.

The Guru handed us a packet that had chants with sporadic English subtitles in it. The next chant was for the Mother/Goddess, and I chanted along with the parts I could read. After it was finished he explained the significance of the chant. "Everyone has this infatuation with God, and it's because we all come from the same light. God, like our own mothers, created each of us and the bond between mother and child is something that keeps us." As I stared at the multi-handed mother statue I smiled, picturing my own mother, who was always so good at juggling so many things at once.

Another chant began; this one didn't have words to follow so I sat with open eyes as I admired all of my surroundings. After this chant, the Guru asked for us to all take a look out the window at the blooming roses. The last chant was a prayer to the light in God and the light that lives within us. "See that rose outside? Do you think that two weeks ago it got out its laptop and sent a message to all the bees and told them to come down in two weeks and pollinate it? Of course not; roses do not do that! The rose is filled with light and purity, and the bees are attracted to what the rose possesses. If you are filled with the light of God, then good things will find you as well, and people will flock to you to seek the goodness within."

Then, very quietly, a humble man walked up towards the front of the room and grabbed the white conch shell from its stand. He blew a mighty gust into the shell that echoed through the horn so loudly that people covered their ears. It was amazing. As he filled his lungs again and blew louder, a little boy scurried to his bongo drum on the floor and played a beat along with it. The two continued as a little girl danced with bells on her feet, creating a chiming tambourine sound. With that, the celebration chant began. Everyone was singing, clapping, and chanting. The smiling faces around the room gleamed pure happiness. One by one people came forth and grabbed a small shiny tray that had five small lit candles on it. They moved the tray clockwise three times at the feet of the Goddess as an offering to her of their light, and in turn to be blessed with hers. The Guru urged me to step forward and partake in this ceremony as well, and he said "Go on! Go on! Everyone is welcome!"

Afterwards, there was a feast. The Guru said that the food was prepared out of love and offered for all. He smiled and said, "Now is when the real party starts!" There was a prayer for the food and then we all ate together seated upon the blankets on the floor. I happened to sit next to the man who had greeted me at the top of the stairs on my way in to the temple. He said, "You lucked out coming today. We don't do this all of the time." I didn't know what he was talking about, but apparently today a special tour was set up for a few college students that were studying theology at a nearby university. This man happened to be the theology professor at a large university in Portland and was there with his group of students. He went on to say that he had lived most of his life in India, and had studied the vast majority of religions. Just recently he and his wife had adopted a child with special needs and decided to move to the U.S. to ensure proper schooling for him. Then he looked at me and said, "What about you, what brings you here?" His response to my story…How serendipitous!

He said that when/if I do go to India, I should call him and his wife and they can help me as far as where to go, stay, and places they recommend that I visit. I enjoyed the rest of my meal, which was homemade delicious Indian food, said thank you to the Guru, and walked barefoot towards my car.

Though I don't fully grasp the origins of all of the Gods yet, I do connect with the concept of one God, and being connected through energy. Not so much that there is one God, but that all Gods together equal one unified light. I would like to learn more about the concept of energy cycling, reincarnation, and karma, but I suppose that will come to me when the time is right.

July 9, 2013: A Visit from Mom

This evening, I had a vision while riding my bike through a canopy of trees. Cotton was blowing through the gusts of wind like summer snow. I was upset about money, stability, and what lies ahead of me, so I went for a bike ride. I stopped at a vacant park to swing, reflecting on the simplicity of childhood. When there was no pressure or worries, just the goal of achieving butterflies in your stomach. The sun was setting and realized I had been gone awhile so I got back on my bike and began to ride home. As I coasted down the hill a burst of sunshine pedaled up next to me, young and smiling. Carried by wheels of light, my mother joined by my side and said, "You are not alone." In this sincere moment of excitement I wanted to tell her everything that has been going on in my life, but I didn't have to. She let me know with just a glance that she already knows, and she has seen it all, as if she has been glancing over my shoulder the entire time.

We conversed without actually speaking, just smiling and reading each other's thoughts like some telepathic telephone line that only mother and daughter share. Our thoughts bouncing like electrons in a lightning storm, or presently a summer snow storm. She let me know she is proud of me, and everything will be just fine. I saw her start to fade back to the beam of sunlight that brought her and pleaded, "Please! Don't leave me, Mom!" She smiled and said, "I never have, and I never will," and just like that she was gone. Instead of stopping to reflect on what had just occurred I pedaled faster for some reason. I smiled the entire way home, and felt a new sense of serenity from that point forward.

July 12, 2013: Judaism

I'm more nervous about attending this place of worship than I have been with any others; possibly because it's a Friday night, and I'm not in my typical "holy" mood. The synagogue is huge and occupies an entire block downtown. I arrived a half hour early to make sure I had enough time to snap a few pictures and find parking. I circled the block like a suspicious outsider peeking between block-shaped bushes trying to find where the actual entrance was. I finally found a break in the bush fortress and caught a glimpse of the courtyard first. Inside the plush green courtyard I saw band equipment, aisles of white wooden chairs, white summer-like tents, and a table with fresh lemonade. It looked like a wedding could be taking place soon, and I may have not received the memo.

This is the type of day in Portland that deceives all first-time visitors. The breeze feels like warm silk on your skin, the sun is shining, and there isn't a cloud in the sky. The summer in Portland makes it worth putting up with the rain all year long. It's like a mini paradise, and if you make your way up to the waterfalls or to the ocean for the day, it somehow becomes more magical.

The sunny streets became flooded by the minute with smiling "fresh out of work on a Friday" faces, and the energy outside of the courtyard was buzzing. Everyone that entered the courtyard was smiling and dressed in cute summer clothes. I was supposed to be meeting a Jewish friend of mine there for the service and just minutes before the service started he called to tell me I was on my own. Panicked, I asked all in one sentence, "Will I fit in? Should I have worn some kind of Jewish hat...will they know I'm an outsider? Will they check my taxes, and know that I'm both poor AND a faker?!"

He laughed and gave me a few pointers on the service including "just be normal and watch everyone else and whatever you do...DON'T CLAP!" He said people will get up and read poems, sing songs, and other things that are incredible, but no one claps, he doesn't know why, they just don't do it.

Just below the monstrous, gothic, wooden chapel doors picnic blankets were spread across the courtyard lawn. There were white canopies shading the rows of wooden chairs, and I decided to sit in a vacant chair I had just spotted in the back of the garden. I grabbed a book off of the small shelf in the center aisle, and made my way back. I flipped the book over a few times, slowly catching on that the Hebrew book read back to front and was bound on the right. Numerous people sounded like Jerry Seinfeld, and the man next to me, wearing a Larry nametag, looked a lot like Larry David. Was I in some kind of *Curb Your Enthusiasm* episode? Was the black swan suddenly going to walk out and take a seat among us? I wish.

At least I knew the safety of the back row and could easily watch others in front of me for what to do. Surely no one would find me out back here. This idea was flawed; I had managed to sit next to the head of the synagogue board and her newly converted Jewish friend. These two women reminded me of my mom and my Aunt Linda both in demeanor, dress, and overall attitude (these are all good characteristics). Not to mention, they both talked equally as much. The two women next to me were longtime friends and since the service was so casual, they talked...a lot. I felt like I was at a family reunion because everyone was hugging, kissing cheeks, tossing babies, petting dogs, and drinking (lemonade).

The two women also managed to ask me about my entire life story. Within the hour I had told them why I moved to Portland, where I was from, why I was there, how old I was, level of education, love life, where I get my hair done, and if I was Jewish. I decided to take the honest route and tell them that I wasn't raised with any religion and that I was just trying to find one that suits me. From that point on they slipped into mother mode and guided me through the entire service.

They explained that the ark in the front of the garden was there for a special occasion, today being the celebration of someone joining the Jewish faith. The ark (or wooden cabinet thing, as I called it) contained the first five books of the Torah. They went on to tell me that we all were to stand in of honor of the ark and its contents whenever the doors were opened. They also told me that there were several other arks inside the synagogue and if I would like I could come back another time and take a tour to see them. The women also told me, via a loud whisper, the meaning of words like *mazel* (celebration) and *shabbat shalom* (peace on your day of rest). They could tell I was puzzled by the words when everyone turned to their neighbors and said *"Shabbat shalom,"* and I just shook their hands and said, "Hi, nice to meet you." I felt like I had two Jewish coaches, strongly resembling family members, helping me through the service, making sure I didn't mess up or do something ridiculous.

I asked what was happening next as a young teenage girl moved to the front of the garden and took her place between the rabbi and the rabbi's husband. They opened the ark again and wrapped her in a white cloak. She was about to take an oath to convert to Judaism. The rabbi said that everyone from babies to adults has been wrapped in this cloak, over the decades and across the world. This was a very important event in this young girl's life, and it was nice to witness someone finding her faith here. I was smiling in awe of the moment and then the woman next to me, who looked a lot like my mother, whispered again, "The good thing about this synagogue is that it is a reform synagogue. Some of the people here don't even believe in God necessarily, but we all believe in the power of unity and the power of peace and love, and everyone is given the choice of what traditions they want to follow." I thought, have they heard about Buddhism? I looked around the garden at generations of old and young, yarmulke-wearing, smiling, peaceful people and thought about how close they all were and how much love was seated around me. The woman next to me noticed me smiling again and said, "See, everyone is welcome here no matter what religion, this is a place of love."

The tent in the front was where the rabbi and her husband set up their musical instruments consisting of a few guitars and four singers. The music that came from just the four of them was beautiful and ancient sounding, as I suppose it was. I was taken aback by the amount of clapping that occurred, as I was specifically told not to clap. I could tell the first clapper took a big risk and started it almost like a movie slow clap. The woman next to me explained the outdoor services are much more laid back and completely different than what I would normally see. She also said the lessons were typically different and today's gathering was more for the kiddies. This was fine with me since sometimes I get more from the kids' lessons than I do from formal adult preaching.

This particular children's service started with the rabbi holding a large soup pot. She said that a long time ago there was a very poor traveling man that came to a city. When he got there he took his empty pot and put it over a fire. The city folks said, "What are you doing, there is nothing in that pot! You are just heating up an empty pot!" The poor traveler took three stones out of his bag and said, "Well, I am going to add these stones and I am going to make a delicious soup!" The city folks were shocked, and everyone knew that he would not be able to make a delicious soup with just stones. So, one by one people came to the fire and added ingredients to the pot. As she said this, little kids skipped forward to the pot she had and added in carrots, bread, olives, chicken, and love. Eventually with all of the ingredients and added love from the people, they had enough soup to feed an entire city. All of the children gathered around the pot, proud of what they had accomplished together. The rabbi added that together with faith and love we can accomplish anything. There may have been more said at this point but the women next to me were talking about my hair saying, "Oh yeah, beautiful hair, just beautiful," and I missed what else may have been mentioned because I was returning the compliments and saying thank you.

After the service the two women marched me hand in hand up to the rabbi. She asked me what brought me there and I explained briefly. She took down my information and invited me to get coffee sometime to talk more. I have never been invited to coffee by anyone religious, but now a minister and a rabbi have both offered to meet with me. I feel kind of bad. This is how I envision Desiree feels on *The Bachelorette*. She goes on all these incredible dates with different men, all possessing appealing qualities, and she ends up liking them all. There is no kissing involved in my story, of course, well except for today I received several cheek smooches. Is it bad that I am starting to like several religions? It makes it so hard for me to try to pick one because so many people have opened up their hearts and arms to me. Today I feel it wasn't the religion that I cared for so much, it was the people. When it comes to Judaism, I have a lot of unanswered questions still, and feel quite uneducated. I don't even know who some of the people mentioned in the scriptures were like Adonai. I imagine it is another word for God, but not sure. I am not sure why they do not believe Jesus has come yet, and do they know he was at my Reiki session? All kidding aside, I do plan on sitting down with both the rabbi and another person I met that has offered to speak with me about their faith and learn more about what it is that they believe in.

July 19, 2013: A Dream

There is a movie showing. I am going to meet my mom there at the theatre and can't wait to see her. When I approach the gates of the theatre the person taking tickets tells me I don't have enough money to get in, so sadly, I turn away and leave. I begin walking my dog Olivia back across the bridge to where we came from, and as I look down I see a great flood coming. A lot of people are saved, and have boats. Others are drunk and playing in the water, while still others are scared and running. My dog and I find a boat nearby and walk aboard. We keep walking and notice we have walked right off of the deck of the boat to a boardwalk on the other side. I find an Indian-run supermarket, and the dog and I go inside. Two women are extremely happy to see me. There is someone there named Jesse that I never get to see, but know he is there. The two women hand me lots of yellow items: blankets, silks, and flowers, and lay me down on a table in the store. They are smiling and rejoicing I am there. One woman hovers her hands over my face and a dot appears in the middle of my forehead. She smiles and says, "There is so much creativity, joy, and peace in there…you just need to find it." She moves to my feet and shows me lines on the soles of my feet, laughing how I don't understand them. It looks like a foreign language I can't read, or a treasure map of some kind. One line she highlights with a ray of light and it says 6xauthor; she shows me just that one for now. She moves back to my head and removes a thick fog with her fingertips. I cry out because I think for some reason she is removing God. She assures me she is taking out the fog, not the God. The price for the session they gave me is $17, and again I don't have the money. The man behind the counter says, "I already ran your card, silly. With all the times you have been here, we just put it on your father's tab." I look and see the name on the receipt is David, and though I know I have no money to pay them, I inform them of the error. The man still insists that it is paid for and tells me to stop worrying about money, and that he is praying for me to do that. I leave the shop with a little Indian girl instead of my dog and we go on our way as the water begins to recede.

I woke up and began to pray. I'm not sure why. I felt scared, as if someone took God away from me, and I needed to let him or her know that I need him back. I asked for clarity and purpose. I said I am sorry to Jesus…as if he is offended I have been searching all religions for the right way to "God," and then asked that he never leave me. I fell back to sleep with my hands folded tightly, and wondered if I will ever just have a good night's sleep.

July 21, 2013: The Book of Mormon

If you ever wondered why it is that the Earth is overpopulated, I will tell you now, the answer lies within the Mormon Church. There are about six babies to every one person, and the choir in this church is that of wailing children. I am still reading the Book of Mormon, and have not yet reached the part about unprotected sex, multiple children, or caffeine limitations, but I plan on fully understanding how all of these are justified.

I had a tough time researching which place to go to for Mormon Church, and discovered that there is a difference between temples and meeting houses. The temples are for those who are members of the church and in good standing (not sure what this means yet), and the meeting houses are for everyone. I am a little bummed about that, because the temples are absolutely breathtaking and the meeting houses are…just meeting houses.

I chugged my coffee before entering, and made my way inside. There was a blank room with no furniture, just a stage, red curtain, and picture of Jesus. It felt a little creepy because the lights were off. I decided to follow the music to where I thought the service would be. As I got closer to the soft music I discovered its source was a room of children. I decided not to turn in here and instead continue down the corridor to the next room that had voices coming from it. I turned in and found myself the only woman in a room of seated men. Awkwardly, I smiled and backtracked to the hallway. I was followed out by a nice older man in a black suit, and he ushered me down the hall to the women's service. I am not sure why men and women are separated, but they are.

As a fresh face I stuck out like a sore thumb. I decided to sit in the back, but much like the Jewish service I ended up sitting by one of the leaders of the church. She wore a heart-shaped necklace with the word "mom" in the middle and gave me a book to keep called *Teachings of Presidents of the Church: Lorenzo Snow*. She also had a handwritten card with her that she read aloud to the group. The card talked about how it is important to keep an open heart and you will get something meaningful out of each service. She also made sure to point me to the right people after the service, and made sure that I felt welcomed and comfortable.

They had three different sessions today. The first was separating the women and the men into individual worship groups. The women related different scriptures in the book to that of hardships in their lives and getting through tough times. The lesson: things are not always done the way we would like. We must have faith and let God's will guide our lives. Some women related this to losing a job and coping, and others to how their husbands sometimes do the laundry and fold the towels the wrong way, but they can't control that, and they should be thankful it was done at all. Each woman had a different way of relating to the lesson, and everyone talked about how that specific lesson applied to their lives. Myself, I thought about how I had ended up in all of these places and much like them, was just trying to let go, and have faith that it would all be all right. Is it this shit economy that has so many people turning to the "have faith in God he has a plan for you" view of life, or has it always been this way?

I liked how interactive the first breakout group was, and how everyone acknowledged all points of view. There was an older woman leading the service and she had on an old-looking colorful dress somewhat resembling the dresses my great-grandma used to wear in the '80s. Like my great-grandma, she also passed out chocolates to everyone she met. I wondered if everyone knew that chocolate has caffeine in it. Is there some kind of chocolate loophole somehow worked into the Book of Mormon? As all of the questions piled in my head I noticed my face had also warped into the puzzled expression giving away my outsider-ness. Four women all surrounded me and started firing away at the questions: where was I from, why was I there, where do I live, and was I going to the next session?

I honestly told them my story. Then I picked my head up to look upon the faces of the women around me. To my surprise, all of them were smiling. One of them said, "I am so glad you are here, and I really hope that you find what you are looking for. I think if you stay here long enough you will find we are good people and there are messages for everyone in each service." I thought about how there have been messages in every service, from every church, that I have visited so far that I really like, or at least take note of to reflect on later. So how am I to find one religion that "fits"? I do know that I love both caffeine and wine, and there are other things in my life I can sacrifice and be happy about giving up just the same if that is an option here.

They guided me to the next room down the hall where the men and women were joined. This session was a group service where we watched videos and listened to an elder read a few scriptures from the Book of Mormon. The videos reminded me a lot of the same videos from the Scientology church. They all showed happy people finding joy in things like dancing in the rain, laughter, and swinging on swings. There was no purchase pressure at the end or propaganda of any sort. Instead, a young man (who was an "elder") promptly flocked to my side and asked how he could help me, and what questions I had. Questions fired out at random like "Is the Book of Mormon different from the Bible? Who is Joe Smith? Why no caffeine? I notice there is water and not wine in the communion, why?" With all of the questions he decided it would be best to give me a book of my own to read. I accepted it and didn't tell him I already had a collection at home from the door knockers that have come around. He also set up a time for two or three people to come to my house to discuss questions I would have. He mentioned that it would most likely be two men and a woman; because of my gender it would be required for a woman to be present for this visit. The young elder had that awkward teen-ness to him and seemed almost like he may have had a crush on me. I was after all in a red velvet dress (Jessica Simpson), appropriate, maybe? Maybe not...the last time I wore this was on New Year's Eve. Nevertheless, he helped me from that point on.

After the videos concluded, all genders and ages migrated upstairs together. I was offered a second Book of Mormon by another "elder" that was probably half my age. He didn't see I already had one, and was really pumped up that I was accepting both the book and an appointment to have people stop by. I found it odd that he was that excited about life without caffeine. He made a very bold statement to me before we moved to the service upstairs, "This is the Book of Mormon, this is the true book of the Lord and you will find that after you read it. We are happy to have you join us." There was an awkward silence between me and the other four people left in the room. I didn't know what else to say except for thank you, and then headed for the door quickly.

The elder that had taken a liking to me asked if this was the longest I had ever spent in a church. I laughed and said, "You have no idea. I felt like I was in the Scientology church all day, but I think it was only two hours." He looked puzzled at why I would have been there in the first place, but didn't say a word about it. He sat quiet, proper, and at a closer distance than that of normal strangers. I wondered if he was envisioning us having twenty kids together, and scooted down the pew. There were so many screaming children in this service that I could barely focus on what was being said. From what I gather there were two young boys telling stories about their "pilgrimage." Apparently when boys and girls hit fifteen they are sent on a journey to a holy place. They said "Zion" but I am still not 100% sure where they really were. They were given tasks like cross a river holding hands with your group, and carry buckets of water from the bottom of the mountain to the top. The larger kid said he "overheated" so I am to assume they were somewhere other than Oregon, or he's just not in that good of shape. Regardless they got up and told the congregation of the journey they went on and the lessons they learned. Four to five additional people got up and shared stories about their individual pilgrimages and how they have become closer to God through scripture. Some of the stories seemed completely unrelated and just ended with some odd tie-in to the scripture.

I was growing irritated by the screaming herds of children and tried to find some sort of happy place where I could drown it all out. I'm sure that a Buddhist would have some life-changing insightful way of altering my thoughts in this predicament, but none were present. I took deep breaths, collected my thoughts, and remained open minded. The young boy next to me took this opportunity to ask me if I would like to set up a time to have the elders stop by and answer more of my questions. An appointment was set for the following Thursday at 3 p.m.

July 25, 2013: Meeting with Pastor Amy

Very few people I meet strike gold with me, and leave an impression quite like pastor Amy from the First Church of Christ. After meeting me very briefly at the Christian church I attended, she invited me out for coffee to learn more about my project. Amy had been up since 1:30 a.m. due to some kids setting off fireworks down the street, and since she couldn't fall back asleep she stayed up. At 3 a.m. she drove her husband to the airport, and at 5 a.m. she dropped her car off to the student that was staying with her and her family. Despite being up for nine hours, and it only being 10 a.m., she still had a glowing smile on her face and bounce in her step.

She didn't look like you would imagine a minister; she was pretty, young, fun, and had on a cute outfit and jewelry. Her wrists were stacked with what looked like wrapping prayer beads, and her fingers were graced by a combination of silver and obsidian rings with crosses both engraved and voided from the bands.

We casually walked to the coffee shop down the street, and took a seat outside. She seemed to brighten every person's day she came in contact with through genuine, kind conversation. Even the already perky baristas seemed happier just by talking with her. After we had our coffees and she had finished telling me about her quite hectic morning she said, "Okay, Stacey, now tell me about you." I corrected her and said, actually, that's not my name, but oddly enough when I was baptized the minister called me Stacey too…so I always wondered if it really counted. She felt so bad, and buried her face in her hands, raising it back up to show how tired she really was. She laughed and said, "See! It's God's fault! Just kidding, it's been a long morning!"

Holding back no details for oddness, I began telling her about my dreams and how I felt like my grandpa had appeared to me in a series to help prepare me for the day when he would come for my mom. I believed he had shown me indescribable beauty that was on the other side of the bridge and that when the time was right, my mom would no longer be in the picture with me, and instead would be in this place with him. I glanced up at Amy to see what kind of face she was making in response to this story, but there was only simple listening and compassion as she began to tear up a bit.

I told her about my mom and how she loved hummingbirds, and when I had knee surgery I was alone without anyone to take care of me. The odd thing, I said, is that a hummingbird kept coming to my window to look in; odd because it was a rainy November week and I lived on the tenth floor of a high-rise building. Without hesitation Amy said, "Well that was your mom!" That's what is so confusing to me, and I have trouble with what lines cross between religions, and that perspective seems to line up with Hindu or Buddhist beliefs doesn't it? What came next from her was the best way of responding to my complex mash-up of beliefs, "God is God, and no one religion can own him, or put him in a corner. God is all around us, and there is so much beauty if we open our eyes, we can catch a glimpse of its entirety." She made an Indiana Jones reference, you know, the part where the men see the face of God and their faces melt off. She said God is literally that magnificent that if we were to ever look face to face with him that we would be so overtaken we would melt into his glory. A bit different than good old Indiana Jones, but I get it.

Next, I asked her how or when she decided to become a minister. As it turns out, Amy's husband, Christian…the Buddhist author…inspired her. She was raised among a family of love and encouragement, and by ministers. Her husband had quite a different story. He was a questioning boy in Bible school who pushed the limit with too many questions; one day a teacher threw the Bible at his head and told him to get out, so he did, and never came back. Together Amy and her husband decided to found a church in a small home in Colorado for those who had been wronged by the church. As time passed the group outgrew the home, and they acquired an actual church. She led that church for a while, and then Amy's mentor saw an opening in Portland for a minister. Without her knowledge, her mentor submitted her for the position. She said she didn't want it and honestly thought that being a minister wasn't for her. She ended up going in for the first interview, and then the second, and finally found herself here in Portland. "I always tried to resist it, but God always won," she laughingly said as she looked to the sky.

She insisted we go back to me, and so we began talking about where I have had so many questions…scripture. Don't get me wrong, I do believe in Jesus, he even showed up to my Reiki session (story followed) but really, I find more comfort and coherence in Buddhism. Amy smiled and said that for the most part people can deduce just about any meaning from scripture. Some people have tried to say that slavery is supported in the Bible, but again she always asks, "Is it loving, is it life giving, and is it kind?" Slavery is none of those things. I said that I've deduced a lot of great meaning in most of the Sunday services I have attended, and despite not fitting with each religion, I have felt closer to God week over week. She also added that if you look closely at the Bible there is a chunk of Jesus's life this is not documented from age 12 to 30. Some scholars believe that in that span of time the Three Wise Men had come back for him and he left with them to study Buddhism and enlightenment. So if I was wondering if there is such a thing as a Buddhist Jesus, yes, there is.

She had me tell her more about my dreams, and more about the impressions the other churches had left. We began with Scientology and how they tried to force me to pledge my faith to them on a contract after only a few hours there. No need to explain anything further. I described my recent encounter with the Mormons, and she suggested I go see the Southpark-created play *The Book of Mormon*. It was so nice to have a candid conversation with someone about everything I had been doing. I said I didn't really jive with the whole no caffeine, no wine, no women, unkind to black people thing. She laughed and just said, "I grew up with a lot of Mormons, nice people, super nice people, but weird people." Not in the "keep Portland weird" way either!

Then there was a pause and she glanced over at me like she was about to tell me I had food on my face or that my hair needed to be fixed. Then she said, "You're a mystic." I didn't know what that was…an adjective? Verb? New religion? She said, "It's an ancient term that dates back to Greek times of Goddesses. Mystics are very in tune with intuition, feminine nature, dreams, and feeling things before they happen. Most mystics long to connect with God or discover an intimate connection…though most have a hard time nailing it down to one and just remain spiritual beings." That just about summed it up! I went home and looked it up and there it was, almost word for word what she had said with an addition: see Wiccan.

My friend Jan said she used to be Wiccan and not to dabble in that. She also said she did a spell to find a man with a big penis, and days later she could barely walk. I'm not really interested in penis spells, dances, or rituals but I suppose going to church every Sunday is a ritual, so maybe I should be more open to what Wiccans have to offer.

Amy and I finished our coffee and headed back to the church. Along the way a homeless man approached us and asked if we had money for food. I remained silent as I waited to see what the holy one would do. Without hesitation she said, "I have plenty of food, follow me back to the church!" She made sandwiches and then some for the man and his pregnant wife. She truly did care about helping every living thing she came in contact with.

Before I left she guided me up to the church library and had a few books she was going to give me, but couldn't find. We searched for about twenty minutes and she said, "Oh yeah! You're an author, what's your book about?" I cringed as I spilled the beans and told her the first book I published was an illustrated book about private parts. She laughed and without delay asked if I had an extra copy she could borrow. I felt so awkward handing her a copy of it while standing in the church library! It was too late; the handoff was made. She walked me out, gave me a hug, and sent me on my way.

Mormon Part 2

It was a muggy, 85-degree, Wednesday evening. I had just gotten out of the shower and put on a very light skirt and bra top to wear around the house, and then there was a knock at the door. Standing outside, at 8 p.m., were two teenage boys in matching outfits. What were the odds of another group of Mormons finding my apartment in the maze of 600 tenants in this complex, or are the Mormons not good with calendars? Their demeanor was very serious and questioning. They looked me up and down and asked if they had the right house or not. I told them they had the right house, wrong day, wrong time (given that we had agreed on Thursday at 3 p.m.). They both seemed awkwardly frazzled and very suspicious about my intentions with the meeting in the first place.

First, they asked me what meeting house I had gone to. I didn't remember the name of it, or even the street it was on, but just said that it was about five minutes away from here and in the Southeast. They both remained emotionless and stern. They then asked what business I had there, and why I was looking to have a meeting with them. As the judgmental questions began awkwardly stammering from the two teenage boys' mouths, I noticed myself crossing my arms and becoming a tad defensive. I felt like they were insinuating that I had no business meeting with them or learning about "their" God, and when I said I had been searching for a fitting religion for the past six months they looked at me like you would look at a stripper applying for a nanny position. Instead of adopting a defensive tone, or mentally pointing out how their ties were too short for their stupid white shirts, I decided to just invite them in.

This too was out of line because "a man wasn't home." They said it is just a rule that a man needs to be home if they were to come into my house. I said there wouldn't be one here today or tomorrow, so if they would like to carry on this conversation with me that they should either send a woman or change the rules. They said they would come back tomorrow and they would be bringing another man with them, so three men is all right, but not two? That seems a bit off, but fine.

Immediately after they left I felt both angry and offended. How is it that people who preach about being "holy" and kind can intentionally pass so much judgment on others that they don't even know? I sat down in my normal oversized writing chair, and as the words surged to the pages I began to just feel sorry for them. I wonder if they misinterpreted the term "written in stone" (stupid attempt at gold plate joke) at some point and now believe there is no other way than their book. How can people honestly think that their religion is the only correct one, and not have any open mindedness for others? Don't they realize that there were other religions created before theirs and that other people aren't passing such harsh judgments on them (other than me right now). Trying to "convert" someone and tell them that their belief systems are wrong is not something that I imagine God intended religion to support. There have been enough wars and downfalls of societies over religion; isn't it time that people just adopt the basic principles of humanity and just be kind to each other? (End paragraph with exhale and punch to question mark key.)

I have been reading out of my Book of Mormon every night since it was given to me and have a bit of questioning to add to tomorrow's discussion. The beginning of the book states that the founder, Joseph Smith, was on a search for the right religion much like me. When I read that, I had so much hope for what was to follow. I thought, maybe this man was a lot like me, and this religion is something that I will be able to relate with. The next line destroyed that hope, "Then God spoke to him and told Joseph not to join any of the churches, for they are all wrong, and they draw near to me with their lips but their hearts are far from me, they teach for doctrines and commandments of men, having a form of godliness, but they deny the power thereof" (Joseph Smith – History 1:19).

I am not writing this book to find flaws in any religions, but rather to find one that is for me, and fits with my nature and spirituality. I find that the word faith has a different meaning to Mormons than it does to a majority of other people. Faith, to me, is believing in something without logical proof or supporting evidence. Faith is something that differs from one person to the next. I have faith that my mother is still alive in the "spirit world"; do I know this for a fact, no, but I have so much faith based on dreams and other occurrences that support my beliefs. Mormons are not allowed to question their religion, and faith to them has a different meaning, and becomes something unquestionable, like having tunnel vision though you see there are gardens on each side of you. In this example the gardens die from lack of sunlight, and somehow it is justified. To me, I will not find a home within Mormon principles. I will never look down on someone else's faith or question their spirituality. I believe that people can find light in their own ways. A wise woman once said, "God is so magnificent and everywhere, who are we to try to corner that and label it our own" (Minister Amy).

The next day at the appropriate time, two boys showed up again in what looked like the same clothes from the day before. I wondered if their closets were as boring as their meeting houses. I invited them in with slight hesitation, and reminded myself to stop watching so many vampire movies. They asked again if a man was home, and again, I said no. I suppose I wasn't a good listener at sixteen either, but still I was annoyed they kept stopping by my house and not doing anything but stand there and be awkward. They said, "Well, we'll have to reschedule then." I asked them why the rule of a ratio of men to women applies. They explained that in the past Mormons had been falsely accused of sexual crimes, so they would rather not come in if a man wasn't home. I made a cringed awkward that's-odd face, and said, "Well, why then would you reschedule to come back and bring a third male with you? Wouldn't it be worse to be raped by three men instead of two? Is there a rule about that in your book?"

Void of laughter, the boys decided to reschedule my lesson for August 4. This time four boys showed up, and opened the lesson with a prayer. They also made me turn off *Shark Week* as it posed a distraction. I poured waters for everyone as they made themselves at home in my living room. I will admit that part of me really thought about swapping out the waters for *sake* and seeing what would happen. They thanked me for allowing them to meet with me, and asked me if I knew about Jesus Christ and more so, what my relationship with God is like. I replied, I have visited a variety of churches over the past six months and all of them worship "God" in different beautiful ways. I find that God and I have a strong relationship, and when I go to bed at night, I still say prayers and give thanks for blessings. I think that a lot of people have taken the Bible and try to comprehend it, and make sense of God or call him/her theirs, or corner him into a "correct" religion. I don't do that, and I think that would be a mistake on my part to do so. I read your book, and I think that it is so discomforting to see in writing that someone claimed their religion is the only way. He clearly hadn't seen all the others. If he had, he would know that God is everywhere, not just in one corner every Sunday.

There were blank stares on their faces, and then they all began flipping through their books in search of scriptures to read me. I said, I met with a pastor and she opened my eyes to the fact that scripture can be interpreted in many ways, to all people, based on where you are at in your life. Some people have even tried to justify slavery from scripture. I told the story of the years from 12 to 30 where Amy said Jesus may have studied Enlightenment and Buddhism, and that is also up to interpretation. I asked if they were all raised Mormon or if they had found it on their own. All were raised that way, and one of them said he left for a period of his life when his brother passed away and went to Hindu temples. The others looked at him surprised, like he just said he had a third leg and they never noticed before. He said he had questioned where he was supposed to be in life, and if God was real or not. He wondered if God was just energy and not a male or female being. I said, well that's very Buddhist of you. He said that he really finds that without questions there are never answers, and that on the anniversary of his brother's death, two missionaries showed up at his door and he decided he was going to join the church again. I believe that there are no coincidences and that maybe he did all that so that he could add to this conversation, or maybe he needed to learn more than he was taught as a kid, maybe both. Wait...aren't Mormons taught not to question their faith? They said that they were taught to question everything. I didn't reply with more than a "hmmmm," but that is not what their book teaches.

I then asked, if you follow the Bible and your founder was just a prophet of God, why not just continue on following the Bible and remain Christian? They said that in a way they are Christian, and that they are sure that there is proof that this is the only way. The ex-Hindu remained quiet for most of this talk. They jumped around a bit, and even at one point said that this book was just made to teach based on Geography. Questioning, I said, well that seems very arrogant to think there was a religion created just for Americans. That's probably why other countries dislike us. They took this back, and said, well, here's an example instead. Picture a glass table, held up by thirteen legs. Each leg represents a disciple of God. One by one when the disciples were killed for their teachings, the table grew unstable. Eventually what do you think happened to the table? I said, the glass shattered and people tried to pick it up and make sense of it. One of them said, "Okay, here's where it gets simple, turn to Ephesians 4:5; it says 'One Lord, one faith, one baptism.'"

As scripture can be interpreted by everyone differently, this one had been misinterpreted. In my eyes I think that this means there is one God, for everyone, no matter how you chose to worship him or her, it is just One. To them, they think this means that this book is the only way, and that all others are wrong. They said that it is very black and white in this regard.

Speaking of, what are your thoughts on black people? I asked. I heard that Mormons don't like black people, or women, or homosexuals for that matter. They all looked at each other to answer the questions. One of them said his best friend is gay, but he doesn't think that he represents what the Bible stands for and the meaning of family comes from a man and a woman. I highly disagree with him and make him aware that family can be any gender, age, or color, and what the Bible stands for is love, not judging. Of the few stories in the Bible I do know, there is one where there are little kids trying to get closer to Jesus, and his disciples are shielding him from all the kids because he is so holy. He tells the disciples that if he shields even one person from getting closer to him that they may as well put a boulder on their feet and head for the river. That's the problem, that people took the pieces of glass and cut their own ways that they labeled holy, but missed the thousand other pieces that help make sense of the entire thing.

They asked me if I knew what a prophet was. I explained my definition as what it means to me, and my interpretation is different to me than it is to others. Just like my beliefs on homosexuals and women, but I digress. I believe a prophet is someone who has been touched by the light of God and spreads the word of love and God to the world. Am I a prophet, no. I am just a person on a journey trying to connect with God, and find a faith I can incorporate into my life day to day. Was Joseph Smith a prophet? Maybe. Were there gold plates with the Book of Mormon written in every language on them in New York that disappeared after they were read? Maybe. That would be a lot of gold if it was written in every language, and would also not make sense if it was only written for the Western world.

They asked if I had any other questions for them and knew that I would keep coming back to the initial unanswered question, "Isn't God love? I just don't agree with the idea of there being just one correct religion; if everyone believes in God, how you can say that is wrong?" So we moved on to the other questions I had:

Question: Why does the Bible only mention Heaven and Hell but Mormons believe in three kingdoms? They said that we can discuss this another time, but Celestial means not of this Earth. (I know what celestial means, but why separate it from heaven?) They said I had to set up another session with them to discuss this topic.

Question: Why do you not drink caffeine but eat chocolate? They said that the body is a temple and that most Mormons know that caffeine is addictive and don't consume it. Others drink it and eat it. It is not a rule that is set in stone. (Or gold.)

Question: Blood atonement? If the Bible says thou shalt not kill, and only God will judge us for our sins, how is it that a man can shed the blood of someone that they believe is a sinner and that is justified by your religion? Part B: If killing is justified, then why not homosexuality? They said that there are websites out there that say Mormons believe in blood atonement, but it is written nowhere in their book. They also said that killing is not justified. They still do not support homosexuals, even if the homosexuals believe in God. This conversation could go south quickly, as I support human rights for everyone, and think it is wrong to pass judgment based on a book that preaches doing good. So we move on to my next question.

Question: Explain polygamy, and why women can't do the same? Well…back in the 1800s men supported everyone in their family with hard labor and trade work. Women often relied on the men to supply for them. There were so many women that often times men would marry multiple women to help support them.

Question: Now that times have changed, why are men still marrying multiple women? For example, nowadays I make more money than most men I meet, so the need to be taken care of doesn't exist in the modern world. They said in their church family comes first, and no one in this church here is married to multiple people. That may be the case in other churches.

Question: What advice would you give to someone who believes in God but has not found a religion yet? We suggest reading the Book of Mormon and praying before you read it so that you can really understand its meaning. We also think that you have been doing a lot of research and that we can't tell you what to believe. Only you can find what works for you.

Final Question: I heard there is an "underwear suit" – what is the meaning of this? Well after we complete our mission we are given a suit to put on every day under our clothes. It's not "magical" or anything like you suggest. It just reminds us to be men of God every day and live our lives that way. I asked if they ever thought about just wearing a cross necklace or something besides a full-blown undergarment, but they said it is just their religious ritual.

So, it seems the Mormons have their rituals just like the Pagans, Christians, and every other religion. I think it's funny how they can wear underwear suits as a ritual and not think that's odd, but criticize homosexuals for simply loving others of the same sex.

After hearing what they had to say I reflected back on the simple meeting house void of murals, stained glass, carvings, crosses, or candles. The explanation was that they don't like to picture Jesus "hung on a cross and suffering"; instead they like to envision him alive and living in all of us. They also left me with a post-it note with a passage to read: Alma Chapter 32 p. 288. After they left I read the suggested chapter and at first thought they were insinuating I was poor, haggard, and void of faith like the example in the book. Then

I read forth and found new meaning in the passage. It seems the person in this passage was so poor that they were not allowed in any synagogues, and so they grew weary. Then they found that it was a good thing they weren't allowed in because they ended up finding something far better. In this chapter the person speaks of a seed of faith that became planted in his chest. With nourishment and light the seed continued to grow, and eventually turned into the tree of knowledge and eternal light.

This was actually the best thing I learned from this experience. I felt exactly like the person that was different and not allowed in the churches, but then found that you don't need to be in a church to find God. Also the visual of the seed already being within us and only needing nourishment and light to grow into a tree of enlightenment teaches what I already agree with. Though, I am not sure if they read that same story and gathered the same meaning.

August 3, 2013: Pagan

Today I'm having coffee with a Pagan woman by the name of Sorcha that I connected with through a website called "Pagans of Portlandia." She said that she is a witch *and* a Pagan, and she can also talk to me about Wiccan beliefs. There really aren't any places that they all go to or worship, whatever it is that they worship, so I joined this group online and posted on their page. Sorcha, the leader of the group, kindly responded that she would be more than happy to meet with me for either a pint or coffee to talk. To avoid asking questions like "are your tits really cold?" I decided coffee would be best.

Her profile says she has been a practicing Pagan for over fifty years, so I am wondering how old this person is that I'm meeting today. We arranged to meet at a good, dog-friendly, outdoor coffee shop in Sellwood, but it turned out there was only one dog-friendly table there, so we looked for another place to meet. Two days prior to our meeting I went down to my favorite gem store (it's Portland) and picked up a baby sage and a black Obsidian necklace. Since I have been wearing the necklace I've been lightheaded and dizzy. I'm not sure why. Obsidian is said to (to name a few):

> expose flaws weakness and blockages needing to be released, dissolves destructive or self-sabotaging behavior, heals past lives and emotional trauma on a deep soul level, protects from negativity, grounds you from the base, strengthens, blocks psychic attack, blocks geopathic stress and pollution, spiritual integrity,

anchors the spirit into the body, growth and exploration, clears confusion and constricting beliefs leaving clarity, absorbs anger, expands consciousness with confidence and ease, helps you know who you are while integrating your shadow characteristics, aids compassion, insight to cause of disease and healing (www.consciousjewelry.com).

The word Pagan makes me think of negative things, unfortunately. Though I know nothing of what their beliefs are, I somehow think of spells, evil, some sort of ram-horned thing, and the devil. This woman may be nothing like that, and here I am shallowly thinking back to movies like *The Craft* and picturing her yanking a piece of my hair out over coffee for a spell later. Over email conversations she seems funny, nice, and open to giving information to help clear up questions I have. She even made a pointy hat and broom joke, so she can't be too bad. Sorcha did say that she loves theological discussions, and is quite interested in what I'm writing. Also, one of her favorite hobbies is debating with fundamentalist Christians. I don't want this conversation to be debating with me about religion, and swaying me one way or another, but rather an informational discussion about her beliefs.

Sorcha picked a place called the Pied Cow to meet; it's a hookah bar with eclectic decorations both inside and out. The patio has a gravel floor, iron and wood benches, curtains draped from the trees, mirrors, and fountains throughout. I ordered a lavender steamer and sat there anxiously waiting, wondering if I had made a mistake dabbling with someone who calls herself a witch. After all witch is not a religion, but Pagan is, so I assured myself to relax and this would be educational. To calm my mind, I took out a book from my purse called *The Tao of Pooh*, a simple charming book that explains Taoism to Winnie the Pooh. I began where I left off, "sooner or later we are bound to find out things about ourselves we don't like, but once we see they're there we can decide what to do with them." What wise words for such a simple bear.

I heard the paws of a dog approaching as I saw feet shuffle through the piney walkway. A woman with long auburn hair and fair skin sat down at a table near the entrance and began looking around. I walked over slowly and said "Sorcha?" It was indeed. Sorcha didn't look "craft-like" at all; in fact she was a kind-eyed, fifty-something (I think) with Scottish traits and a kind smile. She had on Birkenstocks, jeans, and a small purple blouse. Her jewelry consisted of beads, moons, silver, and ivory – all meaningful to her in regards to her own faith. The moons represent the cycles of energy and seasons, and the bone…well that was carved into the shape of a moon as well (possibly because bone is permanent). She ordered a small honey wine and salmon plate that she shared with her large schnauzer, Mojo.

I don't know if I will do this woman justice explaining her in this story, she is wise beyond her years (tbd), and the two hours we spent together filled up a huge portion of my notebook. I didn't ask what she did, but instead began with my story and how I found my way to her. We dove headfirst into the nitty-gritty of witches and Pagans. Sorcha said she actually was a witch before she was ever a Wiccan or Pagan. She used to be a Wiccan but found it was not for her, and offered to introduce me to a practicing Wiccan if I would like. While many Pagans view their religion as secretive and typically don't discuss it with others, Sorcha likes to help others and answer questions for those interested in learning more about her religion.

She was quick to add, "But we don't proselytize, we just like to clarify misconceptions." Like Christianity, there are hundreds of sects of Pagan as well. Sorcha is a Celtic Pagan, but she said she speaks only for herself, and not for all Celtic Pagans. I reiterated my lack of knowledge on the matter and she went on to explain. "Pagan is an umbrella term; not all Witches are Pagans, and not all Pagans are Witches. Wicca is a denomination of Paganism, and they usually refer to themselves as Witches, but not all Witches are Wiccans. Clear as mud, isn't it?"

In 1954 witch laws were repealed and people were able to openly practice witchcraft in England. Sorcha had a bit of a different upbringing than most. She recalls her mother taking her at the age of five to see ghosts walking on the rooftops of buildings on foggy nights, although now her mother says, "That was just a woman walking around in her nightgown." As a small child, people, typically older women, would look at her walking down the sidewalk and tell her mother, "there's something special about that one." She said, it was actually pretty scary but as she grew older she realized that she could take negative energy or feelings of anger and turn it into something good. I interrupted the story and asked if she was referring to good spells.

> Take for example, that one is angry about something, one harbors all of this energy in response to a situation. What one chooses to do with the energy and feelings from the situation is up to that person, not only this situation, but everything that is encountered in life. You take that energy, hold onto it, and cast that out into the world at another time for something good. There is one rule that many Pagans follow: Never cause unnecessary

harm to yourself or others. So you can store energy and cast it out for good at a later time in life.

I urged her to go back to when she was a child; I wanted to hear more about seeing ghosts on rooftops and partaking in rituals. We didn't talk much more about that, but only that other religions have rituals they follow, and that she was exposed to different rituals as a kid. At age sixteen she heard Celtic music for the first time and was so deeply moved that it filled her soul with indescribable joy that she compared it to how people who are invigorated from religion must feel. Speaking of which, I added, "Christians have the Bible, do you...have a book you follow or believe in?" "We don't need a book to show us the reality of our path," Sorcha explained:

> You don't need a book or faith to see the beauty of nature, or the cycle of the seasons; they're tangible; they're all around us; they're part of us. We are part of them. We believe that everything in the world is connected. Many Pagans are Pantheists, and believe that God/Goddess is an infinite "Force" that is immanent in all of us, animals, plants, all of nature, all of Earth. So, God/Goddess is part of us, and we are part of them.

Native Americans believe in these principles as well, and there is a famous response in regards to "our book," Sorcha quoted, "If you take the Christian bible and put it out in the wind and the rain, soon the paper on which the words are printed will disintegrate and the words will be gone. Our bible IS the wind and the rain" (Herbalist Carol McGrath as told to her by a Native-American woman). I thought what Sorcha described was very Buddhist, and she told me that every religion that is not Jewish, Christian, or Muslim is technically considered "pagan" with a lower-case "p." How-so? "That's just the dictionary definition. Pagans, like me, with an upper-case P, are part of a diverse group of faiths that are usually earth-centered, believe in Gods, Goddesses, and believe in self-responsibility, not in being forgiven for sins." I pondered a bit and saw how that fit with Hindu and Buddhist, shrugged and continued on the conversation.

> Did you know, there is a garden in Scotland, called Findhorn, which grows in a salty sand dune, because they utilize elemental energy? The owner of this garden had a vision, and started a garden where she meditated every day and focused on the blueprint of the land. There are plants that grow in this garden that are not supposed to be able to grow in Scotland, and certainly not in a salty sand dune.

So, it seems, Sorcha was a witch before she was a Pagan. Maybe a bit of what we are taught as children imprints in our minds, even if it does become morphed by our own encounters as we grow older. I asked her when she discovered that she wanted to be a Pagan over any other religion to choose from, and she smiled and reflected back to when she was a kid at the doctor's office. She picked up a kids' encyclopedia, and read about Roman Gods and Goddess, about Venus in particular. Sorcha was so excited that there was a female God, she instantly began studying the Goddess, and then found a religion that recognized Goddesses. Many Pagans perceive the Goddess as a triple deity of Maiden, Mother, and Crone.

> Did you know that the biblical God had a wife at one time? It was edited out of the current version of the Bible, but her name is Asherah. There is a lot of ancient text actually in the book of Kings, it speaks of Asherah and Yahweh/YHWH (which is the biblical God) being worshiped as a pair. Also pushed out of the Bible was the story of Lilith, Adam's first wife. Lilith was banished and demonized because she refused to be submissive. Did you know that?

No, didn't know that, I said. "Uppity women often get demonized by male chauvinists." She also added that people often think that they are born of sin, but she disagrees with this as well.

> When confronted by bible-waving evangelicals, I tell them I have no need to be saved because I am not subject to their concept of "original sin." Not being of Semitic blood, I am one of the "Other People." [Oberon Zell came up with this concept.] In the biblical book Genesis, it tells of Cain being banished for the murder of Abel, after which he was sent "East of Eden," out of the sight of the Lord, and he goes east – that's what it says in Genesis, anyway – and ends up in "The Land of Nod." In the very next paragraph, he has a wife. Apparently, Cain's new wife came from the Land of Nod, from the "other people" not descended from Adam and Eve. This does help alleviate the awkward "incestuous" answers to "Who did Cain marry to have babies?" So, even in the Bible, it allows that there were people outside of Eden, who are not descended from Eve, so therefore, we are not subject to original sin, so

we don't need to be saved. I don't really care what the Bible says, it's not my book, but it's a great discussion point with people who DO believe in the Bible.

I had never had discussions like this before, actually, when people like Jehovah's Witnesses came by the door, I remember my parents telling us to shut off the lights and close the blinds.

"I think I know why," she said. "I've had a lot of conversations with Jehovah's Witnesses – nice people, I like them. As you know, they go around door to door, well prepared for debate with a list of questions, and try to convince you to join their church. I often invite them in my house." She chuckles.

> My house looks like the cover of *Better Homes and Cauldrons*. Anyway, the JWs have their list of questions, and are prepared for the answers that normally follow. A lot of people don't question the religion they're brought up in, and so they certainly don't want to be questioned about spiritual matters when they aren't prepared to answer. That's why they hide, or slam the door on JWs. I think about spirituality a LOT, so I am always prepared to respond. They don't come to visit me much these days.

She tries to fake a frown, but it's clear she finds it amusing. "A lot of people don't even know where their important holidays originate. For example, do you know where the name 'Easter' comes from?"

Well, I said, I imagine it is related to a saint or something and relates to Jesus rising from the tomb and back to life after three days? I felt foolish for not knowing more, but I didn't.

"Don't worry about it," she said, "I've never actually encountered any Christian who knew: The word 'Easter' comes from the Anglo Saxon Goddess of Spring, Eostre. She represents fertility and rebirth – so that's where the bunnies and eggs come from. Spring is when the Earth is resurrected after winter, so it also would make sense that it would correlate with Jesus rising from the tomb." She went on to explain how all Pagan holidays focus on cycles of nature. There are several that relate to the common holidays in other religions. Sorcha's views on what people have done to religion is something that seemed quite similar to what Pastor Amy had said. Sorcha pointed out, "Christians and several others form beliefs about the Bible (which by the way is a lot of men just betraying each other), then they try to compartmentalize what is right, wrong, male, female instead of just living by the simple lessons taught." Sorcha added, "People do this so they can try to understand what infinity is, because God/Goddess is infinite; and the infinite is almost impossible to comprehend."

Then I realized that Sorcha wasn't a God-hating or Christian-hating woman. She was a peaceful, centered, spiritual, Goddess-loving woman, who just hated people trying to label God, or Goddess in her case, as "theirs," and was tired of them trying to make everyone conform to Christian rules. "You see, many Pagans feel everything is all connected. Most of us don't have a problem with Jesus' teachings (though we don't like the dogma from 'churchianity.') His Golden Rule is much like, "don't cause unnecessary harm."

I noted how Buddhist of her that statement was, and she told me, for what it's worth, that she has Buddha statues all over her house. Q'uan Yin is one of her favorites because She is a Goddess of Compassion who helps you even if you don't believe in Her.

I felt like she had an answer for everything I had misjudged about her, so…I asked about black cats. Of course, Sorcha has a black cat, but she also has a black and white cat, and a Schnauzer. Wouldn't you know, that America is the only place in the world where black cats are deemed as bad luck, and actually in England they are considered good luck. Of course. And broomsticks??? She has several. They hang over her doors and are symbols of sweeping out bad energy, and help keep a clean house! Well, what about witches flying on brooms then??

"Back in the Middle Ages there were a lot of hallucinogenic herbs used in 'Witches' Potions.' Witches used to anoint their broomsticks with these herbs, ride them in a ritual, and the herbs gave the sensation of flying. At least that's the explanation I've heard; I have no empirical knowledge of that particular method of flying."

Hallucinogenic drugs? So now I'm confused on the differences between Pagans and hippies! Again, an answer, "There is a lot of overlap. Hippies think outside the box, Pagans live outside the box, and both groups are full of environmentalists who like to wear bohemian clothes."

I asked her to tell me more about the Pagan holidays so I could know what it was that was valued, celebrated, and even misinterpreted.

December 21st is Yule, a day celebrating the rebirth of the Sun God. Scientifically, this day is known as the Winter Solstice.

Solstice means "sun stands still," which it appears to do for about three days. "So, while you celebrate Christmas Eve, we're finishing our Yuletide celebrations." Around her house, Sorcha displays all the typical holiday trappings, there will even be a nativity scene present but in the center you will see a baby on a glowing golden sun image.

"So, we DO have a God – several actually, too many to get into here. The two main God archetypes are the Sun God, and the Horned God, who is not the devil (the Devil is a Christian concept and not part of our pantheon at all). Our Horned God is the spirit of Nature, and the spirit of Animals. His horns are usually actually antlers."

"February 1st is called Brigid, a fire festival which celebrates the beginning of the return of Spring, and honors Brigid, a Celtic Goddess of poetry, blacksmithing, arts and crafts, medicine, livestock, and spring. This holiday is also called Imbolc, which means something like "when the ewes lactate.""

"March 21 is the Spring Equinox, also known as Ostara. Spring is coming back strong now. We celebrate the rebirth of the Earth after the long winter. This holiday is rather like the Pagan version of the Christian Easter."

"May 1st is called Beltane (in some Pagan traditions, all the holidays have many names). The God and Goddess unite to give birth again to the Sun Child at Yule. Definitely a fertility festival, and many Pagans like to partake in their own fertility rituals, sometimes in the bushes. You will see lots of flowers and maypoles. Here in Portland we have a dance around a maypole at dawn, and Morris dancers do ancient British folk dances."

"Next is the holiday of Litha, or the Summer Solstice on 21st June. This holiday is exactly six months from Yule, which is the Winter Solstice."

"August 1st they celebrate Lughnassadh. Lugh is the Celtic God of the sun. It is then we also celebrate the first harvest festival. Lughnassadh is when the God is symbolically sacrificed (e.g., the grain harvested), only to be born again at Yule."

"September 21st, Pagans celebrate the Autumnal Equinox, also called Mabon, the second harvest festival."

"November 1st is Samhaim. This is the third harvest festival. People often think this is a day to worship ghosts but really it is a day to honor our beloved dead, rather like Memorial Day. Some people will even set an extra plate at the feasting table for their passed-on loved ones."

Speaking of the dead, I said, how do you view the afterlife if you don't believe in Heaven? "I believe in a Heaven, it's just different than the Christian concept. Whilst the Christian heaven may be full of streets paved with gold, harps, and Jesus, that wouldn't be my idea of Heaven. Mine has Celtic pubs, misty weather, a wild ocean, pints of really good beer and mead, excellent food, my friends, and pets, and never ending Celtic music. We Celtic Pagans call our heaven 'Tir na n'Og,' the land of youth; it's also called The Summerland." Pagans also believe that souls cycle back through reincarnation, after a time of R & R in Tir na n'Og. "Like a drop of rain returning to the ocean."

As we finished our honey wines and rounded up the conversation she pointed out that she liked my necklace. I gave a brief rundown of its purpose, and she laughed and gave one last bit of advice. "Just go hug a tree if you want to feel grounded mentally and spiritually, no need for stones, although they're lovely, and can certainly help with grounding."

I collected my things, and headed to the park to write under my favorite tree. There was no hugging involved, not today at least. I'm so thankful I sat down with her today and learned about her religion, and cleared up all of my misinterpretations of Pagans.

At this point in my journey, and after meeting people like Sorcha, I feel more connected with myself and my relationship with God. I've also removed God from my association of one religion to that that of many. I think that God is the same for all religions, just worshiped in many different ways, and I think that's rather beautiful. The idea that we try to create a male or female version of God so we can better understand "infinity" also is a present thought in my mind. I am starting to just believe that God is neither male nor female, and is a being of infinite love and light. If we want to worship this being as a male, that is fine, or a female, that is fine too.

August 10, 2013: Spirit Guided Friends Christian Spiritualist Church

This morning, I went to a church recommended by both Pastor Amy and Sorcha called Spirit Guided Friends Christian Spiritualist Church. The church is Christian, but focuses primarily on spirituality and a sound mind. They stress that spiritualism is a way of life that combines philosophy, science, and religion, and only through practice and studying can you begin to understand it in its entirety. They offer meditation sessions once a month and I happened to be attending one of those sessions today. Their website says they also have readers/mediums that can offer a message to those who wish to receive one at the end of the service.

I pulled up and parked behind a car with a bumper sticker that read, "Something wonderful is going to happen today." I looked around for a church, but found only a white two-story house with a wooden sign in the lawn with an angel faintly painted on it.

I walked up the sidewalk to the front porch and stopped with a halt. There was large spider web blocking the entrance to the house. After five minutes of maneuvering an awkward limbo around the web I made it inside and took a seat in the dimly lit living room. I could tell by slightly changed mannerisms that I was beginning to grow in a way: respecting other living creatures. Tracy of the past would have swatted that thing down and stepped on it.

Only natural light and candles lit the room, and inside sat a humble older man with a soft gray beard and kind eyes. I was early, and so we sat and talked until others came to join. There were about ten folding chairs arranged in a circle around the living room. At the head of the circle was a table cloaked in lavender silk with a picture resting on it of what looked like a person inside of a glass bottle, and a beacon of white light entering into the crown of his head from above that radiated out into the universe. Beside the table was a wooden piano with several pieces on it including a blue sapphire goblet, three candles, Native American statues, crystal angel figurines, and a picture of Jesus. There was a simple wooden cross nailed to the wall, and two other pictures of Jesus to the left and right. In the time we sat and talked, I learned that the leader of the session today had studied Eastern religion and world studies for over twenty years. He knew a lot about meditation practices, breathing techniques, and suggested a few books for me to read. He also gave me a freshly printed pamphlet that detailed the story of the Essenes, and how people began preparing their world for the coming of Jesus before he was even there. He wrote on the bottom the name of a book called *Bhagavad Gita* for me to read as well.

As others began filing in the room we faded out the conversation and began relaxing and preparing for the meditation session. Outside, it was a typical gray Oregon morning and the sound of light wind and soft rain remained constant throughout the session. He rang his Sangha bell and I began to soften my gaze and relax. This meditation is what is described as guided meditation, where the instructor gives you visuals to help guide you through relaxing, breathing, and calming. We began with relaxing each part of our body and slowing our breath. The breath was counted, one in one out, two in two out, and so on. After mentally picturing each part of my body relaxed individually one by one, there was a light that shone above my head. This light represents the light of God within me. It hovered above my head for the rest of the meditation, and I inhaled this light into each of my chakras one by one. After envisioning the light filling my head, throat, heart center, hips, and entire body, they all breathed together in one breath of light. The light was inhaled and exhaled, filling my body and cleansing out any negative thoughts or feelings. Then I envisioned the light of the Earth below me sparkling in crystals below my feet. The light surged down into the center of the planet, grounding me and reflecting in the stones, then shot back up through my body to the light above my head. I inhaled and exhaled this cycle several times and then I saw an egg. I don't know where the egg came from but I saw it, acknowledged it, and continued breathing. "Seeing" things is not really like seeing a physical entity. It's more like all of a sudden an image pops into your mind in supreme detail and once you acknowledge its presence it fades away.

Next, he guided us to visualize a lavender flame that represented cleansing, healing, and forgiveness. I inhaled the flame and slowly envisioned the nourishment and healing it offered and let it fill my body. I could see it surging purification into my soul and flushing light within me. We were then guided to send out this energy in the purest form of love to all beings in every direction. A dog barked in the distance and a car horn beeped. I didn't feel angry that my visual was disrupted, but instead acknowledged it happened and pictured the light above unmoved.

I had a very nice moment of stillness. I felt like my body was full of kindness and light, and then the bell rang. I thought I had only been there fifteen minutes, but it had been an hour. I opened my eyes and felt so dizzy I thought I was going to fall over. I looked at the ground and it looked as if it was moving. I promptly told the teacher how I felt, and he told me to put my feet flat on the floor and reground myself. He said sometimes in meditation we have such energy changes that we sometimes feel like we could just fly away, and anchoring our feet to the ground helps bring us back to Earth.

Everyone sat silent for a few minutes, and then he asked who would like to receive a message, and everyone smiled and was open to receiving one. When he came around to me he said:

> When I come into your vibration I really gather a lot here. Ever since you stepped into the room there was a female that was here, maybe a mother, she has long dark hair and is carrying a bundle of Easter lilies. I am not sure if this is your mother or not, but she has been here the whole time. I see this journey you are on and it is not unfamiliar to you; you have been on this for many lifetimes as a nun, a monk, and so on. That is why when you go to explore each of these religions you pick up on them quickly and gain the message from each. I do see that there is a light shining on you from above and that there is much to see inside you. You should focus on what's in the soul and you will learn much more there. I also see that you are very familiar with this feeling, and when you feel the light, take it in, and put it out all around you, and then…you will be surprised the great things that will happen.

Apparently he was not the only gifted one in the room, and message time was for others to share messages as well. A woman sitting across the circle from me said that she too had a message for me:

I see you are thinking about getting another tattoo and I suggest that you not be so quick to do so. Your tattoos are all in places where you have had fatal wounds in your past lives. You have a tattoo on your foot, right? [I do] That is where you were crucified and nailed to a cross and in a life before that a soldier stabbed you there when you were just a child. Though it seems you tattoo yourself after a hard time in your life, you are just sealing these wounds from past lives and keeping them on your body.

I had a dream a week ago where I was inside a house at Christmas time and my family was there inside preparing a great dinner. At the table sat my mom, Grandpa, Aunt Bobby, Great-Grandma, and two other dark-haired tan men, that looked like twins that I didn't know. All of the people inside the house at the table have passed on. My mom and I were preparing another chair at the table, and she was asking me for my help with something else that I told her I didn't have time to do because I had to wake up soon. Across the table my grandpa showed me a glass picture of both a horse and dragonfly, and I knew that from now on in dreams dragonflies are significant.

I have been seeing a lot of dragonflies lately. Yesterday I hiked six miles in the Columbia River Gorge to a place called Angel's Rest. At the top was a breathtaking view of tree tops, waterfalls, and the river below. While I sat there catching my breath and soaking in the view, three dragonflies kept flying by me, and I thought, how fitting that they would be all the way up here at Angel's Rest. I pondered getting another tattoo of a dragonfly just under my right arm on my side. Maybe I'll pass on that one.

I left there feeling calm and peaceful, and decided I would be coming back next week for the actual service. It was nice to be in a place that embodied spirituality and Christianity at the same time, though nothing was discussed today of Christianity. I will have to see what lessons next week has in store.

For the sake of interest in the meaning of the dark-haired woman with the bundle of Easter lilies, I did a bit of research on the origin of them. Here is what I found:

> The Easter lily: For many, the beautiful trumpet-shaped white flowers symbolizes purity, virtue, innocence, hope and life—the spiritual essence of Easter. (http://www.appleseeds.org/easter-lily.htm) (Possible correlation with egg vision)
>
> The pure white lily has long been closely associated with the Virgin Mary. In early paintings, the Angel Gabriel is pictured extending to the Virgin Mary a branch of pure white lilies, announcing that she is to be the mother of the Christ Child. In other paintings, saints are pictured bringing vases full of white lilies to Mary and the infant Jesus. St. Joseph is depicted holding a lily-branch in his hand, indicating that his wife Mary was a virgin.
> (http://www.appleseeds.org/easter-lily.htm)
>
> Since the beginning of time, lilies have played significant roles in allegorical tales concerning the sacrament of motherhood. Roman mythology links it to Juno, the queen of the gods. The story goes that while Juno was nursing her son Hercules, excess milk fell

from the sky. Although part of it remained above the earth (thus creating the group of stars known as the Milky Way), the remainder fell to the earth, creating lilies. Another tradition has it that the lily sprang from the repentant tears of Eve as she went forth from Paradise.
(http://www.appleseeds.org/easter-lily.htm)

I have been considering donating my eggs for money lately. It pays very well and seems like a fairly simple process. The other night I had such a terrible nightmare that I couldn't fall back asleep. In the dream there was a spinning hole in the middle of my bed, it was a circular, fuzzy, black and white static that kept spinning and trying to suck me in. I physically got out of my bed while still asleep and ran into my closet screaming. My boyfriend jumped out of bed trying to wake me up, and I kept screaming that someone was grabbing me from this black and white image. I woke up in tears with a burning sensation on my arm. There on my wrist were three nail marks too close together to be from my boyfriend's massive hands, and not at an angle where I could have done it to myself. The next day I went to the reproductive center for my consultation, and had to do an ultrasound, and there on the screen was the same image from my nightmare in black and white static.

Since then I have decided that whatever transpired that night made me feel like I should not follow through with the process, no matter what the pay.

I'm not sure how Easter lilies and my own fertilities correlate fully, or if I am missing the message here altogether. Maybe the woman with the lilies stepping forward was my mom, and the lilies represent her relationship to me as mother. Maybe this was a sign to protect my own eggs and fertility. Maybe I'll never know, but I do know I won't be getting any more tattoos anytime soon or donating my eggs.

August 14, 2013: Dream

I've had the same dream two nights in a row now.

In the dream, I'm in my bed dreaming, though I think I'm awake. There are separate doors that appear at the foot of my bed and they are all different paths to the same place. A voice says, "There are as many ways to God as there are hearts of men." After the first dream I thought I should write this down but didn't. Then it happened the following night and I decided to take note of it. Also, when I wake up from these dreams I see green bushes around my bed and my bed is warped into the base of a tree. I wake my boyfriend up and tell him I am seeing green and I'm scared. He says, "Yeah, sounds terrifying, go back to bed." He is normally the voice of reason after most dreams that tells me that everything is all right and it's safe to go back to sleep.

August 18, 2013: Spirit Guided Friends Christian Spiritualist Church #2

This was my second visit to the Spirit Guided Friends Christian Spiritualist Church. There were about ten people present today, all in good spirit, hugging and sharing stories before we began. We opened the service with a prayer by Reverend Dan and then he welcomed individuals to come up for energy healing. He saw the puzzled look on my face and explained that this is an optional energy healing session and its first come first served, and if I want to partake in the energy healing to come forward and he would place his hands over my shoulders and crown of the head, and that he would transfer energy for healing either spiritually or physically. This is very similar to Reiki I believe, though I am under the impression that the healer is just a conduit for God to come through, and the healers themselves have little to do with the healing.

Dan is an interesting person; he's an astrologer, reverend, medium, and writer. He is also one of many people at the church who conduct special classes once a month for people who are looking for spiritual guidance and on how to channel their abilities.

Two people went up for healing before I did, and finally I worked up the courage to come forward. I sat down in the wooden chair, with my long white skirt brushing my ankles. I had been having a bit of pain in my back between my shoulder blades so I adjusted my seat to sit in a more comfortable spot. I could feel his hands shaking as he placed them upon my shoulders. I closed my eyes and began to feel like I was on a rocking ship on the ocean. I opened my palms towards the ceiling and allowed myself to open up to all positive energy that may pass through. I tried not to think of anything at all, just allowing myself to rock back and forth in this sea-like motion. He then moved to my right side and placed his hands above the crown of my head. The rocking continued and my toes grew cold. He didn't place his hands on me, only moved them within about an inch distance. I could feel heat from his palms sporadically throughout the few minutes I was in the healing chair. He then whispered in my ear, "God bless you," and it was finished.

I returned to my seat feeling a bit off balance and cold. The service began with several songs that were all inspirational and centered on being thankful for your blessings and gifts. Then a member from the congregation was called forward to lead the service for the day. Ed is a kind older gentleman that somewhat resembles Larry David in appearance. He is hesitant and humble, and takes his time to speak when conveying messages. Last week and this week he carried a small water bottle, book, and pad of paper. He is extremely nice, and just seeing him makes me smile. Ed did a reading from a book he brought with him that I think was called *Guardians of the Gemstones* and focused his lesson on the benefits of quartz. After listening to what he had to say about the properties of the stone, I went home to research it on my own. This is also one of the stones that I was told to pick up during my Reiki session.

> Quartz is said to be a grounding stone and when placed back on the Earth it restores its own energy. People wear quartz to replace negative energy with positive and in turn protect from harmful entities.

When people speak about crystals they are often times referring to a six-sided prism of pure light and energy containing the entire color spectrum, known as Quartz, or the perfect jewel. In the metaphysical world, Clear Quartz crystals are the supreme gift of Mother Earth. Even the smallest is imbued with the properties of a master healer teacher. Ancients believed these stones to be alive, taking a breath once every hundred years or so, and many cultures thought them to be incarnations of the Divine.

Today's healers agree, believing crystals are living beings, incredibly old and wise, and willing to communicate when an individual is open and ready to receive. Wearing, carrying or meditating with a Clear Quartz crystal opens the mind and heart to higher guidance, allowing the realm of Spirit to be transmitted and translated into the world of physical form. (http://www.crystalvaults.com/crystal-encyclopedia/quartz)

After Ed finished his lesson, Reverend Dan led us in a few more songs, and then began the message service. He started with the people he gave healing to first and gave each person a message they both understood and could relate with. Then he moved to me, and said, "When I touched your back between your shoulder blades I could feel pain from your past that you need to let go and forgive yourself for." I begin to tear up a bit, and Dan continued, "Have you heard the saying about forgiveness? To forgive is to set a prisoner free and realize that prisoner was you" (Lewis B. Smedes). He took a few paces back and forth and rubbed his hands together a few times, and continued to say:

> You have so many gifts, and a lot of what you are searching for is inside you already. I know right now it seems a lot of your friends are just living for the moment and having so much fun, but you're different and this journey you are on…connecting the dots, asking questions, taking time for yourself on your own…it's going to help you…and most of all it is going to help many others.

I noticed the messages he gave others were in turn helpful to me as well. He told one man that he is on a thousand-step journey and is only looking ahead thinking about how far he still has to go, and if he would take the time to look back and acknowledge how far he's come he would change his perspective. I realized I should be more like this in my own life too.

Reverend Dan sat down and then another woman named Dianna, from the row over, stepped up to the front of the room and addressed everyone. She looked almost directly at me when she gave this blanket message to the room. "Spirit is so delighted you are all here today with open hearts, and that you are taking these messages and applying them to your lives and sharing with the world." Then she froze and rubbed her arms with her hands, she said she had just gotten extreme chills. She paused for a few seconds as if to let the chills pass, then continued on to say, "This is something that the great Jesus did in his life on Earth as well, and people threw rocks at him and were naysayers, but he went on to carry out what he was meant to do with his time here, and a book was created then as well.

Someone is writing a book." She looked away, and never gave me a direct message but I really feel that she meant that one for me. She could have meant it for Dan; he's a writer too.

She walked towards the back of the room and asked another person who the bride was that she was seeing. The woman responded that her niece had just been married a week prior. Dianna said the joy that she has from events like that floods into her being. Dianna suggested that she could try envisioning herself in the middle of a canyon with palms pressed to the walls next time she feels overwhelmed with good energy. Then picture the energy as water flooding the canyon and going through her, and on the other side of her body envision compartmentalizing that energy…for example this part is going to flood my bank account, and this part is going to flood my marriage. I really like this image and want to apply it next time I feel overwhelming positive feelings (especially in the bank account area).

Dianna retired to her seat and we ended the service with a prayer, songs, and announcements. Reverend Dan said that classes would be resuming next month, and the first class will focus on reading vibrations and energies of others. I plan on attending at least one of these courses. I also noticed today that I sang aloud in church without caring how bad my voice sounded. I was just happy to be in a room with like-minded individuals. I think because I really liked the messages within the songs I had no problem singing along no matter how stupid my voice sounded.

After the service I shuffled around the room and shook hands and introduced myself to everyone. Someone said, "I hope to see you again next week" and I thought, I look forward to coming back. This is one of my favorite churches so far, though they didn't talk much about any scriptures or beliefs. I'm actually glad that they didn't. It seems like the common belief there is that there is a greater being and that through gifted people like those present, we are able to receive messages to positively impact the world. I walked outside into the warm sunshine and felt a feeling I can't quite describe; it was a very light, almost dizzy, sensation but I was extremely happy. I just looked up at the sky as the breeze passed between my open fingers and said "thank you."

Dreams

Since I was a child I have recorded my dreams, most of which took place in lush green gardens with a boy named Matthew. I wrote them down in poem form, and turned it into a stapled book called *The Boy in the Garden*. When I grew older I felt the need to continue recording my dreams, along with a vast fascination with the "who, what, and why" of the subconscious. With age, the dreams became a bit clearer, and though I knew nothing of biblical figures they would often come to me in dreams.

Through the teachings of the Spirit Guided Friends Church I have learned a lot about vibration. Everything on this planet caries a vibration…even the planet itself. There are things we can do to raise our vibration, and in turn, things that lower it. Stilling the mind, dreaming, meditating, and even prayer can help raise the vibration. From what I understand, and I am still learning every day, Spirit resonates at a very high frequency. By quieting the mind and expanding the heart, we can become more in tune with the source. So, it is no wonder that God often used dreams to communicate with those who were open enough to receive when their minds were still.

From my own personal experience, not all dreams are profound, or messages from Spirit. The ones that are exquisite are just that. They are extremely detailed, real, and have distinct sounds, tastes, time periods, and teachers. When I wake from these dreams often times I see gardens around my bed, or tunnels of light on both sides of it. Some dreams I wake with tears in my eyes. And on few occasions I awoke to the spirit of who I believe is St. Peter standing by my bed. Though I don't fully understand the why yet…I do say thank you to the One that showed it to me. If I didn't keep a journal on my nightstand I would lose much of the information that was presented; the symbols, languages, and details all need to be written down immediately.

I am sharing with you two recent dreams I had, which left me in a state of awe when I awoke. The symbols are unique to my own interpretation, but I thought that I would share this with you.

Dream #1: I meet an Indian man while swimming in a river or wading pool. He is in a bold chariot, and I immediately replace his horse and begin to pull him through the water. I feel like his servant, though the unspoken love we have makes it more than what it appears. I drop his chariot once, and he cracks his tooth out. I feel really bad about it, but we make up immediately. He exudes royalty and seems to be either Indian or Egyptian. I drop him at his destination and watch him as he steps into a larger fountain that I am not to go into. It looks like there are two golden angels on both sides of the towering fountain. The angels blow fire at him, something goes wrong, and he drowns among all the people who seem to be jumping into the fountain as well. Because I love him so much I retreat to an underwater cave to mourn. In this cave there is a statue of a horse, a golden vase, and scroll. His family finds me in the cave and gives me a gift, which is a scroll I have been painted into, though I look different than I do now. It depicts us as a family, happy and seated together on a large throne. I am also handed the following things: a golden vase with two angels on the sides of it, and a letter from him that is rolled up in a tube of some kind. I see two hummingbirds as I sit with these objects under a blossoming cherry tree. One hummingbird is blue, and I know that one is my mother. The other, which is a bit smaller, flies close to my face and hovers there. We lock eyes for what seems like minutes and I know that my love is safe, and his name is Ram (sounds like Rahm).

Dream #2: I am in an old ancient tomb; I feel it is the underneath the Sphinx. I am taken first to one room and here there are several bodies placed on the shelves. They look like the tombs of royalty. Dianna is there, and she can communicate with them and bring them back to life. I follow her through the tunnel so I can be sure to learn from her. I can see that this room I am in is at the end of a long corridor and is the fourth room on the right. She raises her palms towards the walls and pure white light shoots from her palms and onto the walls of the tomb. I know that all parts are connected. There is a family tree that is drawn onto the walls, and Peter's name is highlighted for me to take note of, but it is only a small part of the bigger picture, which is shaped like a pyramid. I feel this is part of my family tree, but the names are many. I go into a room and there is a very handsome man with dark skin and black hair. I kiss his stomach. He is very wealthy and drops me at a place with a lot of shops that I know I don't have the money to explore. I find a really expensive pair of shoes and jeans that fit me perfectly and slip them into my shopping bag. I find another dark-haired Egyptian woman here and she is very kind. I tell her of the error of the goods falling into my bag and she stops me and points towards the white robe that I have on. She asks me what the tattoo is on my chest and at first I am confused because I know I don't have anything tattooed on my chest. But when I look down I can see through the white garment I am wearing and the mirror image of the family tree from the tomb appears tattooed upon my chest. (I have this actually drawn in my journal.)

At the top of tree there are wings. The tree appears golden like a treasure map. The woman picks up a yellow marker and adds to the drawing on my chest. There is much more that I cannot see yet. She doesn't complete what she started. I go to take my shopping bag and leave but it is now empty. I walk outside the store and take a seat on a stool, here someone hands me a bowl of fresh basil to eat. My mom appears with open arms. She tells me she has a gift for me, which is a surprise buried in my chest. I see her old cedar chest and then wake up.

August 25, 2013: Spirit Guided Friends #3

Today was my third trip to the spirit guided friends church. I normally don't gravitate to one place as much as this, but I just feel so drawn to the feelings I develop here every Sunday. I feel a bit sad that this is my last visit here, well for now at least, until the book is finished. Everyone at the service understands where I am headed, and what I am doing with my journey. I took a bit longer than normal to say my goodbyes today. I felt like I was at a family reunion drawing out repeating hugs that I know have to last me until the next time we meet. The magnitude of knowledge and positive energy among the people in this room is compelling, and is something I will be seeking out again down the road.

I didn't take part in the energy healing today, but sat back and watched as Ed came forth to perform the healing for the day. There is a different healer every Sunday. Ed is usually very quiet and a little flustered but today he had a bit of a different demeanor about him. I didn't know that he too was a reader and healer, but everyone there seems to surprise me week after week. I wonder what it feels like for two mediums to "heal" each other. Do the others in the room see the energy or feel what is being transmitted between them, or do they see colors or images? I asked some of the people who have been using their spiritual gifts to heal others for quite some time and they said that they can feel the other person's energy, and yes, sometimes they see colors and pick up on messages as well. It is different for everyone. I decided with the amount of people in the congregation today that I would let others partake in the healing and sit this one out.

After the session Reverend Dan got up and shared a lesson from the Bible that Spirit encouraged him to share. Because I am still learning, I assume that when he says "Spirit" he means the Holy one. He turned to the beginning of Genesis One. He read about the creation of the world and covered the first three days of creation where God created land, sea, day, and night. When he got here, Genesis 27: "So God created mankind in his own image, in the image of God he created them; male and female he created them," he noted that the Bible states they are created together, and he clarified that this meant God created them in Spirit first. So we were in spirit form before we were placed in these shells/bodies. After God created the spirits of man and woman as a mirror image of himself he then created them in the physical; man first and woman thereafter. I love Dan's interpretation of the scripture. Others have seen this same scripture and thought either 1) The Bible contradicts itself by saying they were created together first and later notes man was created first then woman, or 2) Men are superior to women. I side with Dan's interpretation.

Dan went on to say that because of the way God created us as mirrors of himself, that we too have instincts to create, and not only to create but to love as he did, and seek companionship. So in turn, when we create something, whether it is a sculpture, building, writing, painting, or any other creation…we are mirroring God. Our creations should always be made for the greater good and what we put out into the world will circle back to us in positive energy. He stressed that we should not create things with the mindset of expecting things back in return. Sometimes we create just so we can help other people in their lives, and the things we want in return may not be the things we get. If we are happy with what we already have and are thankful for our existing gifts what we create will be pure and of positive energy. This reminds me that when I write I should not expect anything in return, only to inspire others and find my own connection to God as I originally planned.

After he finished the service, Dan walked straight over to me and asked if he could give me a message. A woman in the front of the room clarified that they have to ask each time if we will accept a message because it interferes with, or intrudes on, our personal energy. Dan said that when I deal with negative people or someone who I'm in an uncomfortable situation with that I don't need to carry that negative energy around with me, and instead to just learn from it, acknowledge their feelings, bless them, and move on with my life. I didn't know what he was talking about at first, but after a few seconds I realized exactly what it was.

I thanked Dan for this message, it really meant a lot to me. Others received messages from Dan and after four readings he sat down. An older woman whom I had never seen before stood up slowly with a shaky cane, adjusted her glasses on her face, and said she had a few messages to give too. She gave several and then turned to me and said:

> Young lady in the back, you have some loved ones on the other side that want you to know not to worry about them and they are just fine where they are. Also, when you dream of them, record the dreams because often times they communicate when your mind is still and they use a lot of symbols instead of words. If you are confused about what the symbols mean, just ask them aloud before you go to sleep and they will clarify for you.

I'm going to try this method, specifically with the images I've been shown recently of a family dinner, dragonfly, and bathtubs, and see if some clarity comes about. She also suggested I try Reverend Dan's class on Billets (explained later).

"Billets are a good stepping stone for those trying to harness spiritual connections and gifts. It's a safe way to begin, because once you have that connection it never goes away!" she said with a bit of wit and excitement. I liked her message to Reverend Dan as well; she congratulated him on all the writing he's been doing and advised him to pick a day and time and make a date with spirit to work on his writing, and spirit will come through and help guide his mind to get the lead out. Usually I write in the park every Sunday around the same time, and I love the concept of making a date with spirit to create in a positive way.

She did three total readings and took her seat. Afterwards a woman from the congregation told her that while she was giving messages baby's breath appeared and kept growing and eventually the white flowers turned to crystals and radiated out beacons of light to all in the room. This gives new meaning to the phrase "she lights up the room," but she really did. She was a pleasant woman that made me smile just looking at her. I love this visual and will try to incorporate it into future meditation. A few more people stood and gave messages and then the reverend asked me, "Young lady, do you get messages?" I said, No, I don't...but I want to. Then the elderly woman, Reverend Lucille, spouted out, "OH! You Will!" On that note we concluded, and this time I stayed and talked a bit with everyone. I told them I would be gone for a while and was headed back East to Ohio for my sister's wedding and then on to a few other churches to fulfill a creation of my own. Dianna (reader from last week) got chills and said "Yep! You sure do, I just got confirmation of your journey." She also pointed me to the upstairs library and suggested a few books that may help me until we meet again.

I followed Diana and David upstairs and stood patiently by the bookshelves as they both selected a few books for me to borrow. One book is called *Chariots of the Gods?* and though I haven't started reading it yet I get the idea that it is about linking extraterrestrial beings to unexplained structures on our planet. The other book is by Edgar Cayce, otherwise known as The Sleeping Prophet. I had never even heard of him before, but it seems that Reverend Dan is an avid fan of his and has about thirty books in the library reflecting his work. I began reading it last night and could hardly put it down. Edgar Cayce was able to self-induce unconsciousness and while "asleep" he gave over 14,000 medical diagnoses, readings, and dream interpretations. He is one of the best documented sensitives in the history of psychical research. One of my favorite quotes so far is from the preface:

> He saw the collective or universal subconscious as a vast river of thought flowing through eternity, fed by the sum total of man's mental activity since the beginning. He maintained that this river is accessible to any individual who is prepared to develop his psychic or spiritual faculties with sufficient patience and effort. (*Dreams: Your Magic Mirror: With Interpretations of Edgar Cayce*, p. 13)

I realize the themes of the day: creation, mirrored images, dreams, and the beginning. I can reflect on all of these in different ways, and center them all into one general thought: This is the beginning for me, letting go and seeing others as mirrored images of God walking different paths. By using my gifts from God/Goddess to create purely, and with an open mind, I will be able to understand my dreams and messages clearly. The ultimate goal, once I get past the hindrances of the ego and self-doubt, is to help others.

August 28, 2013: A Dream

I am around a family dinner table with lasagna being served to everyone seated. My grandma had prepared it and is serving it to all the children there, none of which I know. The meal appears dry and someone says it needs more water. I'm now on the Oregon coast (one of my favorite places) walking down a sunny street. I can smell the salt in the air and hear the soft roar of the ocean in the distance. Off to my right I see a beautiful mansion that I recognize, and realize it is a dollhouse that I had from when I was a kid, though this time it is made of wood. I get to go inside and it is beautiful. Once inside I am back in my existing apartment and looking up at the high vaulted ceiling. There is a canvas tarp stapled to the ceiling that has the sky and all the constellations painted on it in abstract colors. Once I realize this is not the sky and I am looking at a fake the tarp becomes unstapled from the ceiling and falls down. Behind it is the real sky in all its majesty. The stars are brilliant and bright, and the sky is a deep hue of blues and deep ocean colors. As I admire its beauty two constellations light up like Lite-Brites. One highlights a ballerina dancing holding a bouquet of flowers and the other is of a heavyset beautiful person sitting in a chariot looking down on the world below. I try to show others in the house the pictures within the stars and no one can see them but me.

September 1, 2013: Muslim

I am really nervous, anxious, and apprehensive about today. My interpretations of this religion are based on the news, terrorist attacks, and things I have read reflecting Muslim people in a negative light.

I put on my most conservative full-length dress with sweater over it (despite the 80 degree weather) and a pair of black Converse shoes. I packed a head scarf in my purse to wear, possibly, but I had no idea how to put one on besides what I had seen in old '90s rap videos and in the movie *Friday*. I wasn't sure if I would stand out more in my makeshift Muslim outfit, or without the headscarf with blonde hair shining for all to see.

I also read that you are to remove your shoes, clean your feet in the footbath, and never point your feet in the direction of Mecca. I am unsure what direction that is, so I plan on following the direction of other's feet or look for a sign. Also, their website says to never shake hands with the opposite gender, and if you are greeted by someone they will say *Assalamu 'alaykum* (Peace be unto you) and you should reply *wa alaykum us salaam* (peace be upon you also).

The service today is actually a class for people interested in learning the Muslim faith, and on Friday and Saturday they have the actual prayer service.

As I walked up to the mosque there was a woman in a beige silk robe sipping tea seated outside by a lavender bush. I asked her if there was a class today and she said, "Well, yes, but it is for the children who are learning Arabic and the Qur'an." She was more than happy to show me around though, and speak with me about the Muslim faith. She happened to be there that day because she was meeting someone to bring food to a friend who had been in a car accident. I saw the look on her face when she saw me reach into my bag and pull out my head scarf, and shyly ask if it was all right if I put it on. She smiled ear to ear and was delighted. I said I didn't know if I was putting it on right, and she reassured me however I put it on was just fine.

Inside there were twenty-plus children all dressed in bright colors of silk with wide eyes and big smiles. I looked at all of them seated patiently around an African American man seated cross-legged within the center of their circle. What is he teaching them? I asked. "Oh, he is a very talented man and knows the Qur'an by memory; he is reciting it to the children, so they too can learn." We left the children's side of the mosque and went back outside and through another door labelled "women." All of the women studied and prayed together in this room (just not today). She showed me the main room where they all pray and then we continued on into the library. She said that on Friday at 1 p.m. they would have a prayer session specifically devoted to praying for our parents and loved ones. I told her the story about how my mom passed away and she teared up a bit before she spoke.

> Now when you pray to Allah you will become closer to where your mom is. When we pray to Him the veil comes up and it is a direct connection...No prophets, priests, or middle man to go through and there will be two angels on either side of you recording your prayers and life on a long white scroll. When you do meet Allah,

and all humans do, that scroll will be read back for judgment.

I told her about a dream I had where I was on an empty sun-soaked beach and there was a white scroll laying in the sand that spread down the shoreline into the distance that I kept trying to read but the wind kept blowing it over. She smiled, "That is the very scroll I am speaking of. There are reasons why we are led places and Allah is guiding you." She also added that this was my new home if I wanted it to be. We slipped our shoes back on and went outside by the lavender bush to speak more. She told me that all the books of ancient prophets, Jews, Christians, and unrecorded/lost books are what make up the Qur'an. I had no idea. She said that it is written in Arabic, and if I could learn the language I could begin to study the Qur'an as well. She also said that they recite the prayer of Jumah on Saturdays and this ensures that all of our sins are wiped clean for the next week plus three days. Why three days? Because Allah tacks it on for making the effort…like extra credit I suppose. I told her that I might be back on Friday (work permitting) but for sure on Saturday. She said she wouldn't be there but to tell everyone I am new and seeking to learn about the Qur'an and I will be aided.

We parted ways and I headed to Powell's to buy a copy of *Arabic for Dummies*. I also left my scarf on my head for the rest of the day. It made me think about why people cover up their hair or why Buddhists shave it off. Is it because things that are dead weight on our bodies don't serve us, or do they cover up everything so that everyone looks the same…just mirrors of each other?

A Dream

I keep having nightmares of a single black boot hovering above my bed, and if I look at it, it will swallow my soul. I wake up and panic, then fall back asleep. I slip into a more pleasant dream where I am watching two white horses with beautiful white wings. They are illuminated with sunshine spilling through their feathers as they fly. There are swings in the sky hanging from clouds that I climb onto and sit up in the air to watch the horses and admire their beauty. The world below can't see us. I realize I am not alone as I see a second swing. The name David rings through the air and I realize he is with me. We sit on the swings and look down on a visual of the inside of my head. It looks like landscaping is going on and people are clearing bushes away and making room for the sunshine. I see windmills and wake up with a song in my head that stays there all morning.

September 6, 2013

Because my sister is getting hitched in a few weeks I decided to drive downtown and pick up some shoes for her wedding. I had a déjà vu feeling as I remember that she was a ballerina for a long time and recall the stars from my previous dream. I snapped out of la-la land when I heard the song that I woke up with in my head come on the radio. Almost like an eerie coincidence I looked up and there, just ahead, were windmills on the top of a building. I realized that where I was at this exact moment is in front of an enormous gothic looking chapel, and decided to pull over and go inside. I figured since it was Friday that no one would be there, but something compelled me to go to the doors and knock.

There was a woman inside at the front desk who was very nice and gave me a paper with information about the church and what Presbyterians believe in. She also told me that they have a beautiful service here on Sundays at 10:30, and if I live nearby I should come down. I decided that tomorrow (Saturday) I would go to the Muslim women's class and then Sunday I would attend the service at this church.

September 7, 2013: Muslim #2

I showed up again at 11 a.m. as instructed, void of makeup and covered from head to Converse. I walked in through the women's entrance into a room of about eight women all seated in a circle around a woman in a black silk garment. All of the women were covered up from head to toe in different colors of silks and scarves. Most of them had on fun jewelry that accented their attire. As I walked in hesitantly, feeling somewhat like I was interrupting something, Mindy stood up and said, "Oh I'm so glad you could make it! Everyone, this is Lisa, she is studying Islam and is interested in learning the Qur'an." I corrected her and said, actually, my name is Tracy, but thank you for the introduction. She said, "Oh, well, Tracy, we started at nine today so we are just wrapping up." I was kind of disappointed as I had come all the way down there again and missed the entire service. I could hear the ringing of children echoing through the walls from a room over. I contemplated simply joining children's hour since it had just started, but instead decided to hang around a bit longer and chat with the various women.

Mindy asked how my day was going as we began walking together. We stopped in front of a glass case holding a massive book with clean white pages covered in Arabic writing. "This is the Qur'an, isn't it beautiful? Now this one is unable to be touched by those that are not pure of heart, or have Wudu." I assume that Wudu is a state you must be in that shows that you are clean and pure of sins. "Also, women who are menstruating can't touch this book either." I am not sure why a menstruating woman would be labeled "impure" and for that matter it makes me think that only three weeks out of four is she able to interact with their scripture. I didn't ask any questions because I was still trying to comprehend this in my mind before speaking or asking something that might be offensive. I was picturing loopholes and ways around it, like rubber gloves or a long stick to turn the pages. I refrained, and followed in silence down the hall towards the library.

We stopped in front of a large wall of books, and here she explained that there are other Qur'ans that *can* be touched, and the ones that have equal amounts of English in them are able to be touched by us Westerners. I was unaware that there were other versions of the Qur'an, but there are. According to Mindy, other prophets have read the Qur'an in Arabic and then rewritten it in their own interpretations for others to read. This is interesting to me. "It is best if we don't use others' interpretations and instead that we learn the language for ourselves and deduce our own meanings from the original version." Well, I said, I fully plan on learning the language so that I can read and interpret it for myself, I even got a book called *Islam for Dummies*. She looked extremely offended as if I was saying that Islam is for dummies, and I quickly realized my error. I explained it is a book called *Arabic for Dummies*, which explains the basics of the language, and that I had already learned a little bit just in the past week.

She looked relieved, and assured me that most people that are diligent in their studies can learn it in about three months. Once I understand the language I will be able to read the Qur'an and also understand the prayers, which they do five times a day. I am not sure why they pray five times a day, but each prayer throughout the day washes away all of the little sins we have committed between that prayer and the next one. I am not sure what or who measures what is a little sin and what is a big sin. As I pondered the sin wiping we walked into the next room, where she showed me a pantry of canned foods and kitchen supplies. They have food on hand at all times to help those in need. Then she lit up in shocked excitement like she just remembered something great, and she had. "Have you tried any of the dates up in the main room yet? I have been waiting all season for these dates! Finally they are ready to be eaten." We walked back up front to the small table by the door as she smiled and reached for the large bowl full of fresh dates. "Now hold out your hands, dear," she said as she filled my cupped palms to the brim.

Mindy looked delighted as we ate dates and carried on our conversation. "These are just amazing aren't they?" I nodded with a full mouth. "Do you know why we eat the milk and dates?" I shook my head back and forth as I hurried my chewing. "Whenever there is a marriage, it is custom for us to eat milk and dates. Are you married, dear?" I finished chewing with a forced swallow and finally responded with a hopeful no, but added that I hope to be someday. I also told her that my oldest sister was getting married next week, and I would gladly eat some more on her behalf. She smiled and said that what I need to do is just write down about four to five sentences detailing what I am looking for in a husband and then either a Wali or a Sheikh (learned person or scholar) will take my list to the brothers and select a mate for me. Once they find the man for me, the Wali will then act as a go-between person and conduct all of the negotiating and arranging. I didn't want to break it to her that I already had a boyfriend, who is not a brother, and that there would be no written contracts or list of demands to be negotiated for us. This seems so odd to me that people select mates in this manner, but I suppose they probably think dating websites are just as weird. To each their own.

They confirmed the date and time for the next women's session, September 21st at 9 a.m., and invited me to come back for the actual service. Mindy also recommended I pick up a copy of the Qur'an that has English translations, to read while I am learning Arabic. There is an entire section on women which she said would be beneficial for me to read between now and then. I wondered if I had done something wrong and she was suggesting I read about how women are to act so I don't do it again. From what I have experienced thus far I think that the Muslims are really great people. I like that their book contains several books within it, and really embodies several religions tied into one massive entity. Mindy, and the other women I have met, are very kind, loving women that have gone out of their way to help me on my path. They seem like they have a strict prayer regimen, and are very devoted to God. The kitchen and all of the food that they give to others in need also shows how kind hearted these women are. I am eager to read the book for myself. I headed home to put on makeup and summer clothes, and went to the park to reflect on the day's lessons. I know it is frustrating that I keep going there and missing the services, but I suppose everything happens as it is supposed to and when the time is right that door will be opened.

Sunday, September 8, 2013: Presbyterian

Today I went back to the gothic looking cathedral that I stopped by on Friday. The garden outside was breathtaking and all of the plants had been planted in soil from the Holy Land. The garden was enclosed by black iron gates and had small paths winding throughout the greenery. I walked in through the garden and into the enchanting church. The balconies, altars, pews, and chapel were made of very detailed carved wood. It was absolutely beautiful. The pipe organ stood about sixty feet tall and wound through the wood carvings in the front of the room. The stained glass spun rainbows onto the upper balconies that looked down over the pews below. I felt like I was in a holy log cabin that occupied an entire city block. Opposite of the organ was an entire wall of stained glass. The sun pushed through and cast rays of light over the choir standing in the balcony across the room. It was heavenly and beautiful. To my left and right were Easter colored stained glass windows with what looked like flowers and grapes painted on them. Like a church tourist, I took several pictures before I took my seat.

Today's service was titled *Reshaped Into a New Future*, and began with several songs and prayers, and then a declaration of pardon. "The God who calls us is the God who created us; the God who formed us is the God who forgives us. This is the good news, that in Christ, we are a new creation."

Then the children were called forward for the children's lesson. All of the children gathered around as the woman in the front of the room took out a jar of play dough. She asked the kids if they knew what it was, and they did. She asked them to tell her something to make, and one child yelled Tiger! At first she just made what looked like a head with ears, and the children told her that it didn't look like a tiger yet. She continued on and formed a body and tail, and then the kids said that it looked more like a fox, but pretty good. She asked the kids if they knew what a potter's wheel was and if they knew what clay was. Most of the kids knew what she was talking about, or at least they acted like it, and she continued on.

She said the good thing about creating on a potter's wheel is that we can start with one thing and with God's help we can mold and create something great and useful. Sometimes if we don't like what we have created we can put it all back into a ball and start over, using the same clay as before. She went around and handed some play dough to each seated child. "Do you know what you will create with your own clay in order to help others through God?" One kid yelled out "Bowl! So others can eat!" A few other copycat kids repeated his idea. A couple other kids said they would make hearts, to just give love to others. I thought of my own creation of this book and how I want so badly to help others in one way or another. Even if one person can become inspired by my journey I would be happy. Like the clay, I started shapeless, and just over the past six months I too have been molded into something of God's work. I pray at night that when I write the right words come out and the right messages come through, and I just hope that what is created is ultimately something pushed to paper by God's hand, not my own.

I was at a cookout last night and began discussing my writing with someone and they intervened and said, "Wait, you believe in God?" and I thought back to the beginning of this journey when I didn't know how to answer that same question, and now, I said without any hesitation, "Absolutely." Someone else chimed in and said, "Well not in the stupid way, what she is doing is different." I don't think there is a "stupid way"; there may be people that I don't agree with, or people who worship in ways in which I don't prefer, but I think in general if people are good to one another and become better people based on what they are worshiping, that isn't such a bad thing. It only becomes stupid when you mix in ignorance and judgment. I refer back to the checklist Pastor Amy told me: Is it loving, life giving, and creating, and decided that things that embody these elements align with what I support and believe in as well. I have also been trying to make a conscious effort not to judge others. Judging my own character is all right, and developing understanding and knowledge based on what I am learning is too. So, if others I come across believe something different than me, I am simply acknowledging it, looking at it from their point of view, and not judging. Everyone sees this world from a different perspective, which is how we learn.

The minster came forward and began with the first scripture Luke 14:25–33, called "the cost of being a disciple." In this scripture she talked about what would happen if you set out to build a great tower and didn't think first about the cost to create it, and then realized halfway through the project that you didn't have the means to complete it. In this scenario, she points out that the creator would be viewed by others as a failure if they are worried about what others think. The point she made was that no matter what it is that we are creating, we need to think of how we will successfully be able to create without fear of failure.

The scripture also said that sometimes you have to give up everything in order to become a disciple, and these sacrifices are for the greater good of mankind. I am assuming disciple in this sense refers to any dedicated student or follower of Jesus. I began to daydream a bit, and for some reason I pictured a child walking home from school. Every day, the child would stop at his favorite large evergreen tree and hug it. Day after day the child would come to the tree, admire its strength and glory, hug it, and go home. One day the tree falls, and the child is heartbroken, but then he realizes that behind the tree was a church that he was never able to see before. So losing something, or letting go of something you love, can lead to greater things. And sometimes, those things can be for the greater good of mankind. The word selfless comes to mind.

The overhead bubble popped as a tray passed in front of me. I scrambled for a crinkled up dollar I had stuffed in my pocket and relaxed back in my seat. After the music faded the pastor began a second lesson from Jeremiah 18:1–11 called "at the potter's house." In this scripture the prophet Jeremiah was instructed to go down to the potter's house and there he would receive a message from the Lord. When Jeremiah arrived he found the potter there molding his clay but it was marred. So the potter started over, again and again. He had set out to create one thing, but then the clay became spoiled and he was not able to. The pastor compared this to our lives, and said that sometimes God has plans for us that are good and sound, but that does not mean that he will not change his plan for us if we do not act faithfully. The potter had envisioned the sculpture he was creating, but because of his ways the clay became unusable and the plan changed. The lesson reminded us to live righteously every day and not take for granted what we have laid out ahead of us. I immediately reflected on my own words and thoughts, and reminded myself that I had been blessed with my passion for writing and helping others, and not to take my gifts for granted or misuse them.

She went on to describe a new sensation to her, autumn. As fall begins there is a unique energy in the air as the leaves begin to turn. With the pastor's recent move from Australia to Portland she was encountering fall for the first time. To her there was a celebration of new changes and energy that came about and helped her reconnect to the direction that God intended for her, and in turn convey God's direction to others. She circled back to the topic of prophets, or the "chosen people." Jeremiah specifically was called the weeping prophet, because even at times of great distress he passed on messages that the people may not have wanted to hear. When the great temple was destroyed in Israel, and the people were in distress, it was Jeremiah who conveyed that it fell due to the people's own ways. The people questioned the exile, quite similarly to people mulling over the financial crises of present day.

Jeremiah went to the potter's house and admired all of the soft clay that could be used for something useful and beautiful and then something happened to spoil the vessel in his hands. She explained that sometimes the flaws can be worked out, and sometimes there is no hope and it all must be put back to a ball of clay to begin again. When a flaw happens in the clay of life it is God that can mold and remake the vessel of our lives into something beautiful and useful. She asked us to think about where in own story God used calamities of our lives to reshape it. In times of strife we see the hand of God at work bringing a new shape out of chaos. Sometimes it's when our life falls in on itself it can be remade with the help of others who have walked this path before us. This pastor had just lost a family member of her own, and said that she was taken aback by the generosity of a group of people who brought meals to her house every few days, and never wanted or accepted anything in return. They too had suffered a loss and in the time of chaos in their lives someone had done this for them.

I remember when I lost my mom, and the days all ran together. If it wasn't for someone doing the exact same thing for me I probably wouldn't have eaten for an entire week. This person brought over casseroles and pots of chicken noodle soup for my family, and I will never forget her generosity and how much that helped our family in our time of loss. My boyfriend just lost his aunt this morning, and I am going to be doing the same thing for his family this evening. People who have walked this path before me have helped guide me through, and showed me how to respond when others are faced with similar heartaches. What an appropriate service for the day. As I reflected on the appropriateness of the service and my own remolding, I pictured my life before as clay on the wheel. When my mom died it spun out of control and collapsed. When I gained the courage to allow for reshaping, I made room for new creation and beginnings – knowing it will never be the same as the first piece, but could better serve others in this new form.

She left us with a poem by Wendell Berry, called "Work Song, Part 2, A Vision." The poem is quite beautiful and makes me visualize a ruined land that becomes nourished again and rebuilt; not only for this life but for those in generations to come. The pastor ended with this:

> This is the vision of a world reshaped by the potter's hand. There is one that came upon us that was born like us of dust and clay, and whose life we see the potter's own heart and hand making all things new. May we all

find our own place and part in the new life that God is shaping here and now.

I left the service feeling blessed and thankful. It is hard to view loss and tragedy as a stepping stone for creating or molding our lives into something new. I remember one of the last things my mom said to me, "Everyone has to die so that everyone can live," and I wonder if she knew that her passing would change my entire world. If she was still alive I would still be living in Cincinnati, I would have never met my boyfriend in Portland, or become an author, and I would have never connected with God. I guess mothers really do know best.

Reading of the Qur'an: Attempt 1

Yesterday I was supposed to attend the Muslim women's session from 9 to 11, but realized it had been replaced by a fundraiser they were having that day. To keep up with the education I decided to go down to Powell's and pick up an English translation of the Qur'an by Abdullah Yusuf Ali. I began reading it at a nearby coffee shop and though I am only on page eleven of the book here is what I deduced thus far. There are a lot of threatening messages in the first nine pages, all listing out consequences of not believing in God/Allah. I have been watching a lot of documentaries lately about the Dalai Lama, and I have noticed his compassion for all humans, races, religions, and genders. The first nine pages of the Qur'an seem semi-violent and harsh for those who are nonbelievers and I can't help but reflect on the views of the Dalai Lama, who recognizes all religions are different but all worshiping the One Creator. His nonviolent beliefs enforce that peace and harmony can triumph over those who wage wars to overthrow countries violently. Even when his country was taken over by China he remained nonviolent and encouraged prevalence through peace.

At first the Qur'an made me think that Muslims only welcome those who believe in Allah, and those who worship as they do, then I came to page 10, section 113: "The Jews say: The Christians have nothing to stand upon; and the Christians say: The Jews have nothing to stand upon. Yet they profess to study the same Book." Mindy told me that the Qur'an actually holds several books within in, so I suppose that this book encompasses a lot of religious principles within one book and welcomes all faiths, just as long as you have faith. Wishful thinking maybe? Then again, I'm only on page 10.

I skipped to the section on women which I was encouraged to read, and had to read aloud some of the phrases to make sure I had understood what I had just read accurately. This seems outdated, sexist, and harsh. One section describes how to deal with your inheritance should you pass. In every situation the men get the amount equal to that of two females. The limits are set by Allah and "those who disobey Allah and his Messenger and transgress His limits will be admitted to a fire, to abide therein; and they shall have a humiliating punishment." This passage also bothered me, "If any of your women are guilty of lewdness, take the evidence of four (reliable) witnesses from amongst you against them; and if they testify, confine them to houses until death do claim them, or Allah ordain for them some other way." I am not sure what lewdness meant back then, or if the definition of lewdness has changed from then. Could this mean that a woman could be sentenced to death for simply flirting or showing too much of her body? Also the part that says "if any of *your* women" labels women as property. Maybe when slavery was around this was thought of as acceptable, but that kind of treatment of others does not follow suit with human rights. It also bothers me to think of the other way in which they would be dealt with.

I believe in freedom: freedom of individuality, speech, human rights, and expression. The image of four "reliable" individuals judging and sentencing me, or any woman, to death makes me question who really came up with this idea, as it certainly didn't come from God. I believe God is loving, kind, forgiving, and life giving. The section on women was obviously written by a man. I continued on reading and had to stop after this passage:

> Men are the protectors and maintainers of women, because Allah has given the one more strength than the other, and because they support them from their means. Therefore the righteous women are devoutly obedient, and guard in the husband's absence what Allah would have them guard. As to those women on whose part you fear disloyalty and ill-conduct, admonish them first, next refuse to share their beds, and last beat them (lightly); but if they return to you in obedience, do not seek against them means of annoyance; for Allah is Most High, Great above you all.

It blows my mind that people in this day and age still follow this book. I hope that people don't really still follow these rules set by "Allah." Clearly this was written by a man and the rules for women all go to support men ruling them. Anyone who does not love or care for others, or tries to rule or enslave based on something they do not understand, scares me.

While I'm on this rant, I also have read stories of people killing authors who have written out against Muslim beliefs and think about how deluded the minds have become of those who think they were or are the protectors of women…or anything at all. Certainly taking another person's life in the name of "God" has to seem a bit odd to them? I recall the commandment, "thou shall not kill," and wonder how people of the Muslim faith think it is all right to take another's life for not agreeing with their standpoints on what "God" deems correct or incorrect. And the beating? I am a believer in kindness and goodwill. I don't support abuse of any kind. I need to read this in small portions as it upsets me. I am not finished with the women's portion of the book, but can only imagine it is all written in this manner.

I went back to the book later that day. I truly want to find some part of this book that I agree with. So, I prayed. "God, The Source, The One light, please open my eyes to what I need to see within this book. Please allow me the ability to receive your wisdom, and understand what it is that I am supposed to see here." Then I prayed to Muhammad. I asked aloud, "Muhammad, I'm sure you were a prophet as well. I'm sure you had visions and were visited by God…as was Buddha, and the Apostles. If there is something written within your book that you would like me to see please show me." I closed my eyes and skimmed my fingers over the pages of the Qur'an then I stopped when I felt a surge of heat on my right arm. I opened the book to a chapter titled Surah 23, "The Believers." Here in this passage I gained a sincere understanding of a very important message. It began:

> We sent a long line of prophets for your instruction. We sent Noah to his people: he said, "O my people! Worship Allah! You have no other god than Him. Will you not fear Him?" The chiefs of the unbelievers among his people said "He is no more than a man like yourselves: his wish is to assert his superiority over you: if Allah had wished to send messengers, He could have sent down angels: never did We hear such a thing as he says, among our ancestors of old." And some said, he is a man possessed. Noah said, "O my Lord! Help me, for that they accuse me of falsehood."

The passage goes on to give another example of yet another prophet sent down to the people to help, and give instructions, but again was accused by those who didn't understand at the time of his visit.

> Then We sent our Messengers in succession every time came to a people their Messenger, they accused him of falsehood: so We made them follow each other in punishment. We made them as a tale that is told, so away with the people who will not believe....We sent Moses and his brother Aaron, with our Signs and authority manifest...They said shall we believe in two men like ourselves and their people are subject to us. So they accused them of falsehood, and they became of those who were destroyed. And we gave Moses the Book in order that they might receive guidance. And we made the son of Mary and his mother as a Sign: We gave them both shelter on high ground, affording rest and security and furnishing with springs. O you Messengers! Enjoy all things good and pure and work righteousness: for I am well-acquainted with all that you do. Verily this Brotherhood of yours is a single Brotherhood, and I am your Lord and Cherisher. But people have cut off their affair of unity, between them, into sects: each party rejoices in that which is with itself.

So, it seems, there are incredibly wise words written within the Qur'an. As with most books I think that some of that has been misinterpreted. In my eyes, I believe the message here is that there have been many prophets...all of which were regular humans with the ability to open their minds to messages, and for each of the ones that were Messengers for their time they were struck down by the masses that did not understand. The people all hoped for angels, but didn't realize the beauty of what can be within the simplest form of man. This trend is documented for Aaron, Moses, Noah, Jesus, and many others that were sent to enlighten. Muhammad was also a great messenger, and transcribed these words for others to learn from. He also highlights that there has always been just One Lord and Cherisher, but people have cut off the unity between one and instead divided the one into sects. I agree with this wholeheartedly, but I also believe that any way to worship God is just fine. If you are Muslim and want to call God "Allah" so be it. If you are Christian and want to thank Jesus in your prayers, go right ahead. In the end, we are still all just worshiping the One God, just labeling him differently depending on the sect that we have either fallen into or chosen.

I feel like I have a better understanding for some of the wisdom that presents itself within the Qur'an. Rather than focusing only on the portions that I support, I am also taking into consideration that which I do not support, and learning from this book in its entirety. I think that is what we were all supposed to do in the first place.

September 22, 2013: Center for Spiritual Living Science of Mind Church

For a nice change of mood, today I went to a church that welcomes all faiths. They welcome any gender, age, religion, upbringing, sexual orientation, or otherwise. On the walls hang symbols of the cross, Star of David, Islam crescent moon, yin-yang, and several others. What they believe is "there is only one God and that it manifests itself through all creation – in every person, place, and thing. This God is full of Love and is eternally present for us." They believe that "using the power of God, working through our minds, we can create lives that are fuller, richer, and more satisfying." –Reverend Larry King. They also align a lot of their beliefs with Hindu principles. The founder of this specific church said, "We should listen to the wisdom of the celestial currents, like that found in the *Bhagavad Gita* (the same book I was told to read by David at Spirit Guided Friends Church). Spirituality is literally hanging in the air in India." During Reverend King's time spent over in India he didn't see a single face that wasn't smiling. He took a lot of this inspiration and brought it into his weekly sermons.

This church encourages sound mind, body, and spirit. They focus a lot on meditation and prayer, and believe that most problems start in the mind, and create negative thinking, which creates stress on the prana level (vital energy) and causes the problematic circumstances on the physical body and in life. This church gives lessons that offer positive suggestions for viewing life, and helps strengthen the core of all of its members through God. They also believe in the joy of Oneness and Wholeness, and believe that God is one; there is no difference between us and God. God is One Source expressed in a million forms.

Today's service was about faith. I decided not to describe what the physical church looks like because it no longer matters. What I learn while inside and the messages shared are the only factors I am paying attention to now. The choir began and was elegant and soulful, followed by one of the members of the church getting up and sharing a prayer. Here she discussed the significance of creation, and that all creations embody God. There is no end or beginning to where God starts and ends because God is within everything. She then asked if anyone had a birthday today; one person raised her hand, and she went over and gave her a red rose. She then asked if there were any first-time visitors; I raised my hand, and with that she came over and gave me a rose that was mostly pink with hues of yellow around the base. Everyone clapped and then the Reverend Larry came forth.

He was full of energy and glowing. He began with a story about how he just got a new car. Apparently he had been on the lookout for a new car for about a year, and had been putting off the purchase because he didn't think that there was one vehicle that embodied all of his criteria. He was looking for something affordable, electric, and also wanted assurance that there were going to be charging stations between here and where his beach house is. He discussed that for the longest time he had people constantly telling him that it wasn't possible, that he couldn't afford an electric car, and surely there would never be charging stations between here and his beach house. Larry decided after almost a year of driving an almost defeated car that he would say a powerful prayer, asking for some sort of resolution to the failing belts and leaking oil of the car. Within three days he received an unsolicited email from a dealership inviting him to test drive a new electric car. He put this off too because he just knew there weren't any charging stations between here and the coast, and even if he liked the car he couldn't drive it to where he was the most happy because it would never make it. After a few more days he received another email from a friend showing him that two new charging stations were built between here and his beach house. So, he went in just to look at the car. He knew it would be too expensive anyway, but decided to look and give it a chance. Larry found himself driving away in a new car that would only cost him $99 a month on a lease, and would only cost him about $25 in electricity a month. He couldn't believe it.

The lesson he conveyed is that he constantly got in his own way, and if he would have just stopped trying to figure how he was going to make it work, and let the universe do its work, he could have been in that car a long time ago. That deal had been out there for a while; he was prohibiting his own happiness. He looked at us and said, how many of you can think of ways in which you are having faith in anything but yourself and the right things happening for you? Often times we have faith, but in the wrong things. How many people have faith that war is more effective than negotiating with peace, sadly, probably a lot? His assignment for all of us was to try to raise the bar a bit, and try to reach for better things, and have faith in ourselves, and the world, that things can happen for us and for others.

Larry went on to talk about a monk who went into a cave for several years and was seeking enlightenment. After several years the monk returned home to his mother and rejoiced and said, "Mother! I have been enlightened! I am now one with God" She said, oh that's nice son, now let's move on to other things. He realized that she didn't believe him, and so, he showed her that there were such things as miracles and faith, and so…he created a giant flame next to his head that flowed toward his torso, and in the middle of his body it turned to water and flowed to the ground. She was amazed, and then he reversed it and the flame was at his feet and the water above. After she viewed the miracle she believed. Larry asked us how many of us would need to see something in order to believe that miracles can happen, and do happen. Sadly, not too many people believed in miracles.

He encouraged us all to get out of our own ways and open ourselves up to receiving messages that God has been trying to give us. I noticed that at the end of the prayers and services they say "And So It Is" instead of Amen. I like how this church practices principles of positive thinking and deeply cares about enriching the lives of everyone through God and love. I also looked just over the reverend's shoulder to the tapestry hanging behind him on the wall. It was beautiful. It looked exactly like what I picture when I meditate. It was a glowing ball of light woven with threads of lavender and gold. It shone down through several other levels containing smaller balls of light and lavender within them, and below that level was a light shining down to reflect on the entire Earth. Below the majesty of the light the Earth looked so small. That very second I envisioned how small I am on this Earth, compared to the entirety of the universe. It's hard to think that one little speck on this planet even makes a difference at all, but here, they believe that every living thing on this planet is part of God, and every part matters.

After the service I walked with my friend into the bookstore attached, and was happily greeted by one of the church members. She gave me a welcome packet full of books and information, as well as a copy of today's service on CD. All of the books in the store were about spiritual growth, meditation, yoga, and positivity. There were prayer beads, incense, Buddha statues, and scarves for sale (among many other things). This church is wonderful because it just encourages Oneness and connecting to God in whatever way you can, whether through yoga, meditation, prayer, or scripture. I also learned that they choose a different book from the bookstore to cover over a course of a few weeks through a book club that they host. I think that is really nice, so that you can hear other people's interpretations of the same words. Speaking of words, I realized I still had the book from the library at the Spirit Guided Friends Church and decided to drive over there and drop it off.

Billets Class

I pulled up and grew excited, like I was just about to walk in the door at Christmas time to see family I hadn't seen all year. I was well aware that I missed the service for the day and didn't expect to see anyone there except maybe one or two people, who hang around to talk, but I walked in and everyone was still there! They were seated in a circle and when I walked in Reverend Dan said, "Oh, I'm glad you could make it for the class, we already got started but you can still join, I'll fill you in." I didn't know there was a class today, but it was the class on Billets that I wanted to take anyway and didn't know when it was. I realize that everyone here is far more gifted than I am, and that my messages or interpretations won't be as good as theirs, then I remember to get out of my own way and have faith that it will be as it will be.

A bit of information about billets; billets are pieces of paper that are handed out to everyone seated within a circle. On your piece of paper you are to write a question, symbol, or word, and then fold it in half. Then place a symbol on the outside of the paper that you can recognize so that you won't draw your own paper from the basket. Once you have written your question down, and folded it, you are then to hold your paper in your hands for a couple of minutes. While your paper is between your palms, you are to meditate on the question or just pray. After a few minutes, everyone takes their own piece of paper and places it into a basket with the others. Once all of the billets are in the container it is passed around and each person draws one out. The billet you pull out is then placed between the palms of your hands and held for a few minutes.

In these few minutes it is recommended that you recite the Lord's Prayer to yourself, ask for all messages to come from the highest being, and say a prayer for the individual it may be coming from.

> Because our minds are extremely active, thoughts come and go quickly, sometimes at a pace that we forget as soon as they occur. In using psychic gifts the first thought that occurs is usually the right one. This encourages us to slow our thoughts to the point where we are able to catch that first thought, and use it as the foci or focal point. Many times the first thought seems so outrageous that we disbelieve it, or we get caught up in our own lessons and tell ourselves it is wrong. Billets suggest that by picking up on the vibrations on the card in your hands you can receive messages in accord, and through Oneness with God we can convey the right direction. –Reverend Dan

I took my first piece of paper and wrote, "When will I publish my book" and then on the outside I drew the symbol of a sun. The person that draws your paper is not to open it and is supposed to give a reading based solely on what they instantaneously see or feel based on the card itself. When the time came for my reading I wondered what message I would get. Another reverend had drawn my sunshine card, studied it over, and said:

I think this person has experienced quite a bit of the light, and is yearning for more. With patience and perseverance you will experience more gifts and more of the light. Ask and you shall receive. I think what you are looking for will happen when you let more light in. Once you have more light what you seek will happen.

She looked at me without even opening the card and said, "This is yours, right?" I nodded. She opened it up and then read my question aloud to everyone. She said to me, "I see that right now the time is shorter, and when the days are longer in the Spring, and there is more light…then it will be finished."

Next it was my turn. I held the card in my hands that had a star and either the symbol of infinity or an 8 on it and said, well this is my first time so it probably is wrong but what I immediately saw was a huge base of a tree trunk that was providing great strength and shelter to others, and a living room with a small painting on the walls. It reminded me of comfort and home. The woman across the circle giggled and said, "And so it is!" I opened the folded paper and the statement just said "spiritual guidance." She smiled ear to ear and said that it answered what she was looking for.

We went around again, and on the next paper I wrote the word "Destiny" and on the outside the symbol of a V, or flying bird. I love Diane, who happened to draw my paper, and she smiled and said, "I know this is yours." Without opening it or even seeing what the question was she said:

> I see you writing, books, there will be more than one. I see you by the ocean, and can taste the salt water. I see that you draw inspiration to inspire others and you draw it from places with water. If you are by a waterfall, spring, or ocean you are very inspired and draw in that changing pure energy from the earth. I also see you up in the forest by redwood trees, and I know we don't have those here, but you will be writing by redwood trees, possibly a mountain, and a spring. I see that you will be

able to produce the books when you are inspired by these places.

She didn't even open the card, and just handed it back to me. Someone in the circle said, well, what was her question inside? She laughed and said, "Oh yeah! Whoops! Her word was destiny, and I think we answered that."

After the class was over Reverend Dan asked if I had any questions, and said he would be doing another class in November. He also said that there are a couple of books that I may benefit from reading, both on meditation. I plan on picking up the first book, *The Secret of the Golden Flower*, first. I looked at the cover and noticed a familiar symbol. I made a puzzled face and started to say, "That symbol…" and Dan answered and told me that this is the symbol of the chakras. Then he said, you were saying? I went on to tell him that something looking quite similar appears to me in my room at night, and is spinning really fast, and it is quite scary to me. He handed me the book and told me to look through it and see if there is a picture of the one resembling what I see at night. I found one within seconds. He said that most of the time, right after we start to slip into the half-awake half-asleep state, most messages come through. He said he would research this symbol for me and get back to me next time on what it is, or what it may be that I am seeing in my half-awake state.

I watched as one of the members of the church helped Reverend Lucille out to her car and made sure she got in all right. I thought about how her question was related to her rent being increased and she was worried about how it would affect her. She is one of my favorite people that attend this church. I am in awe by her, and struck by sheer inspiration when I hear her speak. She is wise, calm, and one of the most unique people I have ever met. She offers up unique perspectives on life, spiritual practice, and intellect. I haven't known her long, but part of me loves her. I am guessing, but I would say she is near eighty years old. I hate the thought of her not being able to live comfortably or having to worry about financial problems at her age. I promised myself today, that if I ever do come into more money than I need I am going to help not only her but this church. There are a lot of wonderful people in this church, and if I had the means, I would help them all because they have helped me in more ways than they know.

September 24, 2013: A Visit from Peter

I woke up last night because I heard what sounded like paper being flipped through downstairs.

I look to my right, and there standing by my bed is an old man draped in white from head to toe. He has white hair, a long white beard, and a glowing body. His name is made known to me, Peter, without any spoken words. He seems like he has been standing there watching me sleep my entire life. He is stoic, calm, wise, and extremely guarding of me.

Once panic set in, I yelled, "OH MY GOD" and my boyfriend woke up and flipped on the light. I am not sure if this is the half-awake half-asleep state that they were talking about with me at the billets class, and I am not sure if I was dreaming this or if there really was a spirit by my bed. It seemed like he had been there a long time, almost like he was watching me sleep. I wasn't scared of him; it was quite the opposite. I felt extreme comfort from this vision.

I fell back asleep and dreamed again.

I am getting ready for work but can't find any socks to fit my feet. I leave this place and go down the elevator to a place where there is a garden. Within the garden are several ripe tomatoes that look wonderful. I want to eat one but as I get closer to them I can see all of the atoms of the tomatoes bouncing off of each other, and know they were to be observed and not eaten. I also know that somehow this is a smaller version of the solar system, and the atoms all correlate with stars or planets.

I shut my eyes and open them and am standing on a golden beach. There are several unicorns walking along it, and I am ecstatic that unicorns existed. I look to my hands and now have a Polaroid camera to take pictures of them, and with my other free hand I grab for my boyfriend's hand to come with me. He doesn't follow. I begin following a unicorn up a set of glowing white stairs towards a platform made of sunsets, and the unicorn turns into a young girl. The girl is not to be touched, and is so pure and holy that she must be pushed in a rolling bed with silver rails. She allows me to grab her hand, and smiles at me. Her hair is white and her robe was white and shining.

I look down to the ground and see my boyfriend below speaking with a very wise old woman; she whispers in his ear to buy a lottery ticket. He can't hear her, so I tell him what she said. I am under the impression that he will become very successful and ask her if he would still want to be with me after this took place. She nods. I look down at the ground to pick a flower and notice that all the flowers are light bulbs and I am standing in a garden of light. I look back at the girl so we can take a picture together, and she is gone.

Second part of same dream:

I am walking into a large mosque. My head is down because I don't want to look up or be present in what I think is a Muslim mosque. Someone says, "Raise your head; you are not where you think you are." I straightaway think I am in a place that is Hindu, and begin to pick out different things in the room that make me think it was a Hindu temple. Then I realize that neither is correct, and the best thing for me to do is to meditate in this space.

September 29, 2013: Sikh

The next day I woke up to the sound of rain hitting the windows sideways. There were storms coming in and something within me decided that I should go to yoga. I hadn't been for over four months and the thought of it just sounded wonderful. I arrived to what I anticipated would be a full studio but it was just the teacher and I, and I ended up having a very personal one-on-one session with the yoga instructor. Normally the classes are so packed it is hard to put your mat down without being in someone else's wingspan, but today it was just the two of us. He normally just says hi and bye, but today we actually had conversations before and after. I told him a little about my journey and he asked if I had been to any Sikh places yet. I had never even heard of it before, and asked what it was. He said he thought it was a cross between Hindu and Muslim, and he didn't know much more about it. So, I decided to see if I could find any places in Portland that had Sikh temples. After a bit of research I found that the places of worship are actually called Gurdwaras and the term temple is not satisfactory because they possess no sacrificial symbolism. I also found that the first misconception of Sikhism is that it is a cross between Hindu and Muslim. The religion itself is actually quite beautiful and is the fifth largest religion in the world, with over 23 million practicing Sikhs. Sikhism is a monotheistic faith that was founded by Guru Nanak Dev Ji (1469–1539) and was shaped by his nine successors in the sixteenth and seventeenth centuries in South Asia.

I called the Gurdwara the day prior to see if I could speak with one of the leaders, but unfortunately I don't speak Punjabi, and they don't speak English, so I went to their website to gather a little bit of information. The basic Sikh beliefs are very similar to that of Buddhists intertwined with Christianity with a touch of unique spirituality. They believe that God is omnipresent, omnipotent, and omniscient. The sun, moon, planets, wind, fire, water, vegetation and all other things that exist are His witnesses. They believe God is the sole creator, sustainer, and destroyer. He is beyond birth and death, and is self-illuminated. The Sikhs call God Waheguru, meaning the most wonderful Master. They share a lot of the Buddhist principles, but instead of seeking enlightenment, they seek to connect with God and also believe in the Bible. They incorporate a lot of Hindu principles as well, but they only worship one God and don't follow the idea of there being many…even if the many represent or come from the same One.

The religious leaders are also something of interest to me. I wondered if the people that give the lessons are Gurus themselves or if they read from a master book that another Guru wrote?

> The "Guru" is the exalted master who shows the way to enlightenment and union with God. According to Sikh beliefs, there were 10 Gurus in the human form from Guru Nanato and Guru Gobind Singh who developed the faith and molded the Sikh community. Guru Granth Sahib (sacred text) is the scriptural embodiment of over two centuries of spiritual teaching and instructions that became the eternal Guru of the Sikhs, ending the human lineage of Guru. Sikhs consider the message contained within the scripture to be the living word of God, communicated directly through the enlightened Gurus and Saints. Guru Granth Sahib

teaches through divine bani (words of god) that are set to a formal system of Sikh classical music. In the compilation of the Sikh scripture, the Gurus included the hymns of many non- Sikh spiritual guides from diverse religious traditions, making Guru Granth Sahib truly universal.

(http://www.gururamdassgurudwara.org)

I also wasn't sure if I should dress a certain way, but there wasn't any information on that besides the fact that the men wear turbans out of respect to God, and the women typically cover their heads with scarves to show respect as well. I pulled up to the Gurdwara and slowly got out of my car. I saw several men in white clothes and colored turbans under a tent outside preparing large quantities of food. I said hello and they just smiled and carried on. I went toward the building and entered in through the main door. Inside several pairs of shoes were placed on wooden shelves. I didn't see any people belonging to the shoes or any clear signs of where to go. I tried to listen for music or people talking but heard nothing. I removed my shoes and walked back outside to the men and tried to ask them where to go, but again no one spoke English.

Thankfully, up walked a young teenage girl who said, "Are you looking for something"? I smiled and exhaled, saying yes I actually am just looking to find out more information on the religion itself and this is my first time here. She said she was helping prepare the food for the day, but she would gladly guide me around. She instructed me to put the scarf I had on over my head and place my shoes up on the wooden shelf with the others. She led me to a set of wooden double doors and we walked inside the Gurdwara, which was ornately decorated with silk colors of pink, yellow, and red. We walked barefoot down the carpeted aisle that stretched all of the way from the back of the room to the front to what looked like a wooden canopy. There were tapestries hanging on the walls and pretty gold symbols arranged around the room. I was unable to read what was written on the symbols and the various signs placed around the room. We walked together down the aisle and then she placed an offering of a dollar in the offertory basket in the front. She whispered, "You don't have to do that if you don't want to, but we always believe in supporting each other and the community so most people donate at least a dollar." She dropped to her knees and bowed her forehead to the floor, and nudged me to do the same. With forehead to the ground I whispered, "What are we bowing to?" and she said, "To the Bible." I was unaware that they read from the Bible, but they do. Most of the readings came from the Bible today, but were spoken in Punjabi so I had to ask her most of what was being said.

After we bowed down we stood back up and took our seats on the floor to the left of the wooden canopy. A man in white came over and handed us a napkin and their food offering called *prashad*. I had never tasted *prashad* but it is really, really good. It tastes like a moist, sweet, grainy pudding. My new English-speaking friend GiGi explained that everyone typically helps prepare all of the food for the day, and the *prashad* as well as all the other food was freshly made. They had several offerings of food that were handed out during the service, and then afterwards homemade Indian lunch was served for everyone outside in the tent. "Here, we value supporting the community and like to make sure that no one is ever hungry. Speaking of," she said, "let's go to the kitchen and get tea and food."

We exited the main room, and walked barefoot back outside into the rain. She guided me back to another part of the building where several women and children were all seated on blankets throughout the room eating, laughing, and drinking tea. The rain was misting inside the room just a bit as we all sat around in a circle and shared stories. I loved it. It felt genuine and grounded. She explained that this is just what they do before the service actually starts. I think the food was battered zucchini with homemade sauces paired with several breads and pastries, and the tea reminded me of chai, which is one of my favorites. As we ate our breakfast we discussed certain traditions and beliefs that they have; one important one was that they believe in equality for all mankind despite race, gender, class, or religious distinction. This is quite a relief compared to others that believe that women are inferior and still enforce the caste system. Another important belief is that they encourage literacy, individual growth, hard work, family life, and honest living. Sikhs promote education and science as well as doing what you can to make the world a better place for all of humanity. She also told me that when they pray they can face any direction of their liking, because they believe that God is everywhere, and not just in one direction.

She asked me what brought me there and I explained where I had come from and what had led me there that day. She said she had only been coming to this place for a few months because she had just moved here from California, and was going to school here to be a flight attendant. She is only nineteen and seems eager to see the world. I pointed to a picture overhead of a beautiful temple with the words "Golden Temple" below it. She went on to tell me that it is a sacred Gurdwara built by the fifth Guru in the sixteenth century in Amritsar, Punjab, India. She had been there a few times, and asked if I had ever seen anything like it. In my opinion, there really is nothing too ancient or spectacular in America, and if I want to see a piece of history that is 500 years or older I need to go to another country. I told her I wanted to go to India for my second book and submerge myself in the culture for a different viewpoint. Apparently she had been to India several times and immediately chimed in that I should not go alone and it is best if I go with a group or a friend, or at least someone who can speak the language. Noted.

We finished up our meals and walked back into the Gurdwara. More and more people filed in the room, and took their seats on the floor. The women sat to the left and the men to the right. I admired all of the beautiful silk garments seated around me. I felt like I was in a sea of shining silk flags. There were several children there as well. All of the little boys had on turbans and the girls had small silk scarves over their heads. To the right of the wooden canopy was a small table draped in white cloth with two harmoniums and a set of small drums placed on top. The leaders took their seats on the floor behind the table and began playing the instruments in a melodious beat, then one by one, little boys and girls came forward and took turns singing with the leaders and playing the same song over again. A projector screen lit up and showed the words in both English and Punjabi for everyone to follow. It was nice that each child got a turn playing an instrument and singing with the leaders. After each one of their turns they skipped back to the arms of their parents.

The young boys behind me all had handheld games they were playing that helped them learn how to translate Punjabi to English. I thought for a second how more people should teach their children this way. Most American children have Gameboys with war games on them, and nothing educational. I watched these peaceful humble people all hugging and sharing cheer with each other and thought about what happens when these little boys go to school with the American kids. I wonder if they have to explain to others that they wear their turbans because they are showing respect to God, and if other people care to understand. I'll admit I was one of those people who judged due to a lack of education on the matter. Taking a step back and seeing how beautiful this religion is, and the people that carry on the traditions, I realize how wrong I have been. I'm sure I am not the only one, but I am happy to admit I have found change within myself and new perspective. I thought about compassion for a second, and a lesson I was taught at the Spirit Guided Friends church. Someone offered the example of reincarnation, and said "we alternate genders, races, and religions throughout our cycles of rebirth to teach us the true meaning of compassion for all."

After the children sang and played their instruments three leaders came forth and took their places behind the white cloaked table. They began playing beautiful harmonious music that instantaneously made me shut my eyes, exhale, and turn my palms to the sky, as if something magnetic was now present in the room. It was sacred and enchanting, and though I couldn't understand what they were saying, I loved it. I could feel myself swaying back and forth, almost like a pendulum unable to control itself from the forces around it. I felt as if my sit bones (also known as sits or sitz bones, the ischial tuberosity, or lowest part of the bones that make up the pelvis) were part of the floor, and the energy and rhythm of the chants were guiding my body in a swaying motion. I remember this feeling precisely; I had this same feeling when I had my Reiki session: this swaying, as if I was on a boat being softly rocked back and forth in a clean and gentle sweeping sea. At once I began to meditate and didn't envision myself any other place than where I was at that very moment. It was wonderful, and different. I opened my eyes and looked around, and saw every other person rocking together in the same motion that I was. Mesmerized and intrigued, I smiled and was thankful for the purity and sincere unity I felt at that moment. I recalled the story from the Buddhist temple about the man who saw the reflection of one gem within all the others within his web of gemstones and thought about how we are all connected to each other, every being, everything, and though we can't see God, this is the energy that connects life throughout the world. Growing and living, and somehow flowing together through this cosmic energy. This is the closest I have felt to God thus far.

I looked to the leader standing over the book they were reading from, and noticed he was waving what looked like a long jeweled wand with white feathers hanging from it. He waved it back and forth over the book for several minutes. I leaned in to the girl next to me and asked what it was, she said that it was actually a whisk and it is used to fan over the book as a form of blessing and respect. In ancient times they used the whisk to fan the privileged, and now as a form of dignity and honor they fan over the book, and treat it as if it is something that is alive and respected. I realized that I had been there over three hours, and could really feel the soreness setting in my muscles from the combination of intense yoga from the day prior and too much sitting. After the last prayer and song concluded, the leaders walked amongst the seated people with their hands out and placed one final offering of *prashad* within our palms. Everyone was migrating outside to another part of the building to enjoy lunch that was prepared for the day. I had been there so long, and though the food smelled amazing, I decided to head home.

I thought about how the entire service was set to music and couldn't help but become intrigued by the movement and swaying that happened during the chants. Someone once told me that the frequency of the Earth is the same as the frequency of most Indian chants, specifically ones used in meditation. I can't help but wonder if the frequency moving me today was something divine. It's hard to explain. But in that moment I really did feel like I was whole. Bound with love, bound with God, and with something that is present within every other life in the world. I pictured little beams of light connecting every soul, every living thing in the world and vibrating, in tune together. That frequency, that harmony that I felt echoed throughout every person in the room despite language barriers and ethnicity…it felt like, for the first time, God.

October 2, 2013: Reflections

I began reading three books at once. Not because that's my norm, quite the opposite actually, but because I am eager to read all of these books equally: The Bible, The Qur'an, and a book called *Chariots of the Gods? Chariots of the Gods?* was recommended to me by one of the members of the Spirit Guided Friends Church. I started the Qur'an first, and found that I have to read it in small increments because it angers me. I also found that being angered by ignorance and outdated chauvinistic practices is something I need to personally work on. To take a refresher, I opened up *Chariots of the Gods?* This book starts off with a lot of statistics on the probability of life on other planets and surfaces, and odd occurrences on this Earth that remain unexplained. Interesting enough to remain on my Goodreads list I suppose. As of yesterday, before I go to bed I read the Bible. I figure I should read the Bible if I am reading the Book of Mormon and the Qur'an as well. I began with page one, and so far I have realized that people lived a really, really, really long time, and the thought of living to be 900 years old seems both vampire-ish, exhausting, and intriguing. Especially due to the fact that everything we were taught growing up showed that the average lifespan of people has increased as time has gone on, not decreased.

So far, I've read up to the point of the creation of man, and Noah building the ark. (Side note, it has been raining nonstop for the past four days and is officially the most rain Portland has seen in the month of September in history.) I wake up to a text from my sister asking me if I am building an ark…how fitting. I go back to the

Chariots of the Gods? book and explore the concept that if aliens landed on Earth in prehistoric times, would their ships and lights have been viewed to the cavemen as "Gods" and more so, why is it that the cave drawings of men with circular helmets on have appeared in caves all over the world? I never imagined these thoughts would ever cross my mind as rational or possible, but I suppose if someone or something from another planet did visit the Earth from above, flying, with bursts of light and wings on their ships, they *could* have been viewed as a God or Angel. Just as crazy as a talking snake I suppose.

The author then focuses on the beginning of the Bible, which I am reading currently, and discusses how it is possible that these Gods reproduced with man, specifically in the creation of Moses, and suggests that he received instructions from the Gods regarding the Ark. Details around the Ark were specifically outlined as to how it was to be built from God – even the appropriate footwear and clothing to be worn while transporting it. He details an account from 2 Samuel 6:2: "David had the Ark of the Covenant moved, and Uzzah helped to drive the cart it was in. When passing cattle shook and threatened to overturn the Ark, Uzzah grabbed hold of it. He fell dead on the spot, as if struck by lightning."

The author then goes on to highlight his interpretation of the Ark being electronically charged:

> If we reconstruct it today, according to the instructions handed down by Moses, an electric conductor of several hundred volts is produced. The border and golden crown would have served to charge the condenser, which was formed by the gold plates and a positive and negative conductor. If in addition one of the two

cherubim on the mercy seat acted as a magnet, the loudspeaker, perhaps even a kind of set for communication between Moses and the spaceship, was perfect." (p. 40)

This author also suggests the frequent flashing sparks mentioned in Exodus were evidence that Moses made use of this transmitter whenever he needed help and advice.

The spiritual nomad in me doesn't want to explore this option because I have come so far in my own voyage to connect with God, and pondering this theory would set me back greatly. I think maybe that is why those raised with a specific religion put up walls to explore or accept other religious beliefs themselves. What I've come to believe: There may have been aliens that visited our planet and were depicted as Gods, but ultimately there was something that created them…and us…and everything in the universe. Whatever energy that I felt while meditating at the Sikh Gurdwara, and whatever energy orbits the Earth around the Sun, and whatever energy changes the seasons…that is God. God is bigger than this Earth, or other planets, and outside of our gender specific labels. God is and will be something, that whether you try to fathom it or not in your lifetime, will remain as infinity, unmeasured, and unproven with scientific proof or documents.

October 6, 2013: Nondenominational

This evening I went to a nondenominational church around 5 p.m. I arrived to a full house packed with about 300 people all around my age. A person driving by might think this was a concert hall or gallery. People flooded outside to the sidewalks all casually talking, hugging, and drinking coffee. The smell of Stumptown coffee greeted me quite nicely as I approached the building and walked through the double doors. I shook hands with a nice girl on my way in and began making my way through the crowd. Through the main doors to the right was an entire wall of coffee and tea options. There were also vintage lounges and plush armchairs neatly placed throughout the main room. The sun was setting and people began taking their seats inside, but not in the way you would think. There were no two chairs alike in the entire church, and people walked up and down the aisles in search of the perfect chair for the service. Some were wooden, some old school desks, others plush velvet, and the list went on. It made for a very unique arrangement for a church, but somehow I felt as if I was at a friend's house waiting for a poetry reading or movie to begin.

Once I had picked out a perfectly plush blue armchair I sat down and got situated. Others were still sizing up their seats and moving like a 300-person game of musical chairs, and then up walked the girl who shook my hand at the door. "I notice you came in alone, do you have friends with you or are you meeting someone here?" I was taken off guard by the stranger and just said oh…um no…it's just me here. "I've been attending this church for over three years now; you can come up front and sit with my husband and me if you want to." I moved from my seat in the back, and right up to the second row. My new seat was far less comfortable, but it was too late. I spent a lot of the service fidgeting and trying to find a comfortable demeanor, and listening of course.

They started off the service with a band. The band played a few songs, and if I didn't know I was in a church I would have thought that I was at a live concert. Their voices were wonderful, and the main singer sounded a lot like Kurt Cobain and his backup singer a bit like a country Tori Amos. After they finished two songs they introduced another musician. A petite woman with pixie hair and a big guitar came to the stage. She introduced herself and began speaking about her focus on children's music. All of her music focuses around scripture, and is available in several different languages. With a confident smile she said, "Our goal is to help introduce children to the meaning of scripture at an early age and dress the feet of children with the word of the Lord." I not only liked her music, but really admired that she was introducing children to music that wasn't about women, or bling, or whatever rich people think about. She was soulful, passionate, and in her eyes, "tattooing scripture on the hearts of the young."

While the band exited the stage the girl next leaned in and whispered, "the next speaker is not normally the pastor, but he is really intelligent and so passionate about the Bible. You'll really like him!"

A man walked slowly up to the platform with Bible in hand. He had on brown boots and gray jeans with a solo roll cuffed just above the tops of his shoes. His hair grazed his chin in a soft wave and accented his big eyes. He was subtle yet passionate, simple and real. He was a father and active member in both his church and community, and today, he was sharing verses 1–10 from Ephesians 2. First, he read the passage in its entirety:

> As for you, you were dead in your transgressions and sins, [2] in which you used to live when you followed the ways of this world and of the ruler of the kingdom of the air, the spirit who is now at work in those who are disobedient. [3] All of us also lived among them at one time, gratifying the cravings of our flesh and following its desires and thoughts. Like the rest, we were by nature deserving of wrath. [4] But because of his great love for us, God, who is rich in mercy, [5] made us alive with Christ even when we were dead in transgressions—it is by grace you have been saved. [6] And God raised us up with Christ and seated us with him in the heavenly realms in Christ Jesus, [7] in order that in the coming ages he might show the incomparable riches of his grace, expressed in his kindness to us in Christ Jesus. [8] For it is by grace you have been saved, through faith—and this is not from yourselves, it is the gift of God— [9] not by works, so that no one can boast. [10] For we are God's handiwork, created in Christ Jesus to do good works, which God prepared in advance for us to do.

Most churches that read from the Bible take scripture and then try to relate it to our everyday lives through scenarios we can understand. This man, however, took the entire next hour to break down each sentence line by line and tell us exactly what it meant, and why it is important:

> Let's start at the beginning, see, we are not actually dead, not physically, but there are those who are dead with Christ and dead in faith, and have no desire to have it either. This is like someone trying to teach you a language of a country that you have no intentions of ever visiting. Those people are almost like the walking dead, and have no interest in God or utilizing the light and beauty that could be theirs. Let me transition here for a second, to a story from my childhood.

He paced back and forth with the Bible still in hand, as he reflected back through his vault of memories, and began again.

> Every Christmas as a kid, I would sit behind the Christmas tree with my back against the wall peering through the wonderland of lights and tinsel, and that place too was always the mirror of innocence. I was with family and in the arms of something almost magical and traditional which I got to be a part of every year. Well, a year went by from one Christmas to the next and in that time I had done a lot of bad things, things that I'm not proud of, and don't care to share. I was like a dog that kept going back to its own vomit; though I was seeing these things I was doing, and though I knew they were bad I just kept on repeating the unhealthy cycle. And with every instance of immoral behavior that I carried out I felt like someone was taking a hot stick and branding me with it, just enough to singe away a bit of my innocence each time. But all sores become callused and the next time I did it, I didn't feel so bad, and so I carried on.

I really like the visual he gave next of being led down this path and by the time he realized who he was following, the door shut behind him. The following Christmas, when he sat in his favorite spot and tried to look through the once shiny lens of innocence he noticed it was broken, and that place was like a burned down city he couldn't revisit and could only faintly remember. He went back to the scripture and said, "And now, if it couldn't be worse it talks about how by nature we are deserving of wrath." He paused for a second and said, "if this was a *Walking Dead* show this would be the end, when the wrath rains down and those who are dead remain that way and no one is saved but a few, BUT luckily for us, this is not the end, and the Bible goes on to say that there is hope, and not because of anything that we have done, but because God is full of mercy and grace we are saved."

I think that the term "saved" is thrown around a lot. People who have done wrong or sometimes find that they have been "saved" and then are able to forgive themselves for the deed. People in jail say they are saved a lot, but when you are sober and in a cell for the rest of your life in between accidental soap drops or beatings, what else are you going to find to have faith in, or find hope in? Who actually tells them that they have been saved? Does saving mean that you just realized you have done wrong in your life and you have found something that gives you comfort for what may be near in your future? This jail-time soap image was not in the service; this was just a random thought of mine. The bubble overhead is popped as I return to the service, and the pastor says, "And to be saved means to be made alive with Christ and raised up to sit with him in the heavens. To be raised up from the spiritual death and ascend up to the heavens." He mentioned that from the point of being reawakened with Christ that there is then a place within us where he lives, and we can connect, grow, and communicate with this place at any time.

The bubble reappears and I have a thought…is the tree of life within us, and if it is, is this the place where we reconnect with the root of the living spirit of God? Is this the place that I go to every time I successfully meditate, or better yet, when I dream? The bubble spans on, and I think that if reincarnation happens, which I think it does, then does that mean that I have been to heaven already? Maybe several times, and each lifetime this seed or tree just needs to be lit up again? Maybe that is the reason we light trees at Christmas: in celebration of reawakening, rebirth, and making this piece of us alive again.

October 12, 2013: Jehovah's Witness (JW)

God, Allah, Lord, Thetan, Krishna, Yahweh, Jehovah. The same God being called different names, and worshiped through different ceremonies and books. The Bible says (John 14:6): "I am the way and the truth, and the life. No one comes to the Father except through me." Jehovah's Witnesses also believe this, as a matter of fact; they believe everything in the Bible, literally, not figuratively.

I had two women come to my house this morning for my first JW Bible study. We started with a prayer to Jehovah. As soon as the prayer concluded I asked, and why do you say Jehovah, not God or Lord or any other name for God? They instructed me to flip to Psalms 83:18 and read it out loud, "And let them know that you alone whose name is Lord are the most high over all the Earth." With a crinkled eyebrow she said, "Well most Bibles have the word Jehovah there and not the word Lord, and that is why we worship Jehovah because that is the name of God." With that she handed me a book that was described to me as "like putting on glasses to see better, because the Bible can sometimes be misinterpreted." They now have this helpful handheld pamphlet that can make the Bible crystal clear. This is also their interpretation, just like there are different interpretations of the Qur'an.

We could only cover one section today so they had me flip through the pamphlet and pick a topic out. I chose a section called "Where do the dead go?" According to JW interpretations of the Bible, the soul ceases to exist at all once the body dies. They referred to the death of Lazarus when Jesus describes him as just resting. They described to me the image of a candle going out, and after the flame is gone that is it, there is no more. They believe that after we die we are simply put to rest…not in heaven or hell or any spirit realm, but here on Earth in a grave. Because we are doing a little bit of reading out of Matthew today, I highlighted this passage that makes me think that reincarnation is supported in the Bible, and that Elijah and John the Baptist were the same soul:

> Matthew 17:10–13: And the disciples asked him, saying, "Why then do the scribes say that Elijah must come first?" But he answered them and said, "Elijah indeed is to come and will restore all things. But I say to you that Elijah has come already, and they did not know him, but did to him whatever they wished. So also shall the Son of Man suffer at their hand." Then the disciples understood that he had spoken of John the Baptist.

So, what do you believe happens then? "Well, this is just a resting period, and when the second coming of Christ happens God will reawaken all of the dead and everyone will walk the Earth together, restored to perfect health like Adam and Eve were in the beginning." She backed this thought up with more scripture. John 5:28–29: "Do not be astonished at this for the hour is coming when all who are in their graves will hear his voice, and will come out. Those who have done good to the resurrection of life, and those who have done evil to the resurrection of condemnation." And Psalms 37:10–11: "Yet a little while, and the wicked will be no more; though you will look diligently for their place they will not be there but the meek shall inherit the land and delight themselves in abundant prosperity."

I raised a shy quick hand and said, so...like zombies? What you just described sounds a lot like zombies. I also picture my mom having some trouble in this scenario since she was cremated. They said, they could better describe this to me later, and wanted to carry on to the next part of the passage. I also asked about Heaven, specifically because the Bible speaks about the reward of Heaven and that all are forgiven of sins when they repent. So why do they not believe that people go there when the Bible describes it? They went to more scripture and read Revelation 14:1: "I looked and there was the Lamb on Mt. Zion and with him were 144, 000 who had his name and his father's name written on their foreheads."

I interrupted again and said well, wait a minute, are you saying that over the entire history of the world that only 144,000 people are ever going to Heaven? Well how many Jehovah's Witnesses are there? They answered, "Well there are about seven million in the world right now." I gave an awkward smile as I did the math, and said well then I suppose the odds don't look that good at this point, and if the odds are *this* bad, and there is nothing that happens after we die, then why be a good person at all, and more so why go door to door telling about the bad odds?

She turned to more scripture, Matthew 28:18–20, and said, "And Jesus said to them all authority in Heaven and on Earth has been given to me. Go and make disciples of all the nations baptizing them in the name of the Father, the Son, and the Holy Spirit." She also said that God wanted people to go in pairs to gain disciples, and that was the will of God...which they take very seriously. I read on and then said, but in Luke it says "do not go door to door." She paused and said that she didn't see that in her Bible, and asked what version I had. Well, I have the version my Grandma gave me in

1993, and if that much has been altered between then and now what does that say about the alterations that could have been made over 3500 years? It is possible that she had a JW Bible and they took that part out, but I am not sure.

With that, I asked her what her thoughts on the scripture was, and asked her to ponder for a minute if maybe the burning bush was just red leaves in the fall time, and the parting of the sea was a sea of people or there was just a shallow part of the water that was able to be walked on, and maybe the young boy that sat up from his casket when Jesus put his hand on it really wasn't physically dead. Both women sat in silence and one just made a note that said "burning bush." Once again my question was answered with scripture, Romans 15:4: "For whatever was written in former days were written for our instruction, so that by steadfastness and by encouragement of the scriptures we might have hope." So without directly answering my question she said that it looks like the Bible wants us to apply what was previously written here and use it for encouragement and hope. I also came across another passage in Matthew that said, "Jesus spoke to the crowds in parables."

I guess my face looked like I had questions, so she asked if I understood everything so far. I replied, so to be clear, you guys believe that once we die there is nothing? No communication, no next world or spirit realm, and we cease to exist until one day we all are resurrected, and at that point all of the dead and living will together walk on the Earth and they will all be restored to perfect health? That sure will be a ton of people, and I am still picturing zombies. What about mummies? People who were cremated? Then you believe that 144,000 virgins that have never told a lie will go to Heaven – right? So my question is, if you don't believe in anything after death, and really no one knows, and your guess is just as good as all the others coming from all the other books, then…well let me tell you a story.

I went on to tell them about how my mom and I had both seen the Indian girl on several occasions in our house, and that cabinets would open and close on their own right in front of us. She said that that most likely didn't happen because there isn't an explanation for that according to what Jesus said. I also told her about the hummingbird that came to my window when I had knee surgery, and how it came several days in a row…in November, in the rain, to the tenth story of my building. She couldn't explain this either, and of course turned to more scripture, John 4:1 "Beloved, do not believe every spirit but test the spirits to see whether they are from God, for many false prophets have gone out into the world." This passage suggests to me that spirits can give messages, but I think what she was trying to say is that many other religions or people think they are worshiping a God but really it could be something else.

They asked me what I think about other religions and if I thought that God would approve of how they worship. First off I have no idea of what God approves of or not; no one does. I went off on a bit of a tangent and replied that I picture God as a giant umbrella covering the entire universe. Underneath the umbrella I see a lot of people desperately try to make sense of what little piece they have seen. So they label it their own, divide what they think is right and wrong, slap a gender on it and leverage accordingly, and then the conflict begins. The people begin fighting in the name of peace all trying to represent something that they will never understand. So, I think that religion, in a sense, has strayed from what it was meant to be. BUT I also see the good people under the umbrella too, who have open minds and realize they are part of something bigger. They realize that God isn't theirs or anyone's and no matter how they choose to worship…whether it's praying five times a day, meditating, wearing an underwear suit, or going door to door, I think God is loving and he or she doesn't care how you worship, just as long as you are worshiping for the right reasons.

After seconds of silence and a few nods while taking notes I decided to ask the girls what they thought about what I was doing. Scripture followed. Matthew 5:3: "Blessed are the poor in spirit for theirs is the kingdom of Heaven" (my edition). I frowned. One of the girls chimed in that their book doesn't say that, and should have said, "Happy are those conscious of their spiritual need, since the kingdom of the heavens belongs to them." That sounds better. I deduced that this meant that they approve of my spiritual journey and the spiritual need that I have. She wanted to go back to my concept of the soul and what happens to it when we die. I said that I believe the soul goes on to a spirit world and continues on until rebirth, and this happens until we learn the lessons we failed to learn the life prior. As far as where I think my mom is…sometimes she's in Heaven, sometimes she's in my dreams, sometimes she's a hummingbird, and other times she is everywhere else flowing energy into every living thing. I don't think she's gone, and in a weird way, I feel like I am closer to my mom now than I ever was when she was actually here.

"Tell us a bit about your dreams." I told them that I had several dreams where my grandpa would come to me as a white horse and show me that he was coming to take my mom away. I detailed them much more than that, and they remained silent. "Well, maybe that was your way of coping to help accept that she was sick," she said. I countered, and said that I had those dreams far before we knew she was sick. I did reiterate that in the Bible many great prophets were visited and given messages in dreams, and that is a common theme in the Bible that is too great to ignore. "That's true, but most of the dreams in the Bible come from God, and not from other people that are passed on." I think that wherever my mom is, is where God is, and so...I think the dreams are valid, meaningful, and I don't care if they line up with the "rules" of this specific religion. "I'll tell you what, I'm going to do some research to see if what you have experienced has an explanation, and lines up with scripture." I felt the need to quote the great Salt-N-Pepa and say "there's only one true judge, so just chill and let my fatha' do his job," but I refrained. She did seem sincere and willing to help me, and really did seem like she wanted to help bring me peace of mind. I also remind myself not to judge others, for they are just mirror images walking a different path.

Before they left they asked if I would like to set up another time to discuss more sections and answer more questions. For the sake of second chances I accepted. They also asked if I felt like I understood them and could see myself as a JW. (Which, by the way, you have to earn rights to be a JW and I don't know much about how, but assume door-to-door visits and money are involved.) I decided to answer their question with a quote from Sorcha, "Most people don't let Jehovah's Witnesses in their houses because they don't want to question their beliefs and what they were raised to believe." So even though I wasn't raised with much religion, and I don't specifically agree with their foundations I will keep an open mind and allow education to ensue. They asked me if a Jehovah's Witness had told me that, and I said, no actually a Pagan. They seemed a bit thrown off by that, and then got back to the subject of our next meeting. They told me to read up on the next section on Souls and write down any questions between now and then.

After they left I walked upstairs and stood in front of my mom's smiling picture and had a few moments of just silence. I felt bad for some reason, and said, Mom, I'm sorry about that. I believe you are still here and know it is you when you visit me in dreams. I hope you know that these conversations I have with people are supposed to be helpful, and I guess they are because it's helping me figure out what I actually believe in. One day I'll figure it out, until then, please don't leave me.

A Dream

I'm watching myself get ready for an event in a large dressing room. I'm trying on all kinds of head scarves and place a yellow silk sari over my head. It is sheer, shiny, with embellishments. It falls into place over my head and turns into a wedding veil. Once I have the wedding veil on I am no longer a witness in the room, but am back in my own body. I am off balance and look down at my feet down below and realize I am standing on wooden stilts. I run out of the room and onto a beach, and trip over a path of white fabric. I look to the source, which seems miles away, and it appears I've tripped over a bride's gown, or the train of it. I wake up and feel like I am not in my bed. I look to my right and there is a tunnel to the right of my bed, filled with green gardens and white light. I look away and turn to the left and to my surprise the same thing is on the left side of my bed. I shake my boyfriend and whisper, "Do you see that?" He wakes up and the tunnels disappear.

October 20, 2013: Unitarian

When I think of what a Unitarian church may be, the words unity, oneness, and whole come to mind. So, I imagine that this church must be a representation of being "one with God" or something along those lines. It was a foggy October morning; the colors of red, yellow, and rust popped through the fog and piled in heaps along the sides of the roads and sidewalks. Even the immense gray thick bricks of the castle-like church seemed hidden until I was feet away from it. I swooped another round of scarf around my neck as I briskly walked inside.

The church was so full that even the balcony that I migrated to was crowded. I looked around and noticed the wide variety of people present; people of all ages, colors, genders, and sexual preference filled the pews from top to bottom. My gaze centered to the woman directly in front of me who was knitting a sweater or scarf of some kind. Her hands were moving in an almost poetic trance, and I thought Oh no! I've been staring at her hands for several minutes now! I had to have missed anything going on around me for the past five minutes.

The service began with a choir, but not the typical church band choir I've been seeing week after week. It was a tribal beat harmonized with bongo drums and deep humming. Then wooden instruments began and tied in the sounds with maracas. The music sounded like it belonged in *The Lion King* or something similar. The pipe organ blended into the wooden backdrops and looked like gold-painted bamboo shoots with a piano for roots. To the left and right of the organ was what looked like trees from afar, but when I looked closer the entire tree was made of different color wooden blocks. Up close it looked like a waterfall of wood, but from far away, it looked like a pixelated tree, like something out of a video game. I noticed there weren't any crosses, Jesus pictures, or stained glass either. Instead, there were ornate tapestries hanging on the walls that looked like the sun, and simple glass windows with wooden frames. The windows actually looked like an autumn watercolor with the colors of the leaves blurring through the foggy glass.

After the choir finished the first song a little bird perched up in the open window and sang. It was like something you would see in a Disney movie, and couldn't have been timed better. The minister came forward and led us in an opening prayer that started like this, "Dear Creator of Life, and God of many names." I opened my eyes a sliver and smiled. It was nice to be in a place that lined up with my thought processes at the moment. There wasn't a Bible there either; instead there was a book full of poems and quotes from literary geniuses that the church found inspiring.

Today's service was on marriage. A poem by Wendell Berry called "The Larger Circle" was read first and then the minister began the service. He began with the words "by the power vested in me I now pronounce you…" I thought for a second about when I might hear those words, and if it would be anytime soon. He went on to say, that he actually had said those words several times, but one of his favorite times saying it was when he was able to legally marry the first same sex couple in Massachusetts, everyone clapped (this was also the first time he appeared in *Time* Magazine). He sits on several boards supporting same sex marriage and gender equality, and actually sounded a lot like President Obama. I also was very shocked when he said he was on a board for African Americans because until now, I thought he was white. Maybe my vision is going bad. After a quick introduction about his views on same sex marriage he kindly introduced a member of the church to come forward and speak. A petite short-haired woman came forward with a huge smile on her face. She and her wife had found a wonderful home here at this church where they felt welcomed, supported, and loved. This church seemed like a very supportive community-based group that encouraged peace and love through God. They preached modern-day services and kept everything relevant to ongoing world events.

After another short story about two elderly people who were still in love after seventy years of marriage the minister led the congregation in a silent meditation. It was unexpected, but really nice. I also liked that people young and old silently meditated for several minutes together as a congregation. A bell rang to end the meditation portion and then the minister came back up to begin his sermon called "What is Marriage for?"

> Long ago, when people married, it was not for love but for two reasons: 1. You were poor and needed more labor workers (kids) and by marrying you could help support many people under one household, or 2. You were rich, and you were strengthening your house and alliances. In most cases women didn't even get to say 'I do' and their fathers would say it for them. Also, the act of the father walking his daughter down the aisle was to symbolize her being handed from one ownership to another. Sounds romantic right?

He also highlighted the fact that in the Bible King Solomon had over 300 wives and 1000 other women he frequented because back then men could marry as many women as they wanted, or could buy. Thankfully much has changed since then, and he asked again, specifically to the women, who now have the right to not get married and break free of old confinements…Why get married?

Next he asked how many people have seen the movie *Shall We Dance?* A few had seen it. He described a scene where Susan Sarandon finds out her husband isn't cheating, and the reason for his reinvigorated lifestyle is ballroom dance lessons. She sits down with the detective and he asks her specifically why people get married, and her response is:

> We need a witness to our lives. There's a billion people on the planet…what does any one life really mean? But in a marriage, you're promising to care about everything. The good things, the bad things, the terrible things, the mundane things…all of it, all of the time, every day. You're saying "Your life will not go unnoticed because I will notice it. Your life will not go un-witnessed because I will be your witness."

I thought for sure that he would take this opportunity to express that this is what God is for us, but he didn't. He simply added that people need a witness in life, support, love, care, and peace. Now that times have changed for so many people this should be available to **everyone,** no matter the partner or preference. Instead of wrapping this back in with something about God he circled back to his main quote and said, "And by the power vested in me I now pronounce you…" Every person…old, young, gay, straight, male, and female billowed out a resounding clap for him, and he went on to say, "May it be so! And may it be soon!" He dismissed everyone with the words, "Go in peace and practice love," but no one got up to leave. The organ struck up the chords to "When I'm Sixty-four" by John Lennon and Paul McCartney and everyone sang along. It was empowering, and caring, and binding, and loving. I felt like this is the type of church that other old, stuck in their ways churches should model. Not once did he read from the Bible, but instead preached lessons of love, compassion, and equality. It reminded me a lot of Buddhist ways. I am starting to see resemblances of several churches within others, and circle back to think about the Buddhist story about the net in the sky with all the gemstones reflecting one another. I also think I could have many more great life lessons to reflect upon if I had attended more than two Buddhist temples. This church is wonderful, and embodies a lot of the characteristics I adhere to, but something in me is looking for more of a spiritual connection. Maybe that is something I am to develop on my own.

Thoughts on Einstein and Prophets

As I finish up a journal entry something in the background forces me to lift my head up and watch TV. A program about Einstein and "ancient aliens" is playing and mentions that some people believe that Einstein acquired knowledge that wasn't available for his time and couldn't have been learned from life on this planet. I don't believe *everything* I read...or see on television, but it is interesting to learn about the studies of Einstein's brain and some of the findings so I kept the show on. Some people believe that there is a place that some people can tap into, known by Hindus as the zero point field, or the Akashic Record. People who can tap into this place, or state of mind, such as Nostradamus, acquire access to information and thoughts...past, present, and future. This is the same stream of eternal consciousness that Edgar Cayce describes as well. The show went on to examine Einstein's actual brain itself. His parietal lobe was 15% larger than most normal human beings. Some people believe that because of this, he could possibly connect with places or thoughts that most others couldn't. The final thought being, the uniqueness of his brain allowed him to communicate with other realms that no one else could tap into before him. The program went on to say that maybe there are individuals that have similar gifts, and these people are placed here in this world as Mystics and Prophets to influence and provide messages to shape religion in our world, and in Einstein's case to create the theory of relativity and other genius theories.

October 22, 2013: A Nightmare

This dream is displayed as a catastrophe that takes place over two days. Day one: I am in the city of sin, there is overindulgence, gluttony, and too much consumption. Everything here is masked in glitter. The sky turns red and purple and the Earth shakes. I look to my left and see the mountain by my house erupting with smoke and lava spilling from its top. My family and I rush into a very tall building. They have given up hope as the lava floods the lands. I say bye to my dad, stepmom, and real mom, who are standing there in a line. I turn to my grandpa (my dad's dad, who is still alive), who is in line to go up an elevator to a safe place. Everyone is in groups of four. I can't go. I hug him and ask where he's going. He shrugs, China maybe? The building tips slowly after the elevator takes him and the others in the groups of four up. All burns. A large, dark shadow of a man is turning the corner.

I wake up.

Day two: I fall back asleep and go right back to where I was before, but it is a different scenario. I am standing in front of the same building and look into a carriage parked out front. Inside the carriage is someone I recognize but have forgotten the name of. I apologize and he says his name is Peter, and I have only just forgotten his name. He is tan with dark hair, and wearing a white robe. He tells me I have to follow him first before I can go back into the building. We walk into a dark room full of sleeping people in black sleeping bags. The room is full of sleeping cocooned people I am careful not to step on. I have the feeling this is the beginning, and I will wake up many. He guides me to a specific sleeping bag and I wake up a man with dark-rimmed glasses and give him two gifts; one is a circular object, magnifying glass, and the other is something for him to read. We leave this room and go on to another where a girl is trapped and I have to try to be part of something to free her. There are thousands of loose wires hanging from the walls. I am in a black dress and walk onto the set of a video that is being produced, and this video is going to distract someone so that we can free the girl that is trapped. I go back to the elevator with Peter, and he puts me in line with my sisters to go up the elevator. I don't want to leave him. Upstairs it is beautiful. There is a party with champagne and lots of expensive jewelry for everyone to have. All of the gems look so extravagant I am nervous to touch anything. Though celebrating, it seems everyone inside is sad – they have lost loved ones in the fire from the last dream. All of a sudden there is an earthquake and everyone rushes to the large glass windows to look down on the world below. We feel the building tilting and this time it falls the opposite way than it did in the prior dream. The ocean rises up to the windows as it swallows the land below. I ask my sister where mom is because she was here yesterday; she only replies, "Has she been singing to you again? Only you can hear her." Everyone in the room is safe from the flood outside. My dog runs out one of the doors and I can't stop her. Once the flood recedes the doors of the safe room open back up and the sun comes out, everyone cheers and runs into the light. I come to the body of my dog that ran outside and her eyes are gone. Once the sunshine graces her body she can see again and wakes up.

Then I wake up.

October 26, 2013: Jehovah's Witness Part 2

Two women arrived at my door this morning for yet another Bible study. Last time we spoke I left them to explore their thoughts on my dreams and if "they come from God" or if they are to be considered meaningful at all. Within a two-week span they were able to give me a definitive answer on the matter. I had just gotten done placing some fresh fall colored lilies around the room and lighting some spiced candles to make the room more inviting. I offered up some French press coffee to the ladies and then we took our seats in my living room.

They began by having me flip to Job 33:13–16 and read aloud to them what it said, and I read, "For God speaks in one way, and in two, though people do not perceive it. In a dream, in a vision of the night, when deep sleep falls on mortals, while they slumber on their beds, then he opens their ears, and terrifies them with warnings." So, they went on to further explain that yes, in some cases God did communicate with people through dreams. I was always told that whatever someone says before the word "but" never matters; then came the but part. "BUT, turn now to Hebrews One and read that." I read aloud, "Long ago God spoke to our ancestors in many and various ways by the prophets, but in these last days he has spoken to us by a Son, whom he appointed heir of all things, through whom he also created the worlds. He is a reflection of God's glory and the exact imprint of God's very being, and he sustains all things by his powerful word." I stopped here, and looked up at them, so…what you are saying is that nowadays this is not how God communicates? They nodded, and followed it up by saying that it is written right here in the Bible for us to see, and back then the communication that God had with the prophets was handled in this way, but after Jesus, then all communication came through him.

The one girl paused and shut her Bible with a finger placed between pages and looked up at me, "Do you know what a prophet is?" she asked. Yes, someone who receives messages in one way or another to help guide others to see what they cannot see yet. I chimed in with an odd example of two nights ago when I had a dream that someone was repeating two company names I had never heard of to me and I didn't know why, and then the next day my boss transferred two new accounts into my account base and those were the ones I had dreamed of. Does this make me a prophet, of course not. I just wanted to give an example to show them that not everyone that gets glimpses of the future, or messages, is a prophet. I asked, so psychics are bad, and prophets are good? The two girls sat there silent for a second and answered my example with scripture. I had seen this method before with the Mormons; they also believe that their book has crystal clear guidance to the correct way to salvation.

The main conductor of the Bible study said that she did some research on dreams over the past two weeks, and read a few articles that highlighted the fact that our minds are stimulated by our surrounding environments nonstop every day. Like right now, she is observing the color of the flowers, smells in the air, coffee, mirrors, and artwork in my house. She may not be conscious of all she is observing, and later tonight when she dreams, and all of those distractions are gone, her mind will put them into dreams in one way or another. "We all have very creative imaginations, and I would just say that here you probably encountered those names at some other point, and didn't realize it." I gave a simple hmmmm noise and said, so you don't think that my dreams that had my grandpa in them coming to get my mom, or dreams about my mom visiting me, or any of the other ones that seem pretty spot on to what happens…no part of you thinks that these came from God or passed-on relatives? The simple answer was no. They reverted back to the scripture from before and said, "God communicates only through his son." I shrugged and said, well if you think everything in the Bible is to be taken literally, then do you also believe that men should be able to buy as many women as they can, women should always obey their men, and slavery is all right? Of course they said that this is a misinterpretation on my part and that could have meant that people are slaves to God or something else. Fair enough, then I suppose it is safe to say that when God also created the worlds, he could have created other worlds besides ours?

I had a random thought, and asked the girls if we could move on to the subject of the soul. I wanted to know if they believe that every time a baby is conceived that a brand new soul is created. With a very confident nod, the answer was yes. The quieter girl of the two said that in Malachi 3:16 a book of remembrance is spoken of, "then those who revered the Lord spoke with one another. The Lord took note and listened, and a book of remembrance was written before him of those who revered the Lord and thought on his name." That to me doesn't really mean that a new soul is created each time a baby is brought into the world; to me this reads that God is keeping track of those who revere him, and wouldn't you think that if there was only one lifetime it would be easy to keep track of? I could see a book of remembrance being written (or scroll) to record what we learn over the course of our lives, and it is opened and reviewed between each cycle.

To lighten the mood I told the girls that last night my boyfriend and I were lying in bed and said how funny it would be if Jesus came back and expected to see his recycled soul program in full effect and was disappointed that somehow along the way someone dropped the ball. With as "green" as Portland is, you would think that the recycled souls program would be supported here. The room fell silent. I kept talking, and said, well you know…like if he originally wanted reincarnation to keep from overpopulating the Earth, and when he comes back he's freaking out because no one carried out his recycled souls program. Explaining jokes isn't as fun as telling them. A chuckle! The subject was changed again.

We went on to discuss whether or not my dreams did in fact come from a "bad place." We turned to Deuteronomy 18:9, and I read aloud:

> When you come into the land that the Lord your God is giving you, you must not learn to imitate the abhorrent practices of those nations. No one shall be found among you who makes a son or daughter pass through fire, or who practices divination, or is a soothsayer, or an augur, or a sorcerer, or one who casts spells, or who consults ghosts or spirits, or who seeks oracles from the dead. For whoever does these things is abhorrent to the Lord; it is because of such abhorrent practices that the Lord your God is driving them out before you.

They instructed me to stop reading here. I kept reading:

> You must remain completely loyal to the Lord your God. Although these nations that you are about to

> dispossess do give heed to soothsayers and diviners, as for you, the Lord your God does not permit you to do so. The Lord your God will raise up for you a prophet like me from among your own people; you shall heed such a prophet.

They went back to the main point, which is that as long as I don't actively seek out sorcery, or magic, or omens that I am not doing wrong by God. I want to begin the next sentence with "riddle me this" but refrain. Instead, I begin to tell a random story about my first time going to the Christian Spirit Guided Friends Church. Surely we are all reading from the same book (give or take a few lines here and there) and the messages that they read aloud are taken from the Bible, from God, and for the betterment and enhancement of everyone's lives. I described how they knew things they couldn't possibly know unless they had been with me in my most private moments. The entire name of the church highlights that they are Christian and help to guide you through spiritual connection…was I going there to "seek out magic, ghosts, or spirits"? Maybe. BUT isn't the Holy Spirit part of the trinity? A spirit is a spirit, and makes me think that if they don't believe that there are spirits around after we die, then aren't they also removing the Holy Spirit from their belief systems? It seems that the parts that they chose to highlight in their teachings are only those that support the foundation of the JW church; all of the other parts of the Bible somehow seem less important to them, or up to interpretation.

The leader of the session asked if I believe the Bible; I said that I believe in the lessons it teaches, the prophets that came before us, and precautions of what is to come. I believe that Jesus was here, and he was a great teacher among many other things. I also believe that there several other master teachers walked the Earth as well. Also, I don't take everything written as literal, and in the depth of who I am I can't agree with you that there is absolutely nothing after we die. Maybe rest is a misinterpreted word in itself. Rest may mean dormant in the physical, and alive in another world. After all, one of the scriptures of today read that God created the "worlds." Or maybe this is something that we as humans have faltered in understanding all together.

The girls asked me what I thought about today's Bible lesson. A long awkward silence lingered in the room, and I thought in that moment how my book needs more Jews. I answered, though I was raised without much religion, I still have a hard time believing that what I have felt and experienced as guidance and something from the other side is nothing of importance. Again, I think that a lot of what is in the Bible can be misinterpreted and for a long time, people have taken certain parts of the Bible and highlighted what they want to follow and shunned the rest; whether for power or political reasons, or maybe just to feel like they're right. I just don't think that this is working here. Almost like a weird breakup I walked them to the door and showed them out. There were no follow-up Bible lessons scheduled or pamphlets left behind. I wondered if I was just a rung on the ladder to them, helping them get closer to God through the number of doors they knock on. Maybe I taught them something. All up to interpretation.

Fall at the Park

I pulled out my journal as I looked up at the sunshine illuminating the fall trees, producing tones of gold only created at sunset. I thought about how I am writing on the backs of the beauty I am admiring. Hoping to breathe new life into what once looked completely different when these trees were alive.

October 27, 2013: The Grotto

The Grotto is a sanctuary hidden away in Northeast Portland, once built out of an old basalt cavern, now an outdoor sanctuary and altar carved into the side of a cliff. The elevator, worn with my favorite color patina, protrudes from the base of the altar up to gardens filled with biblical statues, fountains, and meditation gardens. The church itself sits below and is called the Sanctuary of Our Sorrowful Mother. The founder once prayed to God when his mother was ill, and he said he would build a sanctuary to honor the miracle if his mother would only be healed from her illness. His mother lived, and so he built a sanctuary in her name and more importantly to Mother Mary herself. I walked in the rain, up winding stone-cut stairs towards the church, of which I had no knowledge of its denomination. I really wanted to go there because I read that the setting itself was something to be experienced and the fact that there was a church service there made it even more intriguing for me.

The service itself was a typical Catholic service with scripture, kneeling, Hail Mary's, and communion I couldn't take part in. At first I thought, oh great another communion that makes me feel like I am not good enough to take part in following God, but then they offered for even non-Catholics to come forward and receive a blessing even if they could not receive the body and blood of Christ (better than full exclusion I suppose). After the service I stood in line to shake the priest's hand. He was a petite, Asian, shiny-headed man cloaked in a green silk robe. His demeanor was humble, and his smile was ear to ear. He spoke several different languages as he shook the hands of the diverse strangers that passed through. When it came time to shake my hand he looked at me and said "stay blessed" and his smile grew bigger than it was before. I have never had anyone say to me "stay blessed"; it has always been the typical God bless you or Peace be with you. A smile grew on my face as I walked towards the enormous cavern altar ahead, unaffected by the weight of the increasing rain on my jacket. I stared in awe as I snapped off a few pictures. I walked further into the cave and admired the walls of red pillared candles on both sides of the moss-covered rocky walls. The light cascaded up the sides of the cave to illuminate the presence of God within nature.

I know that "Portlanders don't use umbrellas" but in this case I flung mine up and walked towards the gate to purchase an elevator token; there's only so much rain I can take. I piled in the elevator with an Asian family and I rode up the cliffside with them. When we reached the top I took a few small steps to the left like gravity was pulling me that way. The view below captured the cathedral popping through the fog. It looked like something one of my favorite artists, Leonid Afremov, would have painted of a rainy fall day. I slowly walked through the garden, past the bonsai trees, fountains, and streams, watching the pine needles rain down and fill in the lines of my footsteps. The pamphlet mentions the presence of God in nature, and so, there are statues from Florence, Italy, placed all the way from the beginning of the garden path to the end depicting the life of Jesus and his prophets. The rain seemed to fade away, and several times I wished it was just a bit warmer so I could take my shoes off. It was peaceful, beautiful, and serene. I continued on, and separated off to a portion of the garden called the Grotto Labyrinth. What looked like a headstone greeted me and I read:

Welcome to the Grotto Labyrinth, a replica of the medieval labyrinth of Chartres Cathedral in France. Use the labyrinth as a meditative walk, a spiritual pilgrimage, or a healing journey. As you begin your walk open your heart and mind in the presence of God. Follow the single path at your own pace in silence. If you encounter others simply step aside to let them pass. The path leads to the center, a place of prayer and insight. Return when you are ready, following the path out. May God be with you on your journey through life.

I started at the beginning of the labyrinth and followed the winding stones into the maze of twisting paths, slowing my breath as I entered. I walked slowly, relaxing my breath, disregarding the rain, letting every ounce of nature seep in. I began reflecting on my own path to the middle, where enlightenment lives. I admired the golden oak leaves that covered parts of the path, thinking about how even when things get in our way they are supposed to be there. I admired the colors of fall, unique each season, and thought that maybe the point of getting to the middle is so that you can lead others there. The path coiled in and out, and times when I thought I was almost done with the maze it drew me back to the center. I began to wonder, how long have I been running or walking this track? How many times have I been to the center and tried to show others how to get there as well? I walked out of the garden of peace and towards the meditation sanctuary.

I walked up a different, more precisely cut set of stairs towards the majesty of the meditation sanctuary. At the top of the stairs water enclosed a single path that led toward the main building on the edge of the cliff ahead. The sky reflected on the water surrounding me where I stood and gave me the illusion of walking in the clouds. The glass door of the sanctuary looked through to glass walls overlooking the city below. Almost the entire building was glass, and looked over the tree tops and into the clouds. Inside the glass doors was a platform with six large brown leather armchairs lined up, all facing a roped-off statue of Mary holding Jesus. I took my seat in a chocolate brown chair and began to reflect on the feelings of the day. The sun came out and the clouds rolled away and here I felt sincere peace. I looked down on the city below sprinkled with blotches of red, orange, and gold, feeling truly blessed, and thought…maybe I don't need a religion at all. Religion seems separate from being spiritual or finding a connection with God, at least for me. Today, I got more out of my walk through the sanctuary gardens and sitting here in the clouds than I did the entire church service. Though, part of me has this draw to the prophets, great teachers, and of course Peter.

Because Peter appears in so many dreams lately I decided to find his place in the Bible and read what lessons he taught. In dreams, Peter makes me feel like he is safe, guiding, and maybe in a past life he was a friend of mine. What I found in Peter was the most helpful thing I have read in the Bible thus far, all in a span of a few pages.

> 1 Peter: 4:12: "Beloved, do not be surprised at the fiery ordeal that is taking place among you to test you, as though something strange were happening to you, but rejoice insofar as you are sharing Christ's sufferings, so that you may also be glad and shout for joy when his glory is revealed."

> 2 Peter: 1:5: "For this very reason you must make every effort to support your faith with goodness, and goodness

with knowledge, and knowledge with self-control, and self-control with endurance, and endurance with godliness, and godliness with mutual affection, and mutual affection with love. For if these things are yours and are increasing among you, they keep you from being ineffective. For anyone who lacks these things is nearsighted and blind and is forgetful of the cleansing of the past."

2 Peter 1:12: "Therefore, I intend to keep on reminding you of these things, though you know them already and are established in the truth that has come to you." I especially like this last part because it makes me envision someone that comes back in different lifetimes, or loses their way from the path of God, and is then reminded with this scripture of the truth that they have already learned, and had only just forgotten. I also like the instruction to support your faith with goodness, self-control, endurance, godliness, and love.

I continued reading, and came to 2 Peter 1:19–21:

So we have the prophetic message more fully confirmed. You will do well to be attentive to this as to a lamp shining in a dark place, until the day dawns and the morning star rises in your hearts. First of all you must understand this, that no prophecy of scripture is a matter of one's own interpretation. Because no prophecy ever came by human will, but men and women moved by the Holy Spirit spoke from God.

This is my second favorite passage. I view it as reassurance to disregard other interpretations of messages or meanings in what I have been shown, and have faith; faith in God and faith in the gifts that have been shared. I propped up my pillow and grabbed the Bible more intently now, as if some part of me found greater meaning in this bedside accessory than before. As if my eyes had been opened to a part that spoke to me and moved me in a way nothing else has in the Bible thus far.

Next I highlighted 2 Peter 2:1–3:

> But false prophets also arose among the people, just as there will be false teachers among you, who will secretly bring in destructive opinions. They will even deny the Master who bought them [apparently Peter was a fan of slaves] bringing swift destruction on themselves. Even so, many will follow their licentious ways, and because of these teachers the way of truth will be maligned.

After reading this it reminded me that this book is really old, and times have changed, to no fault of Peter's. Of course I don't support slavery, but I do gather more from this passage than the fact that slaves are mentioned. I jot down on a pad of paper not to follow in the footsteps of people that believe opinions to be facts, and instead to follow in the footsteps of teachers that help promote peace, love, and compassion. I like that in Peter's letters he speaks of how he was a witness to Jesus and that is why there wasn't much need for convincing on his part, but lays the tracks for others after him to read his words and take heed.

Peter also starts a lot of sentences with the word "beloved," which gives me a warm fuzzy for some reason, like I am reading an ancient love letter or something. Finally, I read 2 Peter 3:1: "This is now, beloved, the second letter I am writing to you; in them I am trying to arouse your sincere intention by reminding you that you should remember the words spoken in the past by the holy prophets, and the commandment of the Lord and Savior spoken through your apostles." He also reminds me of something that one of the women in the Spiritualist Church said, which is that spirits don't really have much concept of time. She had said that if they see a date or event occurring, they don't really know when it is, that is why when/if they see that someone is going to die they never tell them because it could be that they were shown a death fifty years from now, and if the person was made aware of it they would live the next fifty years in fear. In 2 Peter 3:8 he says:

> But do not ignore this one fact, beloved, that with the Lord one day is like a thousand years, and a thousand years are like one day. The Lord is not slow about his promise, as some think of slowness, but is patient with you, not wanting any to perish, but all to come to repentance."

2 Peter 3:14: "Therefore, beloved, while you are waiting for these things, strive to be found by him at peace, without spot or blemish; and regard the patience of our Lord as salvation." I make another note: have patience. I read the very last line, 2 Peter 3:16–17: "There are some things in them hard to understand, which the ignorant and unstable twist to their own destruction, as they do the other scriptures. You therefore, beloved, since you are forewarned, beware that you are not carried away with the error of the lawless and lose your own stability." I shut my Bible and set it back by the bed, full of fluorescent post-it tabs sticking out of the sides. I thought

about how simple Peter's directions were, and specifically to anyone who is having trouble finding which way to go in faith, or what teachers and messages to follow. The direction for me is this, listen to your heart and God, have faith in creation, follow wisdom, and disregard the opinions of people who strike down what they cannot understand. Thanks, Peter.

October 30, 2013: Wiccan 1

A Jew, a Pagan, and a witch all walk into a bar. This is not the start of a joke but the beginning of my Halloween Eve. I took the advice of Sorcha and went to a Pagan meet-up group at one of her favorite Scottish pubs, which is mainly a group of Pagans that all get together to drink beer, converse, and listen to Scottish music. Because last time I met with Sorcha she made it clear that she was Pagan and not Wiccan she said this is the best place for me to…the Kentucky in me wants to shout, catch me a Wiccan! but now that I'm an Oregonian I suppose I will say have a few pints and talk with a Wiccan.

He was dressed like a pirate which made it hard for me to keep a straight face while conversing. At first it was actually a tad stale and almost stuffy, and I felt like I was intruding in some way. I went away from the complex generalities and started at the beginning, "Is this too loud for you?" Yes. So, we exchanged information and planned to meet for coffee or some other beverage to talk in a quieter place. After a few pints he got to talking, "so what is it that you are looking for?" I told him my background and that after sitting down with Sorcha she told me that she is Pagan and not Wiccan, and that there are a lot of differences. I also made him aware that Wiccans are actually kind of hard to come by; it seems like there aren't any groups or gatherings that are out in the open for all to see or read about. Despite the loud music, costume contests, and Halloween excitement we touched on a few topics that I plan on revisiting. He told me that he is Pagan, and mentioned a lot of the same things Sorcha did. As he pointed to the witch, literally dressed like a witch, next to him, he said that she is in the beginning phases of becoming Wiccan and has a long way to go.

Despite the loud music and Scottish hoopla, I managed to touch on a few important topics, which I jotted down on a napkin a reminder to speak about further. I uncovered that a lot of their practices revolve around the lunar cycles as opposed to the solar cycles and they have covens. I also asked him how you become part of a coven, and the main answer was that you have to know someone. It reminds me of the freemasons or a secret society in a way. He also told me that more traditional Wiccan folk would consider what they do not strictly Wiccan. So, if I was to visit a variety of different covens or circles I would find many similarities to what they do, but odds are very good that no two covens "do it" the same way. Their "tradition" might be described as "Wiccan" or "Celtic Wiccan," but truthfully it's more aptly an eclectic form of Wicca. Each member brings their own take to the circle. They value this individuality because each must find their own path to the divine. In the past they also called on Roman, Norse, Egyptian, Greek, and Celtic deities as well as Native American spirits…depending on the occasion or the preferences of the person running the circle.

You also have to go through initiations and different phases of becoming Wiccan before you are actually a Wiccan. I jumped right to the nitty-gritty and asked over screaming Scottish music, do you have a book you worship, and if so what is it? Without hesitation and in a normal tone of voice he answered back, oh yes, I have a book of shadows. I made a constipated face, and he replied, "It doesn't just have spells in it. The book has recipes, instructions, herbs, and remedies. Not everything you think would be in a book of shadows is bad." Also, they believe the same principle as the Pagans, what you do comes back to you two-fold, so for the most part no bad spells are ever done. I played dumb and asked inquisitively, spells? Yes, there are spells. Like magic? Tell me what you mean by magic? I didn't expect this answer, but I really like it. "Magic is a prayer. The fact that we dream, breathe, live, die…the destruction is always the same…it's the journey. No black magic, no white magic, it's a prayer…and what you show people." I asked him then if he believes that magic is just a prayer, then what is the difference between a psychic and a prophet?

We both decided to finish our meals and call it a night. The questions were getting a little too in-depth for the atmosphere we were in. So, he told me that coming up there will be a full moon, when his coven will be meeting, and if I would like to come I can…but I had to ask to be invited. So, I asked, and he invited. I also blurted out, "So you know, I'm not a virgin!" He looked confused; I decided not to follow up with an explanation of my random thought. The full moon would be on November 17th. I am nervous and a bit hesitant to meet a group of Wiccans in a wooded place to be announced on the night of the full moon, but how bad could it be?

November 16, 2013: A Nightmare

I barely slept last night. I had dream after vivid dream about the devil. I don't think I have ever dreamt about the devil, or for that matter had the actual word said aloud in any of my dreams.

The dream begins at the base of a large tree. I enter through a door in the trunk of it, and walk down levels of spiraled stairs through a forest. It is autumn, and the leaves turn more vivid colors the deeper I go. At the bottom is a room, and a woman I know is the devil is standing there waiting for me. I think this is odd that the devil is a woman. Her eyes are black and sunken in, and she is trying to look me in the eyes to get into my soul. All the others around me have burlap sacks over their heads and sunken eyes. She gets into the soul of my fiancé and makes him slit his own wrists, and then stares me in the eyes. To the left of me is Jesus on the cross being whipped and in pain; he has on a radiant blue loincloth. I am draped in white and my hair keeps changing color from bright white to black. There are black cats running around. There is an altar suspended in the air with a pentagram made of sticks resting upon it, and one stick is missing where I am supposed to fit. In my dream I repeat the Lord's Prayer over and over until I feel warmth over my face. I open my eyes and am in deep water. It is happier here, but there is still a looming fear. The pentagram is still overhead. I can feel the female presence again, and I call out for my mom, and then God, and then I wake up. I saw two faces pop in my head as I lay there in bed, one a man, one a woman. Their faces were candle lit and serious.

I got up and reached for my Bible. I cuddled with my Bible until I woke up again hours later from the same dream.

Wiccan Full Moon Ceremony

Do you know what it's like to drive out to the Oregon coast in November at dusk? Eerie. Driving through wine country is normally one of my favorite things to do when heading out west, but at night without any road lights or clear paths for farm roads, it is really quite unsettling. The fog rolled in through the towering pine trees and illuminated a faint hazy glow of the moon above, which I knew was full by now. I had been looking up at it nightly for the past week wondering what tonight would be like. It was pitch black on all sides of the road around me, and if I looked really hard I could make out the lines of the tall pine trees from where the sky ended and they began. One could call this sea of shades of black peaceful; one would call it that if one hadn't been watching *X-File* reruns every night for the past month and driving out to a Wiccan full moon ceremony.

I did some reading as to why Wiccans actually conduct circle rituals and gatherings upon the full moon. According to www.wicca-spirituality.com/moon-phases.html one of the greatest powers of the moon is its effects on the tide. The moon phase affects the tides not only of the ocean, but of the atmosphere and even the Earth. And of course, it affects people and animals too. The full moon specifically is said to give abundance to harvest, wish-fulfillment, manifesting desires, sexuality, achieving dreams, and protection. I also read that because the moon affects not only the ocean tides, but the tides within us, that some women start their periods on or around the full moon. I thought that was crap, until I started my period yesterday.

Because I was so bothered by my dreams last night I decided to go back to the Spirit Guided Friends Church this morning. I feel safety, purity, and protection there and overall just felt like I really needed to be there. The service was wonderful as usual, but I felt like I had this looming fear about me, one that someone there was bound to pick up on. Diane stood up and made a general announcement after the service, that I took note of. She said that we get back what we put out into the world, and if we are putting out fear then we will get that back. I wondered if all of the nervousness and false ideas I had been making up in my head had caused the nightmares, and more so, my bad mood for the day. She also said that sometimes bad things happen to us, but we need to take these events and use them for good, and more importantly to learn from them. This helps us to reassess where we are in life, and where we want to be. Oddly enough, last night I had almost all of my laundry stolen from me. I had been upset about that all day, and instead of harboring anger and sadness I decided to reflect on the principles taught by the monks who take years to create the sand mandalas only to destroy them upon completion. This reminds me to not become so attached to my possessions, and instead value what they have brought to me while they were here, and be able to let go. I felt much better after the service, and after listening to everyone share scripture and lessons. When it came time for messages, I gladly accepted with hope for some kind of reassurance regarding the nightmares or this evening's plans.

A man named Carl who is extremely nice, kind, and passionate about life gave readings to several people...me being one of them. He said that so much energy was coming from me that it was almost like a merry-go-round of energy spinning. Oddly, I felt dizzy this morning. He suggested that I take all of the energy that I have and put it towards helping others, or volunteering somewhere. Humane Society maybe. Another message was given to me in regards to my writing, and he just said that there are a lot people that will benefit from what I have to say, and there are two good changes coming my way. I was going to stay after church for a class on Auras but had to run to the mall to pick up new underwear and such to replace what was stolen the night prior. I told Reverend Dan that I really wanted to stay for his class, especially because I consider him to be a guru of all things interesting. Naturally, he responded with an interesting point of view, and said, you have just as much power and knowledge as I do, or anyone else in this room. Picture seven different planes, and on each plane there is a different life lesson. Well, some people come in to the plane from above, and others at an angle, and others from below. This is the same lesson, being learned and viewed by everyone from different perspectives. Only when we allow ourselves to see from all angles do we learn. So, my point of view is no better than yours. Dan also recommended I read one of his favorite books called *Channeling the Higher Self*, specifically the chapter on writing. I left there feeling positive, reinvigorated, and clear again, as usual.

After a long dark ride toward the coast I arrived at the home of Corby, the Pagan Wiccan. I could feel the sweat beading up on my neck and sticking to my palms. I shyly knocked on the door, and then…I was greeted by two pleasant smiling faces and a neat and tidy home. There was a nice table set in the middle of the room, and they eagerly welcomed me in and showed me where to hang my coat and purse. I was nervous still, and told them I would have lots of questions. They were more than happy to answer anything I asked and just told me to make myself at home. After a few minutes of welcoming and talking, we began with the first part of the ceremony, which took place upstairs. I couldn't help but think what if when I come back downstairs, they are in dark cloaks, or have weapons or something raw on the table for me to eat! I followed the other woman who was there, Brenna, upstairs to the bathroom, where she lit some fresh incense and filled the sink with rosemary and salt water. She instructed me to take my time and when I was ready to dip my hands in the water and cleanse out any negative or impure energy. The smells were soothing, and she recited a blessing over the water before I dipped my hands in. I felt relaxed and peaceful and then I looked to the left of the sink and saw two long ropes and a knife. I thought immediately, OH NO, this is it! I'm getting tied up and stabbed and sacrificed and drained of all my blood! I gently asked what the knife was for. She answered politely that the knives are used typically in cutting cakes and baked goods in the ceremonies, and also they symbolize the male Gods. Typically? I thought that maybe this time was not a typical cake cutting night and maybe instead of cake I was the thing to be cut! I took a deep breath and cleared my rude thoughts, which I tried to wash away in the sink. She picked up the white rope and tied it around her waist. I asked her the meaning, and she said that it was to symbolize her place within the coven. Because she is not initiated fully into the coven yet, her rope is a different color than Corby's. I said, like karate? She looked a bit confused. I explained how different color belts in karate symbolize what level you are in your mastery. In short, yes. The different color belts/ropes distinguish your place within the coven.

She dipped her hands in the water after me, and then we both walked downstairs into the dimly lit living room. Corby went upstairs next and repeated the cleansing. While we waited for him to come back down, I thought about how the Muslims also do this same ritual before praying, except they wash their feet. I also asked Brenna to explain to me the situation of the various items on the center table which we sat around. Because this is a sacred and learned arrangement that is passed on through the years I don't think I should share what all was on the table, or the way it was arranged, but I will say that the items that were there represented the four elements Earth, Wind, Fire, and Water. The smell of cedar filled the air as we sat around the candle-lit circle. I watched as the dagger was again drawn and grew a tad nervous as Corby moved around the table. I remained facing north as he walked behind me and I couldn't help but think THIS IS IT! He's going to stab me now, right in the gut, I'm sure of it, or maybe from behind in the back! This is it! Again, I was wrong. I was very wrong. As he moved around the circle, stopping to give praise to each element, I realized that this part of his ritual is only scary to me because I was an outsider, or maybe being in the company of strangers in the dark as they reach up a dagger behind you in ceremony is really a scary thing. Despite the symbolism, or ritualistic place in the ceremony, the extremely old looking dagger was intimidating, as it cast a long shadow down the walls around. I also thought about how sometimes people do outlandish acts in the name of religion, or ceremonies, and thought that though they might be nice people they still might kill me in the name of "God." I popped the overhead bubble and returned to the present. I felt bad for where my mind had wondered and then began pondering the phrase he was repeating at each corner and wondered who is Brigid?

I interrupted eagerly and said what does She represent? Why do you praise the horned God and Goddess Brigid? Is that the devil? Why is the God horned!? He calmly answered first about the horned God:

We have several Gods include Pan, Cernnunos, Herne, and the Green Man among many others. The god represents the "active" part of the male/female whole and like the Goddess, the God can have many roles. For us, the God is the husband/lover, consort, child, hunter and sacrifice. On the wheel of the year it is the God that is born at Winter Solstice, as is the sun. He represents the new life returning to the world, the grain that rises from the Mother's womb in the spring waxing strong in the summer only to be cut down... "sacrificed" to nourish us through the long night of winter. This cycle repeats each year. As Hearne he leads the Wild Hunt that "harvests" the weak in winter. We recognize that "death" is a part of "life"... a circle. The chant below illustrates this:

- Hoof and horn, hoof and horn,
- all that dies shall be reborn.
- Corn and grain, corn and grain,
- all that falls shall rise again. (Ian Corrigan)

Next he went on to tell me about the Goddess Brigid:

> The Goddess Brigid... She has many roles. She is a Goddess of hearth and home, of the creative arts including smithing. So important was she to the Celts that the early Christian church made her a saint. She is also the Celtic Goddess of all high things, specifically: healing, wisdom, excellence, perfection, high intelligence, and poetic eloquence.

He also let me know that Christianity and most things in Hollywood are responsible for anything horned being depicted as evil. Most of the mythical Gods and Goddesses of other cultures have horns, and most of them have connections with strength and nature in some way. I calmed down again, and felt foolish...yet again. I did note that by candlelight I saw two familiar faces from the night before. I had seen this exact image in my dream, and in a way parts were true...for example there was a horned God involved, there were cats running around, and I was sitting in the south, which represents the element of fire. I looked down, and where I was seated there was also a stick. At that time I decided to tell them about my dream from the night before, and made sure to voice my concerns for the pentagram that appeared in it.

The fact was, the circle we were sitting in was itself a pentagram, and yes, I was sitting where the stick was, but the other fact was that the elements making up this pentacle represented the elements of the Earth, and this circle was used to represent protection from anything bad. He also reiterated that pentacles have always been used for protection. Even the main monuments and landmarks in Washington DC all form a pentagram when connected with lines on a map. There is a lot behind this symbol that people do not know, and it seems Hollywood as well as various other religious leaders in history have used what people don't know much about and transformed it into an evil symbol whether for the benefit of themselves or to give a scary appeal in movies. I looked up pentacles when I got home later, and he was right. Pentacles have been used all throughout history, even in masonic traditions, to represent safety and protection.

One of the parts of the ceremony that I liked a lot was that each person in the circle said one thing they would like to send their positive energy towards. Brenna went first, and without hesitation she said she wanted to send any help or healing towards the

Philippines to anyone there who had been affected by the recent tragedies. She seemed so compassionate and upset, and with a sincere voice added that she would like to send all of her positive energy to fill the hearts of those who are suffering there. Next, I stepped forward and said only that I wanted to help inspire people with my work, and help the people of the world through my writing and positivity. I can't remember what Corby's was, but I do remember it was really nice. The other part that was nice was that they had brought champagne to the table to fill the chalice. They both had lovely poems they recited, and also seemed sincerely happy that I had joined them. Before we closed the circle the dagger was dipped in the chalice one last time and the baked goods were cut. There is symbolism in the chalice and dagger reflecting both male and female deities and the baked goods acknowledge creating through heat…or baking. Corby also informed me that the daggers are never to draw blood…ever. They are symbolic pieces that are pure. I also thought randomly of different landmarks in the US that resemble the pointed dagger and cup, and promptly thought of the Capitol Dome and the Washington Monument. The goddess, Columbia, is also the statue on top of the Capitol Dome, and is said to represent liberty. I wondered could our founding fathers have been part of a secret society as well, where these same rituals were carried out.

We sipped more of the champagne from the chalice as we sat cross-legged on the floor and discussed more questions I had come up with. Corby suggested we migrate to the dining room, where he had a place set for me at the dinner table. Some part of me did wonder if my dish was going to be poisoned and I was to be sacrificed when I least suspected it, but then I mentally scolded myself for thinking such things and took my seat at the dinner table.

How would I ever learn to accept others and grow as a person, if thoughts like this continue to even surface in my mind.

I was more than surprised by the extreme generosity, kindness, and hospitality that was provided. He had cooked an entire vegetarian ratatouille, which was paired with an amazing California wine, and a side of fresh French bread. We sat around the dinner table and casually discussed religion, family, traditions, and even my recent engagement. What I gather from this experience is more than can be written, but their bond to the community that is their religion is so strong and beautiful in itself that it alone should be acknowledged. I also learned that they celebrate the same holidays as Sorcha, given that they too are Pagan. I could see myself becoming friends with them, and really felt intrigued by the history, theology, and Celtic traditions that we discussed.

I asked them the classic question, what do you think happens when we die? Corby and Brenna both believe that after we pass on we go to the "land of light" for a while, and here it is a happy place full of Gods and loved ones. Land of Light…Heaven…same thing…to me. Then all of our souls return to the cauldron and become one with all the other souls. This is not a big collection of individual souls, but a combined mass…almost like a constellation full of spinning stars. I literally pictured a constellation spinning with tiny bits of light shining in it, and then one by one these fragments of light separate off and are reborn back into the physical world we know. When that star dies, it returns back to the mass in which it came from. My mind wandered off again as I reflected on the Buddhist story that was told about the gemstones reflecting each other into infinity, reminding us how we are all connected. I also thought about how many other stories had been told at the Buddhist temple in my time away that I had missed.

I chimed in that I had randomly thought today how weird it would be to write a book in this lifetime, and then read it in another life in years to come. We all laughed about how odd it would be, and then went on to the next subject of magic. Of course, with Wiccans there is going to be magic involved. I wanted to know what they specifically use their magic for, and what the difference is between white and black magic. Someone also told me that if you are talking about spells then magic is spelled magick, and if you are talking about card games or pulling rabbits out of hats then it is spelled without the "k". Corby answered this one, and gave an example of a hammer. The hammer by itself is neither good nor bad, but in the hands of one person it can build something and in the hands of another person it could be used to destroy. Magick is the hammer, and the people decide what it is used for. There is no black or white, good or bad, magick is just magick. He also added that they believe that what you put out in the world comes back to you times three, so in their case, they always put out positivity and protection for loved ones. I got chills remembering how I had just heard this same phrase earlier today.

I also wanted to know how it was that they had gotten started with this religion, and oddly enough Corby was raised Jewish, and then was given some introduction into this practice through the Masonic Temple. I interrupted again, and clarified if he meant the Freemasons. He did, and apparently their rituals are far scarier than daggers and cakes. He left it at that. He went on to say that he was raised Jewish but always admired the Celtic mythology and what each deity represents. He knew a lot about other religions as well, and had been a practicing Wiccan since before I was even born. Brenna was not raised Pagan or Wiccan, but met Corby and was introduced to the religion that way. She loves all that the religion embodies, represents, and how it makes her focus on how to better not only herself but everyone else in the world. We finished up dinner and wine and wrapped up the remaining questions. Brenna also gave me a small silk tied bag filled with different perfumes, gem stones, and candles. Overall I really like this religion, and though the word "magic" has connotations of bad or ill practices I think that what they practice is really quite beautiful and very natural. If magick is simply drawing from the energy of the Earth's elements and sending positivity towards those in need, then I guess I support it. I couldn't help but think how funny it would be if after they shut the door behind me they both shrugged and looked at each other and said, "ehhh, we'll kill the one next month…she was really nice."

November 24, 2013

I had a dream last night I was waiting for a plane. I had overslept for the 8:30 flight and am on the verge of missing the 11 a.m. departure. If I miss that one, there is a flight at noon I can catch. I am pulled into a room and put in front of a council full of people in formal suits. The African American woman in the dated formal suit makes all of the final decisions for the council and is seated on the far right of the room at the end of a long table. She slips me papers covered in red slime; these guarantee my spot for the 11 a.m. departure where I am supposed to be. She makes it known that she pulled some strings to make sure I am on this flight.

I woke this morning wondering what church I was to go to. There was my favorite church with a service at 11, and then…a new church with a service at noon. I felt that if I didn't go to the 11 a.m. service I would be missing out on something that I was supposed to be a part of. I put on my warmest layers of hoodies, leggings, and typical Portland gear and headed out for a jog up through the woods and winding through Reed College. The sun was shining through the clouds of my icy breath that encircled me as I ran. The wheat field around the bend was illuminated with frost and sunrise, and then I took a left and ran up the hill into the woods. At the bottom of the hill there were shadows of trees and foliage, but as I climbed the hill more sunshine graced my face. I had an eye-opening moment and thought, the further I go on this path, the more light I soak in. I stopped and put my palms out towards the sun and stood there in silence. I prayed, and asked God to replenish the light within me. My eyes opened and I popped my headphones back on and climbed further, took another left, and began to cross the bridge. To the left and right of me were dead brown plants and trees. I stopped again, and remembered a dream I had well before I lived in Portland, that reminded me of this exact place except in the dream I started at my mom's house. I remembered the residual thought of this dream was that of cycles, things that were dying and things that were starting new. After minutes of smiling like a psycho at the sun overhead I realized that the clock was ticking away and I had to get home so I could make it to the 11 a.m. service.

The normal overwhelming feeling of love and dizziness overtook me as I walked through the front door of the church, yet again. Simple Christmas decorations garnished the room and brought a humble smile to my face. Today, a woman named Sheila gave the sermon. I had never heard her speak before, but every Sunday she is spouting to the brim with joy and has the type of energy that I wish I could jar and take home to sprinkle around my house. She also reminds me in a weird way of my Great-Grandma Kneipp, who as of recently has begun to appear in my dreams. One dream she was walking down a path with my mom and pushing a baby stroller with a little girl in it. I knew the baby was for my sister Kelly. (Kelly doesn't have kids.)

Sheila bounced up to the wooden podium and looked out to the room. Her nerves butted in on her joy for a second and then she paused and said, "I didn't realize I was nervous, I think I would like to first play a song." After a minute of figuring out a boom box in the front of the room she slid in her CD and gracefully resumed her spot at the podium. The music was tranquil, soft, and reminded me a bit of a meditative CD but with inspiring words added in. My eyes shut without me thinking about what others would think, or without any reason at all for doing so. I felt the sun heating my face through the nearby window as I exhaled. After the song concluded she opened up her own notebook and pulled out a piece that she had written herself. I want to credit her directly for the words that come after this, as she is a huge contributing factor to my inspiration for today.

She painted an autumn visual of the leaves changing in cycles of beauty and then falling away, leaving behind the skeletons of the trees for the following season.

> Do you ever look at the dead trees this time of year and notice the crisp browned leaves still hanging on to the trees? When we don't let go of things that no longer serve us we can't make room for new growth. I'm sure if we look in our own closets we all have items in there that we've outgrown or haven't worn in years, maybe we just keep them around for when we might fit back into them or for when that special occasion might arise, but for one reason or another we have held on to it. Even our spiritual closets which are full of relationships, loved ones, jobs, and life's passions all accumulate after a while. Some of these things may even have claw marks on them from where we have tried to hold them for such a long time. These things…no longer serve us and need to be let go in order to make room for fresh new things to be born and surface in our lives.

Just then I pictured myself running back up the same hill I had ran this morning, asking God to replenish my light, and smiled at her as she continued on.

Keep in mind, that what we think we own is not ours, but God's. Everything is God's. You may have things in your possession, or things that you care for and love, but that is all you can do because when the time comes for those things to go…they do, and they return back to God.

I looked at her, and all of a sudden a light shone all around her, glowing in shades of emerald green down the side of her right arm. Then I became so…either excited or skeptical that it went away. As she concluded her service she reminded us to let go of things that no longer serve us and make room for new growth and life within us, and then the message portion began.

When it came time for messages I received several. The first came from Diane, and she said that she saw me in a football stadium cheering "GO! GO!" which is weird because I don't ever go to football games, and Portland doesn't even have an NFL team. I shrugged, and she continued on and said that spirit would like me to consider furthering my education and if I can't afford a master's degree or formal education right now to maybe take a few classes at the Community College. She also said that she sees me as a teacher and whether it is through speaking, publishing books, or leading others, I am meant to teach others. She also said right now my range of understanding this is very narrow, and it needs to be expanded…a lot.

After others gave their messages I finally stood up timidly and said I normally don't have anything to share with others in the form of messages, but today…Sheila…may I come to you? She smiled ear to ear, as did several others, and nodded. I told her how moving her service was and that I saw a glow around her and then beautiful shades of green down her right arm. Someone spouted out, "like an aura?" I just smiled and said, I guess so! I could hardly speak as I felt this surge of energy shoot up my spine and through my tear ducts and up. I didn't cry or anything, but I felt paralyzed by joy. Reverend Dan said, "This is called Euphoria, and can be compared to what Christians describe as Rapture." I have not researched either, but only envision the higher self, or the feeling of being lifted up.

After I got done giving my very first message I sat down and Reverend Lucille used her cane to turn around and address me from her chair. She said, "I am glad you did that. You see when we talk about letting go and releasing and making room for new, sometimes that means releasing messages. Then you make room for more light to come in. And not every message will come to you like the Fourth of July, well they will sometimes, but it is important to acknowledge all messages big or small."

After the service I stayed behind to talk a bit with Diane, Sheila, and Reverend Lucille. I asked Sheila if she would like to have a specific chapter in my book, because I was so moved by what she said. I thought it would be better to have her verbatim as an independent chapter without my input. She was flattered, but insisted that spirit always guides her and she would have to get back to me. She then suggested that I try something called automatic writing. Diane added in that she got confirmation from spirit that I have the ability to channel and if I was interested she could help me learn how to fine-tune this gift. Let me insert here that I am constantly reminded at this church that we are not the gifted ones; we are only channels allowing God to flow through us. The ego is the part of us that gets in the way, and when remove ego from the equation, we can stay on the right path for us and for others.

I told Diane that every Sunday after whichever church I attend I go to the park and sit underneath the one redwood tree that has become a transplant in the forest and write what comes to me in my journal. I usually edit it later on my computer. I asked if that was the same as automatic writing, and it turns out that what I do is called inspirational writing. Automatic writing is much different. I am a little iffy about the offer to help me with automatic writing because her specialty is in hypnotism. I have seen movies like *Insidious* where hypnotism goes wrong and then it's a hellish nightmare with shadow people messing with your life. Maybe that was another movie, but either way, I am scared of what hypnotism would bring out of me. What if I'm an asshole, and say offensive things or what if I fart, or poop my pants? She assured me that I would be in control the entire time, and we could set up a meeting to answer any questions I may have before we would move forward at all. I am open to having a meeting, and finding out what it is that would occur during the hypnosis sessions.

I have had so many dreams about Peter that a part of me feels as if some part of him wants to come through. I am also starting to recognize a correlation between the dreams I have about Peter and the nights when I wake up and hear someone downstairs flipping through book pages. This has now happened three times. Also, I had a dream, or vision, that I haven't told anyone about.

After the third night of pages being flipped through I woke up and he was standing by my bedside cloaked in white and watching me sleep. He didn't speak to me with his mouth, but rather his thoughts and he said, "Read, you need to read." I wasn't sure what I was supposed to read, and when I awoke my Bible was moved and a portion of the pages were folded over at the corners.

I turned on the bedside lamp and began reading the pages selected for me. These pages detailed the final days leading up to Jesus' crucifixion, and the interactions between Peter and Jesus. Part of me is drawn to what is happening here, and I don't want to dismiss the opportunity at hand. So a meeting was set to discuss the process and what hypnosis would be like for me, and what I could expect to see as a result of it.

On my way out the door I gravitated over to Reverend Dan, and said that I really appreciate his classes that he puts on. He added that last week as I was walking out he got a message for me, but it was answered today…the main point was to tell me to make room for the new. He also gave me a quick bit of advice on my first message and as we discussed my dreams and messages he reminded me that when we get these euphoric messages it is important to remember to stay grounded. When we acknowledge that these messages and gifts come from God and not from us we can stay grounded. If we let our egos carry us away we can easily be led away from the path we are supposed to be on. He also gave me another piece to read about karma and reminded me that there are ways to achieve karma, if it is a concern of mine; one way is through wisdom and grace.

December 6, 2013: Meeting with Rabbi Zuckerman

Today marks the first snowfall in Portland, and is also notably one of the coldest days the city has seen in four years. I bundled up in my warmest layers of clothing and headed over to the synagogue to meet with a charismatic man named Rabbi Zuckerman. I had heard about him through a friend of mine named Cas Kopaki, who had taken an intro to Judaism class that the rabbi taught several years back. Over the phone Rabbi Zuckerman's excitement and tone was that of Rodney Dangerfield. I had anticipated actually meeting someone of similar characteristics, but as most assumptions usually pan out, he looked nothing like him.

His office was decorated with success and passion. Pictures of family, life accomplishments, awards, books, and police badges were sewn into the walls and bookshelves. This seemed more like a shrine to his life and family than it did an office. This is what offices should be like. He even had a pool table for when he wanted to strike up a game. Just by looking around I could tell he was a well-travelled, well-educated, inspirational, loving man with a zeal for family and life. His natural optimism and straight-from-the-hip demeanor made for a great dynamic between my uneducated questions and his very seasoned, yet optimistic, point of view.

He was more interested in what brought me in to see him than he was with educating me on the Jewish faith. I started out humbly, and told him about him about not being raised with much religion and that I was taught the very basics: Jesus was born and we celebrate his birthday on Christmas, and when he died for our sins and rose again from the dead we celebrate Easter. The rabbi came back to this portion after I had finished detailing my reasons for coming in today, but allowed me to finish my explanation and then kindly asked me "What is your book going to be called?" I said it is going to be called *Waking Up at 12:10* because I had these dreams where my grandpa would come to me and show me that he was coming to take my mom. They helped prepare me for what was to come so that I wasn't completely crippled when the time arrived. I considered these dreams to be a blessing, and because of the significance of these dreams I took note of them. I went on to explain that I noticed a number sequence of 12:10 that repeated in several of the dreams, only a few of which I was able to record. I continued on and told him that I decided to go to the Bible and then found a scripture that stood out to me about how God loves to restore people who have faltered in their faith back to Him. As I spoke he walked over to his wall of books and pulled a few down from the shelves and asked me where exactly that scripture was at. I assured him that it came from Genesis, and with that he flipped open his Tanakh and his Christian Bible, and one other book. He turned to Genesis 12:10 in each book and each one said the same thing, "Now there was a famine in the land, and Abram went down to Egypt to live there for a while because the famine was severe." I sat there reading all three books and thought for a second that maybe I had read a different version. Surely the whole basis of my book wasn't an error?! Famine? I can't even tie this mistake back into anything relative to what I have been pouring my soul into for the past ten months of my life. Sure enough, I had accidentally written down the first thing that popped up when I searched online for 12:10 Bible Verses and it was nothing more than someone's interpretation of the verses in Genesis 12:10–

20. I felt like a failure. How could I have messed up the one thing that I finally felt I had a purpose for in life?

I didn't confirm my error until I got home and researched it further, so I was still chipper and intrigued while there. I asked him a bit about his background and why it was that he decided to become a rabbi. The man himself is much more than just a rabbi; he served two and a half years in the Israeli Army, and among the various charitable groups he is a part of, he adds Portland Police Bomb and Mounted Officers units to the list. He has several degrees including an Agriculture Degree, and is also certified in Weapons of Mass Destruction so in the case of an attack or catastrophe he can run towards the accident to help as opposed to running in the opposite direction in fear.

The complex man had a simple honest answer for everything I asked. He said he just wanted to be able to impact the Jewish community and help others in life. He noticed that over time other religions have died off, and when he noticed a number of people leaving Judaism he decided to focus his efforts on preserving the Jewish community here in Portland. He then asked me if I knew the phrase *Or LaGoyim*. I looked at him with a raised eyebrow and smirk just about to guess something completely wrong for the sport of participation. He interjected before my attempt, and told me it is a biblical Hebrew word which means "Light unto Other Nations" and refers to the universal designation of God's Kingdom of Priests: people who act as spiritual shepherds for the world. As a rabbi he is considered one of these shepherds, and carries on his duties of helping others in all walks of life. So with that, we moved on to the next subject of belief systems.

As we discussed the differences and similarities between the religions I have studied so far he began to draw a map. On the top of the page was God, and underneath of it were three major religions: Christianity, Muslim, and Jewish. He drew a line from each religion to God. In the middle of each line there was a halfway mark, and he asked me if I knew what Christians believed you have to believe in, in order to get from point A to point B? I said, Jesus? Yes. Jesus.

Next he went to Islam, and got up again to his wall of books and pulled a Qur'an off of the shelves. He had me read aloud the first passage which, of course now that I read it in my Qur'an it is different, but states more or less the only way to get to Allah is through the prophet Muhammad. So he drew in the middle of the second line a dot labeled Muhammad.

The third line was from the Jews to God. He asked me if I know what the Jews believe you have to follow to have Oneness with God. I shrugged, and said, I don't think anything, right? Correct, he said, we believe that as long as you believe in God you can have oneness with God. He went on to detail how this compares to other religions that believe that you can repent for sins at any time and be forgiven, or live a life of crime and on your deathbed accept God and ask for forgiveness and you're good to go. In the Jewish religion they believe in something called GOOD MORALS and not being a crappy person. He jumped to the topic of Bar Mitzvahs for a second, and said that before the age of 13 the parents are actually responsible for the child's actions. All sins or bad acts are placed upon the parents' shoulders. After the ceremony, when the boy is technically considered a man, all responsibility going forward is placed upon the child. It teaches kids at a young age to be accountable for their actions, and that you can't just ask for forgiveness and be washed clean of your sins every Saturday or Sunday when you pray. Simply put, if you steal, you pay the person you stole from back times two, and so on and so forth. There is no automatic redemption or forgiveness aloud.

Next, we went on to the topic of scripture. I told him that this is actually where I have fallen short of believing any one religion. With all of the hands that religious words were passed through, how am I to know that the correct scroll wasn't destroyed long ago and rewritten by some man to obtain power? He opened up another book and pointed out a verse that said, "You shall not boil a kid in its mother's milk." I looked as puzzled as ever and he asked me what I thought that meant. Like a high school kid I gave a vague thoughtless answer and said, well it seems like a bad thing to do. Why? he said. I put more thought into it and replied, it reminds me of two polar opposites, cooking something dead in something that is life giving, more so because one was born from the other. He said that a lot of orthodox Jews interpreted this so literally that to this day they do not mix meat and dairy. No cheeseburgers, ground turkey and cheese lasagna, chicken parmesan, you get the picture. Others, not so orthodox think…that this comes from a very old book and the scripture can be interpreted 101 ways, and so they go on eating their cheeseburgers. The scripture itself is there, but yes, it can be interpreted numerous ways.

He went back to the topic from the beginning of our meeting, and brought up the meanings of holidays and how they differ for Jews. He asked me if I knew why Jesus died. I was puzzled because I thought that Jewish people didn't believe Jesus had come. However, some sects of Judaism do believe that Jesus was here at one point, and his presence is documented; they just don't believe that he was the Messiah. I intervened and asked well…why not. One reason, among the numerous ones I'm sure he had, he said, "do you know what Jesus' nickname was?" I said with an unsure slow reply, The Prince of…Peeeeacce???? Yes, that's what he was called. Since his documented time on this Earth, how much peace has there been? I remained iffy and quiet, thinking of one good example to give of peace on Earth. Though that was a good analogy I still needed more.

He got up again and grabbed another book from his shelf of infinity and asked me if I knew why Jesus died. I said, um…for our sins? This brought up another conversation, which he started with, "Christians believe we are born out of sin, but how can we be born out of sin, an infant? Infants have done nothing wrong." He linked this back to every person being responsible for their own actions, and no one has sinned until they do so. "Jesus was killed by a man named Pontius Pilate, look it up," he said. He zipped around the room pulling books from shelves and spouting facts for me to jot down. He grabbed one final book and took a seat again. He flipped to a precise page and pointed out the three different sects of political parties at the time that Jesus was alive: the Pharisees, Sadducees, and the Essenes. He asked me, if you were a Democrat and you got to release other people from jail, who would you release? I replied, other Democrats. He explained that at the time the Pharisees were in control of the temple and favored both written and oral law. The other two sects didn't, and back then, the ones in control had the ability to wipe out those that didn't favor their beliefs, and that is why Jesus died, because he wasn't in the right political party. Not because you were born out of sin, or because he was dying for your sins…a person that hadn't been born yet, but because there was a trial and he was accused against the wrong political party. (Because I am still scared of the wreckage the internet has caused me, I refrain from looking up any further information on my own at this time.)

There were many interesting examples given, the next one involved a basket of lollipops that was emptied out onto the table. He picked up one lolly and placed it back into the basket, and said, "See, Christians place one thing in their basket, which is Jesus, and outside of the basket lies all other possibilities." He pulled out the wad of lottery tickets in his wallet and said, see…I'm a betting man, and I seldom lose. These are all for fun, but more of the things I bet on are typically based on research and educated guesses. For the Christians who believe that the only way to God is through Jesus…well they have placed all of their eggs in one basket, or lollipops in this case. What if they are wrong? I cut in for a second and described my trip to the Hindu temple and though I thought they believed in several different Gods, I too was wrong because they believe in One, just One. The different Gods that encompass all of the traits and characteristics we should remain true to are reflected individually in their Gods and depicted through storytelling. I told him how shocked I was to see a marble statue of Jesus in the Hindu temple, and sometimes the misconceptions of religions or people in general can interfere with getting to the original goal, or point B. My point being, no one knows who is right, and who is wrong. So much has been ruined by humans. Through politics Jesus died. Through religion people have gained power, crumbled cities, and slayed entire races of people. Even now, someone has put something on the internet that I thought was an actual Bible verse and wrote an entire fucking novel about. Nevertheless, people seem to be the common thread when it comes to the demise of religion, humanity, and the planet itself. I've been trying to find a common thread that ties this entire book/experience together. So far, the common thing that cuts that thread has been people.

I asked Rabbi Zuckerman when it all made sense for him and without hesitation he pulled out two laminated newspaper articles from the same exact day. The first was an article honoring the life and works of the amazing Dr. Seuss. He smiled as he held the article and said, "I bet when he got to heaven God said to him you have done so many great things in your life and children and parents will read your books for hundreds of years to come; here come sit next to me!" I wondered why he was showing me this article but then he explained that one day he was looking at the sad news in the paper and something just clicked. Everything in this world has balance. If the world was all evil it would destroy itself, and if it was all good, it too would destroy itself. As he pulled out the second article he said, "The day that Dr. Seuss died someone evil was removed from this world." As it turns out Nazi Klaus Barbie aka the Butcher of Lyon, died of cancer within one day of the wonderful Dr. Seuss. The obituaries for both men were published on the same day, in the same newspaper, and that day Rabbi Zuckerman said it was almost as if a light bulb went off and he finally got it.

We decided to migrate to the main part of synagogue so I could see what an ark looked like up close and personal. Before walking into the room, Rabbi Zuckerman kindly said to me in the nicest way possible, "You may want to pull your pants up in the back before we enter into the synagogue." I was in shock!! Somehow between all the layers of clothing I had on, it appeared that the pants had fallen down in the back, thus exposing a pink and black polka-dot thong. I pulled my sweater down as far is it would possibly stretch, and awkwardly adjusted myself without saying a word. After my face resumed normal coloration we walked into the huge empty room through the aisles of vacant red plush chairs towards the ark. He guided me up the steps towards the heavy drawn curtains ahead. I kept feeling the back of my pants to make sure nothing had fallen out of place again. As he pulled back the velvet drapes the majesty of centuries was revealed. I had never seen real biblical scrolls, silver crowns, or breast plates before. Above the scrolls, stretching forty feet or so in the air, was the 10 commandments in Hebrew (though Rabbi Zuckerman told me there are actually 613 commandments). I felt honored to see an actual scroll unrolled and read aloud to me by a rabbi. I insisted on doing a curtsey before we left the room, and checked one last time for my enemy the thong before we exited.

When we sat back down he said, "What other questions do you have for me?" Of all the dumb questions I could have asked, I said, do you believe in spirits? He didn't go to any books this time but instead just answered yes; followed by an explanation of the Hebrew word for cycle. He said that there are different sects of Judaism that believe that we go to heaven for a period of time and are then reborn. I'm not sure if I was more shocked by the fact that some Jews believe Jesus has been here already, or that some believe in reincarnation. I took a seat again as he went on to discuss odd unexplained occurrences that he has experienced in his own life. He described to me instances that he couldn't explain, and is still baffled by. He even told a story about visiting Amsterdam once with his wife, and before he turned the street corner he froze and told his wife he knew exactly what was around the corner on the next street. He described the houses, store fronts, and details he couldn't have known to his wife in complete accuracy. I am not sure if reincarnation happens or not, but I do know that if it does my fiancé and I have made a pact to find each other in every life. That's what makes us soul mates (insert cheesy smile here). Through this experience I have found that a lot of people, despite being a part of an organized religion, are open to the possibility of reincarnation, karma, and cycles.

Before I headed back out into the cold, he gave me a book to read that one of his students wrote, called *Religions of the World: Judaism* by Laurel Corona. In the front of the book is a dedication to him for being such a good listener, and he was very adamant about getting this book back since it is the only book he owns where his name is printed inside. I ensured Rabbi Arthur Zuckerman that this would not be the only one. There are several parts of this book which cover more in-depth fundamental beliefs of Judaism. The passages I dove into the most are as follows:

> A long history of valuing debate, as reflected in the Talmud and other texts, as well as simple disagreements today make it difficult to pin down exactly what all Jews believe, although there are a few binding percepts that are clearly shared by most, or at least acknowledged as central to Judaism. The cornerstone of the Jewish faith is that there is only one God and that God is king of the whole universe. Jewish doctrine holds that because Moses and his followers accepted His commandments at Mount Sinai a special relationship exists between God and all Jews that obligates them to a high standard of behavior. Jews are taught that a truly fulfilling life comes from loving and serving God. This includes stopping to praise and to bless the name of God for things that might otherwise go unnoticed, such as bread on the table, or the act of awakening in the morning, or

bringing light into a dark room. (p. 67, *Religions of the World: Judaism*)

The book also goes on to explain what they don't believe in.

> Jews, on the other hand, reject certain ideas of other faiths, particularly some key concepts in Christianity. In the words of nineteenth-century philosopher Moses Mendelssohn, there is not one single commandment in Mosaic Law telling us Thou shalt believe or not believe. Faith is not commanded. In questions of eternal truth nothing is said of believing, the terms are understanding and knowing. This emphasis on acceptance of the "eternal truth" of God's existence and absolute authority is in contrast to the Christian concept of a God whose existence one experiences personally, or at least hopes to, in some manner or form. To Jews, as Mendelssohn explains, personal realization or acceptance has little to do with the matter. God simply is, and Jews strive to know and understand this. One does not need, as a show of faith, deliberately to put one's life in God's hands, for it already is and always has been there. Jews also do not share the central tenet of Christianity that the messiah came to earth in the form of Jesus of Nazareth. They are certain Jesus could not have been the messiah because he did not fulfill the prophecy of ushering in the perfect and harmonious world of the promised Messianic Age. (pp. 67–68 *Religions of the World: Judaism*)

Also in this book I found a passage called "Holy Sparks," which was really stimulating. This section talks about medieval Jewish philosophers known as mystics who believed that God had used the letters and numbers in the Torah to encode hidden meanings about the design of the universe. They believed "they could find insights into the nature of God, the creation of the Universe, the destiny of human beings, the nature of evil, and the ultimate meaning of Torah" (p. 66). The topic of holy mystics is not unfamiliar to me, and was brought up once before by Pastor Amy. I would like to explore this further, and see if 12:10 might be hidden in the Torah somewhere. This also helps me to not feel so shattered by the recent discovery of "correct scripture."

Rabbi Zuckerman asked me if I had heard the term Kabbalah. With a smirk, I replied, "Like what Madonna studies?" With an acknowledging eye roll he proceeded on to say that it refers to "receiving tradition." There is a portion in the Holy Sparks passage that details how it was used to identify Jewish mystical ideas in general. I remembered Pastor Amy talking with me about mystics and how they are intuitive and strive to find this connection to God for most of their lives. As I sat and read the next few passages I drew another line on my map from God to other religions, including Hindu, Sikh, and Buddhist. Soon all of the dots connected into a larger circle, with God as the beginning and end. Laurel Corona goes on to write:

> Jewish mysticism has two important strands. One is the intense study of the Torah for clues as to God's meaning, plan, and will. The other is the experience of union with God through a form of altered consciousness entered by intently focused prayer and meditation, which sometimes takes the form of dancing, swaying, chanting, or other forms of expression.

I connected more dots including the chanting in the Buddhist and Hindu temples, the swaying and music in the Sikh Gurdwaras, and the meditation practices of many. I felt like I was finally beginning to tie it all together.

On my way out the door he also gave me a little silk baggie, similar to the bag I was given at the Wiccan ceremony, but this bag was filled with 31 inspiring thoughts. He said that he made these to hand out to people, and thought I might like one too. He did add one last comment before I was through the door, saying, "Do you know how many people come through my doors searching for something, and in need of direction, any direction? So many people have come to me for guidance and those people were hungry for answers just like you were. So, famine might mean something more to you than what you originally thought." I went on my way and though I was still a tad apprehensive about my possible incredible scripture error, I thought about the fact that if I had not misread it I would have never written this book. If I had come across scripture that meant nothing to me, about famine, I would have most likely dismissed it and kept looking for something significant to happen on December 10th or at that specific time. I would still be waiting. I do believe there are no coincidences, and with that I exhale, pull up my pants, and say "and so it is."

That night I lay in bed with my hands folded over my chest as I stared up into the dark at the ceiling. I wondered how I was going to start off my prayer this time. I envisioned the map he had drawn and wondered if I was going to go route A through Jesus or route B a path unknown. Do I even mention Jesus? What if the Jews are right, and Jesus was just a man that was here and did good things? What if the Christians are right, and because of my Jesus exclusion in tonight's prayer I don't get to go to heaven? As I stared more intently into the dark my mind drifted and I began to think about my drive home from work, specifically when I turn onto the Ross Island Bridge and see Mt. Hood emerging in the distance, its peak and surrounding clouds mirroring the setting sun. It is always so spectacular to see the mountain reflecting the deepest colors of the sky. Some days the mountain appears pink, other times gold. No matter what my day was like, at that moment, I always forget everything and just gaze in awe. Days when the fog is so heavy and the mountain isn't visible I still smile knowing it's there. I can align my gaze exactly to where I know it is hiding. I don't need to see something all of the time to know it is there. I don't need to label it, or figure out which path is the right way to the top. Someone at church told me, all paths of the mountain lead to the top.

December 8, 2013: Spirit Guided Friends Church

I have found a sincere home at this church, and every time I leave there I feel radiant and glowing. There's something about the energy and wealth of knowledge in the small room that brings me so much joy. Today's lesson came from a man named Larry, and as he opened up his Bible he began to skim the pages with his fingertips until he felt like he was where he needed to be. He put on his large dark-framed glasses slowly and looked out to the crowd. He said, this passage today is from Matthew 23, and it is important for you to know that this is man's account of Jesus' dealings with these three groups, the Pharisees, Sadducees, and Essenes. Jesus was not present when this was written, and this is simply another man's account of what may have happened. The important thing to know is what Jesus intended for us to do, which is love. No one knows what is fact, fiction, or otherwise. What we do know is the messages that were taught, and what we can apply to our lives today. I thought about the odds of this service being taught today after just having a similar conversation with a rabbi about this same exact passage just two days ago.

Larry closed the book for a second as he scanned the room and said:

> There is a lot of great wisdom hidden within the Bible. With such chaos among political parties and people, things needed to be hidden quite a bit. When Jesus said to his 12 disciples, "who do you think I am?" who do

you think he was talking to? There are 12 cranial nerves in the brain. Each nerve has a connection to the center, or the light, which is the brain. Each nerve surrounds the brain and some people believe that he was talking about the light within each of us. The source of it all comes from the center, and maybe there is no such thing as salvation. However, there is such a thing as self-elevation.

I also pondered the temples on the sides of our heads and made note of it in my journal.

I heard someone say, people only live as long as the last person who remembers them. When I started thinking about the legacy of Jesus that has survived thousands of years I reflected back to a message Reverend Lucille gave to someone else today. She said:

> I see a person walking down a pathway scattering seeds to the left and right of the path. Some of those seeds will grow in healthy soil, some in dry unhealthy soil, other seeds will be scattered upon rocks. It is important for you to realize the seeds you have planted will grow…even the ones among the rocks will bear life.

I thought then about all of the seeds that were planted throughout the Bible and continue to grow today.

Maybe it wasn't all true, and the stories were written just to teach lessons, but the fact is that because of the seeds that were planted in so many people over time, it lives. Hope lives. Love lives. Spirituality lives. I imagine all the different seeds are the different religions of the world all taking root and surging life into the tree of knowledge.

The seed of life planted in each and every one of us continues to grow all over the world, in rocks and plush gardens alike. This is why the Bible and other books remain breathing. With that, Larry began to discuss the gift of mortal breath. We don't think about it too much, but it truly is a gift. A lot can be accomplished through breathing like meditation, relaxation, and even connecting with the cycles of the universe. He encouraged us all to try to clear our minds for just two minutes a day and meditate.

I was also handed another piece of information from Diane, which talked more in depth about the Essenes. How timely, I thought. Of the several pages that she gave me, I highlighted this passage:

> Since the archaeological discovery of the Dead Sea Scrolls in 1946, the world "Essene" has made its way around the world—often raising a lot of questions. Many people were astonished to discover that, two thousand years ago, a brotherhood of holy men and women, living together in a community, carried within themselves all of the seeds of Christianity and of the future of the western civilization. This brotherhood—more or less persecuted and ostracized—would bring forth people who would change the face of the world and the course of history. Indeed, almost all of the principal founders of what would later be called Christianity were Essenes—St. Ann, Joseph and Mary, John the Baptist, Jesus, John the Evangelist, and many more. They thought, and rightly so, that they were the heirs of God's sons and daughters of old, the heirs to their great civilization. They possessed their advanced

knowledge and worked assiduously in secret for the triumph of the light over the darkness of the human mind. They were true saints, Masters of wisdom, hierophants of the ancient arts of mastery. They were not limited to a single religion, but studied all of them in order to extract the great scientific principles. They considered each religion to be a different stage of a single revelation. They possessed a living science of all of these revelations. Thus, they knew how to communicate with angelic beings and had solved the question of the origin of evil on earth. The Essenes considered themselves the guardians of the Divine Teaching. They were the light which shines in the darkness and which invites the darkness to change itself into light. Thus, for them, when a candidate asked to be admitted to their School, it meant that, within him a whole process of awakening of the soul was set in motion. Such a soul was ready to climb the stairs of the sacred temple of humanity. The Essenes differentiated between the souls which were sleeping, drowsy, and awakened. Their task was to help, to comfort, and to relieve the sleeping souls, to try to awaken the drowsy souls, and to welcome and guide the awakened souls. (essenespirit.com)

I was so happy that she had handed me this document. It is really inspiring, and also made me smile thinking that what the Essenes did is also very similar to what I have been doing over the past year. It also made me think back to a dream I had where Peter had me walk amongst sleeping people and awaken certain ones.

I haven't mentioned much about this but as of recently I have been receiving messages to give to people during church. I have no idea what they mean, but have been assured that though I don't know the meanings, others do. Last week, while Reverend Lucille was talking I saw a snow-covered wooden staircase with blue light shining down on it. I had the immediate feeling of wanting to slide down the ice-covered banister. As I sat there I could feel my heart begin to race. I felt anxious and like I needed to shout out what was just shown to me. I kept it to myself, thinking of how stupid it would sound to tell her to slide down the ice-covered banister. Just then one of the members of the church stood up and gave me a message, "I know we all get up here and say specific names, dates, and places to people. We have all been doing this a very long time. I want to encourage you to give what you receive and only then can you make room for more light to come in. It may not make sense to you, but it will make perfect sense to the person it is intended for." I was so motivated by his words I announced with a shaky voice the message for her. She smiled and said that the very first message she ever gave was two words: Blue Snow. To her those symbols mean a lot, the staircase meaning a journey, the blue snow relating to her spirituality, and the banister sliding only meant for her to enjoy herself. As my heart rate slowed back down I felt at ease and happy.

A few weeks ago I was out to dinner with my fiancé and as I glanced over his shoulder at the wood paneled walls I saw the name "Daniel" written in cursive, and then it disappeared. I didn't want to ask what it meant, so I just forgot about it. I also didn't want to spout out that I was seeing things in the walls either. Today, while sitting in church I looked up at the wood panel walls and admired how the wooden framed picture of Jesus blended into it, making it look like Jesus was hidden in the walls, or just a silent observer. I quickly pictured the carved cursive words again and as if a little light bulb finally went off, I realized that seated right underneath the picture was Reverend Dan. When it came time for messages I could feel my palms begin to perspire and my heart rate increase so fast I placed one hand over my chest to make sure I was all right. I was going to keep this to myself and once again, I was specifically instructed today that I should continue giving these messages that I am getting. So, I raised a shaky hand again and told Reverend Dan my story. He said thank you, and mentioned that he understood what I was saying and that my message really meant a lot to him. I am assuming it held more meaning with him than he shared aloud.

I also stayed that day for a class on Electro Magnetic Frequencies taught by Reverend Dan. All matter has a frequency, including people, food, diseases, and objects. According to Dr. Robert O. Becker in his book *The Body Electric*, "the human body has an electrical frequency and much about a person's health can be determined by it. Frequency is the measurable rate of electrical energy flow that is constant between any two points. Everything has frequency."

"Dr. Royal R. Rife found that every disease has a frequency. He has found that certain frequencies can prevent the development of disease and that others would destroy diseases. Substances of higher frequency will destroy diseases of lower frequency," Reverend Dan explained. The entire thought of everything having a frequency makes it clear why people in church say that they can feel your vibrations or energy. In the class we learned about EMFs and each got a chance to both read and receive a reading of our own. When it came time for me to give one, I walked into the circle and stood behind the seated woman. I cleared my mind of all insecurities of my abilities and just exhaled and shut my eyes. I hovered my hands above the crown of her head until I started to feel like my fingers were tingling. I opened my eyes for a second almost out of shock and then continued on. I kept my hands within an inch of her body, and the closer I got to her (without touching her) the more tingling I felt. When I moved to her right side I felt a surge of heat into my hands. I kept them there for a minute or so and when I moved to her back the heat went away. I moved back to where I was and there it was again! I walked to the other side of her body and only felt tingling in my fingertips there. After a few minutes I took my seat again and Dan asked me what I felt. I told him that I felt intense heat all along the right side of her neck and shoulder. He asked her if she had any pain or problems right there and she said she has had chronic pain in that area for several years. Instead of getting excited about what I had just done, I took a step back and remembered something Reverend Dan once said, "The readings don't come from the person, they come from God. When people start thinking that they are the ones with the power, then the ego gets in the way and steers them from their path."

When it was my turn to sit in the center and receive a reading of my EMF I didn't know quite what to expect. I could feel her hands above the crown of my head and then moving down my spine. She never touched me, but I could feel it. It reminded me of the feeling of someone watching you, but with more static. I could feel her move up my arm and when she moved her hands over my heart it was almost like every painful memory I ever experienced flashed before my eyes and was washed away. She kept her hands in front of my heart and I could feel myself starting to quiver a bit. I don't know if others could see this or not, but I felt like if she didn't move her hands I would cry from thinking about the image of my mom in her hospice bed. She moved back up to the crown of my head, and then I mentally pictured shutting a door and she was finished. As she slowly walked backwards to her seat in the circle she just said "Whooooooooa." I didn't know if that was good, bad, or scary. She smiled ear to ear and said, "I could feel your heart expanding and opening. Your third eye…It is opening! There is a beam of light that floods into your chakras from above that is about this wide (she measured six inches between her palms) and there is incredible amounts of light within, and oh…you will see so, so much. God bless you." There was no mention of tight muscles in my back or anything like that; in fact she said she felt no pain at all.

A Dream

Before I went to sleep I said, "God, I am open and ready to receive and interpret messages from the other side. Thank you for allowing me the ability to see."

Imagine if you will, a dark grassy field stretching off into infinity. Stuck in the ground are millions of tuning forks. Each tuning fork is struck in a different place, producing a sound unique to all the others. The sounds produced are not that of echoed chimes, but of echoed screams surrounding both sides of my bed. They are all begging for help, all in different pitches of screams. I can hear every single one of them. In one ear the screams continue, in the other ear I hear what sounds like someone smacking the top of a microphone. The drumming and the shrieking chaos become so frantic I cover my ears in fear, as I begin to cry. Then, a massive, 20-foot-tall or greater man pronounces his presence and stands strong at my bedside. He is huge, and his presence alone is intimidating. He billows out the words, "I am Michael," and all of the screams stop. I am unable to look at his face; it seems he is so tall that I can't see that high up. I thank him as I wipe my eyes, and reconsider my bold statement. I lay in the dark staring at the ceiling in awe for an hour until I drifted back to sleep.

Native American: *Wakan Tanka* and the *Tanagila*

The rain poured down in large drops that hung from the naked tree branches and resembled Christmas lights outside my window. As nature continued on its replenishing cycles, I too carried on mine. This morning I arranged a meeting with a man named Naeem, whom I had heard possessed some insight on Native American religion. I thought because of how his name sounded that I would be meeting with a man from India, but much to my surprise he was neither from India nor dark-complected. There were no feathers or papooses, just a normal looking white guy wearing a plaid button-up shirt with a top button that read in fine print "I love Scotch." I was curious how this normal-looking Portland guy (oxymoron, I know) was Native American, or if he was at all. The saying "having Native American in your blood" has always made me ponder if there is more meaning than just genetic family lineage to Native American ancestors.

Naeem was actually brought up in Indiana, and his mother is of mixed heritage, including Mohawk/Iroquois ancestry. His parents follow the Bahá'í religion, which promotes the unification of humanity through one God. Through his upbringing and curiosity about his family heritage he began studying where his blood lines tie, and over time found connections with friends in both Washington and South Dakota who practiced a religion stemming from the Lakota tribe. The Lakota religion teaches a lot about connecting with the Earth, universe, plants, animals, and everything in between. Their ways are much like the Buddhists in the sense of interconnected beings, enlightenment, orally passing on lessons, teaching through tradition, dream interpretations, and realizing that we too are a living part within the whole. The "oneness" is created by combining every living thing, every element, and every life form into a moving symphony of harmony. This song, in its entirety, is called *Wakan Tanka*, or the holy divine, translating more clearly into "The Great Spirit."

Not a lot of what he was taught was ever written down, but through the vast numbers of people he has come into contact with over time he has learned to incorporate a lot of what the religion teaches into his daily life. He has met a few medicine men, or holy men, and joined other Native Americans in both national gatherings and ceremonies year over year. One of the more common ceremonies still practiced today takes place in a sweat lodge. Sweat lodges are underground rooms built from twenty-eight willow trunks, which shine through the twenty-eight different cycles of the moon. The lodge itself represents going back into the womb and experiencing personal rebirth and connecting back to Mother Earth. Hot stones are heated in a fire pit outside, and then placed inside the lodge where periodically water is poured over them to create steam and heat. The intense heat causes both extreme amounts of sweating and personal discomfort. What occurs during the sweat varies from tradition to tradition, as well as the intentions of those involved, so each ceremony will have variations. In some sweats a medicine man may ask you what you're focusing on, and help give you guidance for the direction to pray in, or face. Then through song, chants, and drumming they focus on the healing of those in the room. He said that during the ceremonies there may be colors or directions told to those in the room, and each color represents a direction on the medicine wheel. For example if you were told the color black, you would face west, which is also the direction associated with healing. I smile thinking about how literally I took that when I moved across the country to Portland after my mom had died.

Because there are four parts to the medicine wheel, people hold ceremonies for four days, except for the sweats, which are completed in less than one due to the nature of intensity. There are also four colors, elements, directions, and animals associated with the wheel. He made it very clear that each animal means something different to each person individually. It's not like an eagle means X to one tribe and everyone sees it the same. For example, he said, "Today when I was leaving my house on my way here I saw a hummingbird and then a rainbow." He said it was distinct enough for him to take note of and acknowledge they were there for a reason for him to make sense of later. I told him how much my mom loved hummingbirds and also how she had a rainbow maker, as she would call it, in her window that would spin rainbows around the room every time the sun shone on it. He said, "Those types of things happen all of the time. It's like nature is constantly speaking, but not everyone knows the language." He then taught me another Lakota word, *Tanagila*, meaning hummingbird.

In the sweat ceremonies people often share messages with each other too, that they know they don't know the meaning of, but are just supposed to pass on. I told him about my numerous trips to the Spirit Guided Church and the importance of giving messages to others when you receive them because they really can mean a lot to people. It made my entire day thinking that a piece of what my mom loved so much in life was presented to him today when he was on his way to see me. Continuing on the topic of giving, he told me that all symbolic objects that are possessed by the people of the Lakota tribe are heirlooms, and are never to be purchased. All sacred possessions are made by hand and then passed on to the appropriate recipient. I acknowledge the perpetual repetition of cycles that the Native American people honor and respect, and notice a commonality between the cycles they worship of the universe and their traditions of rebirth and passing on sacred treasures. I imagine taking part in a sweat ceremony is difficult both physically and mentally, and admire those who have completed one. Now that I know this is not one of the four-day ceremonies, part of me wants to try it out.

I asked him about the places he worships at, and if he has a personal place he can go to besides a gruesomely hot sweat ceremony? Besides his personal altar at home comprised of sage, cedar wood, feathers, rocks, tree branches, and herbs, he also spends a lot of time praying in nature, but reminds me that every moment we are breathing we are a part of the living world. You don't need to be deep in the woods to realize and cherish that. His personal altar is for daily reflection and meditation, and represents paying homage to the elements of the Earth. Native Americans see each living thing as equal, so when he says there is a piece of the "standing people" on his shrine, he is referring to the trees. Four-legged ones refer to the animals on four legs, and two-legged refers to us animals that walk on two. Everything is respected and praised as a part of the whole. He also mentioned that most Native Americans pray to seven directions, which includes the four that are in the medicine wheel (visual of a cross within a circle) and then adds in the other three directions: up, symbolized by the color blue; down, symbolized by the color green; and within the self (varies between traditions, sometimes orange or purple).

With that he pulled out a red cloth from his bag and unwrapped its contents: a bundle of white sage; a bit of tobacco, which he said is often used as offerings to others; and four prayer flags. The flags were each a different color and placed in the directions they were associated with. The yellow flag was placed in the east, white in the south, black in the west, and red in the north. I've been working a lot on personally associating meanings with colors so that when I dream a certain color or have a vision I know what it means. I asked why the color red is so important to him. I noticed he had it surrounding his altar, wrapping his bag of sacred items, and he had mentioned it a few other times. He said that red represents the color of the Earth itself, blood flowing through living creatures, sacrifices made mentally and physically, and the importance of the cycle of rebirth.

The prayer flags are used differently for each person. Like me, Naeem is also drawn to the power and connection of the waterfalls here in the Columbia River Gorge and does a lot of his praying in their presence. He finds a peaceful place in the woods and here he envisions standing within the quadrants of the medicine circle. To the north he finds a branch and ties the red prayer flag to it. To the east he ties the yellow, and so on for the remaining two directions. He will pray in each direction, and then depending on what he is praying for, he will end in the direction that aligns with his prayer. So if he was praying for healing, he would end facing west. I like how their ceremonies and prayers focus a lot on Mother Nature, rebirth, and cycles. I circle back to the transformation I have made spiritually because I lost my mother, and the reincarnation of my once dead soul to a new enlightened mind and self.

I asked if there were any books he worshiped or that he had received from others, and then all at once I recalled what Sorcha had said about the Native American holy books, "If you take the Christian bible and put it out in the wind and the rain, soon the paper on which the words are printed will disintegrate and the words will be gone. Our bible IS the wind and the rain." I laughed a bit and told him how I thought it was funny that a few of the religions I have explored don't let menstruating women touch their books. He said that even in Native American traditions menstruating women are deemed as very powerful and almost electric and because of the intense, intuitive charge that women put out at this time they are not allowed to touch any of the sacred objects. Menstruation is looked at as powerful instead of impure, though, and the fact that these cycles line up with the lunar cycles moved Native Americans to make "moon lodges" for the women at this time of the month. I like how their community looks at this natural cycle as yet another cycle of the world, and they respect the life-giving abilities associated with it.

So, if there was a sacred book written, it too wouldn't be able to be touched by a menstruating woman. In fact, nothing much about their traditions and language is written down anywhere. For a long time they communicated through beads and other symbols, and the language of the Lakota's is yet another oral thread woven within their tribe. Thankfully oral tradition and strong ties to community have allowed this tribe to survive.

While reflecting on the steps of this journey I poured myself some tea from Portland Apothecary and soaked in the sweet feeling of humble joy. As I stood there watching the rain fall, a hummingbird with a blue streak down its back came to my window and looked me right in the eyes, and then flew away. I knew then that I was exactly where I was supposed to be, and my mom was proud of me. I am thankful that today I was able to learn about yet another culture and religion that I knew nothing of before, and wonder what else I would capture if I was engrossed in a tribe itself, or in another culture altogether. Perhaps a new viewpoint would be captured if I submerged myself in India, where Hinduism and Buddhism were born.

The rain continued to fall, and soaked into the soil below. I stared out my window looking at the last dead brown leaf clinging to the already naked tree outside. I prayed for it to just fall to the ground like the others before it, but something kept it there hoping for more.

Hypnosis

"I feel your awareness to channeling, and automatic writing. What you understand of this is so narrow right now. I would like to help you so that you can get to where you need to be." I don't have the money right now to pay you, I said. "It's free for church members," she said as she smiled.

My first hypnosis session went something like this. I showed up to the church early and walked around the dimly lit empty room. I wandered through the vacant chairs and to the front as I gazed up to the picture of Jesus. I stood behind the main podium and gazed out to the quiet room. Something here felt comforting. My teacher came down from the upper room and showed me up to her office/library. I made myself comfortable and took a seat in an oversized armchair quite like my favorite one at home.

I came prepared with about thirty questions ranging anywhere from "what were my past lives like?" to "where is my lost Christmas stocking that my mom knitted?"

I remember her guiding me down long a long copper staircase, and then I could feel my body becoming dead weight. I actually felt separate from it, and if it moved out of the way, like a magnet, my soul would return back to the light of the universe, or center of a constellation, and continue spinning on. I could feel my arm become heavy and my hands had a bit of a tingle to them, like a limb that fell asleep but the tingling was on the inside. I remember most of the questions, and the visuals I saw with each one. We began.

"Who were you in a past life?" A writer, I am writing on a scroll spread out over a rock. There are roman numerals on the scroll, which looks like animal skin.

"How many past lives have you had?" Seven that I know of. There are images of biblical times, scroll writing, another life in a structure looking like the Parthenon with an African servant whom I recognize from my dreams, another of me in a long period dress that is blue and white, in a country that feels like Holland, and others I can't recall.

"Who are Michael and Marcus?" Michael is the Archangel Michael; Marcus is from a past life and served me, and continues to do so with my best interest in mind.

"What am I supposed to be in this lifetime?" Teacher.

"Who are the key influencers of your past lives?" Great teachers.

"What does the other side look like?" Light and gardens.

"Do we go to heaven each time we die, or an in-between place?" Yes.

"Is there a correct religion?" No.

"Is my mom still with me?" YES.

"Difference between guardian angels and spirit guides?" Guardian Angels protect, Spirit Guides guide and steer, very much the same.

"Are my dreams about floods meaningful? Volcanos?" The volcano is a past occurrence; life lesson associated with this life was greed. The flood is yet to come.

"Is God just energy, or is God a being?" Both.

"Is the Peter in my dreams the same as the Peter in the Bible?" Yes.

Here are a few questions I didn't write in that she asked:

"How did you know Peter?" I carried his things, followed him. We traveled along the river. The river was to my left. I followed Peter and continued on after he passed.

"Were you present when they rolled away the stone at Jesus' tomb?" Yes.

"Did Jesus appear to you in human form or spirit?" Spirit.

"Are you Male or Female?" Male.

"What is your name?" All I do is make the sound of an "S". I know the name starts with S.

"What is your purpose in life?" Teach, Wake up the sleeping.

"What is the name of your next book?" I don't answer her verbally but grab a pen and write the word "Letters." I feel like it is something of love letters, from others. Letters from Peter? Letters from…Teachers? I felt the need to write left-handed and see the visual of an ear being cut off. The pen moved, though I was not the one pushing it. The word "Letters" was written on the paper, and next to it, the picture of a key.

December 15, 2013: Summary of Project

What started as a six-month project has now lasted most of a year. What started as incomprehensible dreams lacking clarity or connection has transcended into a visual of what I call *the light behind the door*. I remember waking up from dreams at night and only having the light of my nightlight to steer me to my journal. Back then I was afraid of the dark, or what came to me when I was alone in it. Afraid of what was unclear or where it came from. The nightlight was always there to comfort me when I woke up. Any light at all seemed to keep me "safe" from my own visions. I envision myself sitting there in my bedroom alone in the dark and looking over at the closed door with light shining through the cracks and slight spaces surrounding it. This reminds me of being a kid again, when I knew my parents were still up and I was forced to retire to bed before the rest of the family, one of the many joys of being the youngest child. An adolescent in so many ways, that's where I stood at the beginning of this journey.

What I imagined behind the door when I was a kid was my mom dancing and having a ball…eating candy and ice cream while listening to music. That visual hasn't really changed all that much. Only now, my mom is a part of that light, and this time I am encouraged to reach for the door handle and take part in what is going on out there. What I think so far…light is energy, love is energy, God is energy. God surges life into all that we know and don't know, and for years people have searched high and low to find what the "right way" is to live, exist, walk, sing, praise, and raise creations of their own. The universe is like rippling waves, vibrations, balanced perfection, and cycles which most people acknowledge but never fully comprehend. Some do. Most don't. In my heart, or soul, for better words, I know that the source of it all is energy. There is no name, gender, or correct religion. What is correct is how you connect with it all. All that spins in this world is done so by energy, and by looking at all of the different religions that have welcomed me in to them I have been able to see beauty and sincerity living in each one. Every religion, big or small, exhibits different ways to worship the same One God, whether they realize it or not. This is the same God that created the universe, continues on the cycles of life, and expands into incomprehensible infinity. God is in nature, ocean tides, cycles of the sun and moon, written scripture, oral traditions, goodwill, kindness, karma, vibrations, and symbols. God has been distorted by religion, and made beautiful again, divided cultures and people, and despite whether we believe in a religion or not, life continues.

I recently had my first encounter with fundamentalist Christians, who disagree with what I have done. I reiterate that my beliefs are my own, and may not be the same as others, and this is simply a reflection of what I learned along my journey starting as a "religious virgin" to…whatever I am now. I was told, via Facebook, that I was wrong, that there "is only one faith, one hope, one Lord, one baptism, one God, and one Savior for all," that "there is no other name under heaven or Earth by which people can be saved." What he wrote was a replica of the scripture that the Jehovah's Witnesses had me read aloud to them when they told me that their faith is the only correct way. I grew sad. Not for myself or what I have had my eyes opened to, but for them. When the Bible speaks of healing the blind, I now know who it was referring to. These are the people who will not be able to see Jesus when/if he does ever come back. I thought about the scripture and lessons that the Bible taught, and that when Jesus was on this Earth he encountered mobs of angry citizens all telling him he was wrong, and discrediting his proclamation. This man had to encounter all of this to his face, not behind the hidden screen of the internet. That lifetime he worked so hard to develop a following of believers, and now when he comes back, they will be so hung up on what they expect to see that they will miss him altogether. That, to me, is sad.

What I found behind the door is that all doors lead to the same place – whether you come in as a Christian, Muslim, Jew, Hindu, Buddhist, Sikh, Pagan, or Wiccan. There is just one God, worshiped in many ways. I found beauty and parts of myself brought back to life in every religion I became a part of. I found that the religions that enforced a "right or wrong" mentality were not necessarily my cup of tea. It may be for others, but those are the teas I chose to spit out. Religions that literally take portions of the Bible or Qur'an or Book of Mormon or whatever book they venerate and dissect it so that they can direct others how to live their lives are also not something I adhere to. I believe that no one person is higher than another, and since no one knows if the scriptures are all completely true or otherwise, all we can do is apply the lessons taught and educate ourselves enough to make decisions about what it is that we truly believe in.

I never thought I would find a church that encourages channeling God, using spiritual gifts, or that could help me to not feel like a crazy person for having the dreams that I do. I never really ever thought I would find a religion to be honest. With all my qualms with scripture and manmade destruction for the sake of power and politics, I thought for sure that I would never be "convinced"...not in six months, and not ever. After this self-study, I have incorporated the Buddhist principles and ways of meditation and self-enlightenment into my religious and spiritual practices. The Hindu perspective of worshiping many Gods that all represent One is a perspective that I completely agree with, and though I do not worship their specific Gods I do agree that there are many different ways to worship the One that they all embody. The traits that the Hindu religion highlights in all of their Gods resonate with me as well, and I reflect on how to live humbly while keeping in mind the different aspects of the self that need to be strengthened. The Hindu religion has also helped me to put things into perspective when I feel like I am out of control in my life. I have found new meaning in the story of the twig floating down the river, and have learned not to try to swim against the powers that be.

I also believe that there are no coincidences and that everything happens for a reason, and you get back what you put out, unless it's a fire. The Pagan and Wiccan practices of worshiping and paying tribute to nature and the cycles of the universe carry with me and remind me to stay grounded, humble, and always be mindful of my place in this world. Their holidays make a lot of sense, and it is easy to comprehend how their holidays were altered by Christians and others. A lot of what they worship is the majesty of nature, and with that I am reminded of how small I am in the entirety of the universe. I don't know when a volcano will erupt or a star will crash to the Earth, but I do know that in the time I am on this planet, this life, and in the ones to follow, I want to help others and inspire positive change.

What I brought through the door is a better version of myself. What remains in the room behind me is a nightlight that will eventually burn out. Through courage and wisdom I have been able to document this eye-opening chapter of personal growth in my life, and remain thankful. In each religion there is beauty, and in God there is eternity, life, and compassion. All roads lead to the top of the mountain, some just take longer to get there than others.

Tracy's Words of Wisdom

To Those Who Are Searching

As it seems, we are all created from something "bigger." The concept of creation itself is a blessing, "an act of God." The common theme between all religions I have experienced thus far is that all acknowledge the creation coming from something yet to be fully comprehended. The cycles of destruction, death, and rebirth are evident each spring. The falling of the last crinkled leaf gives way to clear a path for the smallest stem of life to blossom. Because of how we were created, raised, and placed individually upon our various paths, we are exactly where we are supposed to be.

I have assigned the different religions individual shades of spectacles. The one was handed a pair of blue-tinted glasses to help teach those to see the depth that is the ocean. Rose, to teach those the bliss of compassion. Yellow, finding sunshine in all that is around even when it is cloudy. When we share our perspectives we are then a part of the moving whole: uniquely reflecting light upon others. And no one color is wrong, but simply a different perspective of the same light. By allowing ourselves to see through all lenses without judgment, only then do we learn compassion for all.

I learned from the Buddhists, Baptists, Muslims, Mormons, and everyone in between. Each sect bestowed the gift of sight, allowing me to see through their colored lenses until I learned a lesson. Back to Corinthians, viewing all the different parts of the body working individually to support the whole. We are all a part of this whole, and all of the colored lenses align perfectly to create…a rainbow of a sort.

Would a rainbow be as magnificent if it were all one color? No, well maybe for a second, because it appears different than what we are used to seeing. The point is, all religions are beautiful, unique, and serve a purpose to those both inside and outside of it.

Advice to the Searching:

Don't search. Sometimes you may be looking for the wrong answer.

Open your mind. Remove the glasses you were informed you needed.

Raise your vibration.

Learn what chakras are.

Read books.

Avoid consuming your time with things that will not help you or others.

Sit with old people and listen; most of them are very wise.

Sit in the sun.

Meditate.

Ground yourself.

Learn what grounding yourself means.

Travel the world and breathe it in.

Share wisdom once you've got it.

Pay attention to the small things, they are what makes up the whole.

Open your mind to the possibility that we learn through trial and error.

And where there is a falling leaf, new life will grow.

Stop caring only about yourself.

Learn to care for others and help the world.

Thou shall not kill includes animals, even ants are alive.

Step outside your gender, religion, and race.

And realize that we are all the same underneath.

And underneath is where you can find your soul.

If you have been told you are crazy, weird or abnormal:

Remember, Einstein, Plato, Jesus, Buddha, and Gandhi were considered "abnormal" too.

So…if you are searching, please take off your glasses. Dive through the clarity of your own perspective.

Only then, shall you see.

Epilogue

I write from the park because here, it's clear and free, and I can lie with my belly pressed to the ground with fresh grass up to my eyes and feel the warmth of the sun upon my back. I am a lioness, under the open sky, primitive, yet grounded. This very spot is where I learned what it means to be grounded. Here amongst the slick blades of grass whispering in the summer breeze, there are no judgments or unclear thoughts. No fear or pressure to be anything other than present in this moment. I flip onto my back and gaze upon the sky, and imagine the view from outer space looking down upon me, a single blade of grass in a field, and feel humbled by how small I am in this universe. Often times, I go back to the same initial thought…are we humans having a human experience…or souls having a human experience?

The immutable drawbridge that is life and death moves up and down in silence, engulfed by tears of joy and sorrow. Life happens when the bridge is down, and when it is raised everything stops to give way to the greater passage. A thought: do we die to let another in, or have we done all that we agreed to do this time around, and it is simply our time to come back home again? More importantly, can we visit the other side mentally, in sleep or meditation? The body, as it seems, is just an instrument permitting the soul to speak. The harp is an inanimate object, but when someone picks it up and plays it, it shows the emotion, passion, and imprint of the human who is operating the machine. The harp, essentially, is the body; the musician is the soul. When life is over, there is no more harp, and I have no idea how to think like a musician because I no longer am, but does this mean I am gone forever, or can I still BE something? What are we now, and more importantly, what have we always been? Yes, there is DNA and mathematical code that formulates our genetics but internally, so to speak, what are we?

The wind blows and I inhale the sweet smells of tree sap and evergreen. I can feel on my skin and in the depth of my soul the simple imprints of God embedded in nature. A calling of a sort, and I call back, I'm listening!

Understanding, and more than just theories or mathematical equations of DNA, but understanding the whole – the why. Where do we come from and what can I do this time around that I haven't done before?

Now, **before**...used to mean before now, before I was 31 years old; somewhere between 0 and 31 was before. Now...now that my soul and mind have opened, **before** equates to a different lifetime. Don't get me wrong *before* that notion sounds crazy! Past lives??? Crazy talk. Prove it! I said. Then I went to sleep. In my nighttime visions, or dreams as they started, I was shown pictures that repeated until one day it was as if someone smacked me and said "Hey! Pay attention!" I realized and took note of patterns, which ironically have appeared in my dreams as the word "Logos." So, I took note, and shared my visions with only a select few. I thought...this will sound crazy to the outside world; no one will ever understand or believe me. The thought of being considered "crazy" never even crossed my mind before, and then I remembered..."crazy" is not such a bad thing. I have learned that Plato, Aristotle, Socrates, Tesla, Jesus, Moses, the Apostles, and all the others that followed in their heavy footsteps were labeled as such...which often led to their demise. This demise often led to studies, which led to laws and further studies, and one day someone said, "Hey, maybe, just maybe, they were on to something?" Which led to temples, and statues, and scriptures, and history books. The most important part, which will never crumble or perish, is the lessons.

The lessons are the seeds, taking root generation after generation. The sun and water are education and compassion, and the growth happens regardless. How we grow though…that is the key. Are you a seed planted among poor conditions? The light you need is not around you but within. The key has always been enlightenment.

I can't tell you what to experience, or what it should look like, or feel like, because everyone is on their own path. Simply put, every single one of us has the capability to be enlightened. There are some of us that open up faster than others. Some of us take our time. Some of us need proof…like me, and beg for it, singing up to the white popcorn ceiling at night, "God! Give me proof!! Anything!!" I'm human, but, honestly, I feel that I have been shown things for a reason, to serve as a lantern to others.

Recently I watched a video of a woman who channels spirit, and allows for people in the crowd to ask questions. That itself is odd to me because I don't personally think we should make money off of God but, hey, everyone has to eat. One of the questions was "why were there so many prophets and great messengers in biblical times, but none since?" Her answer was perfect. People are fearful of speaking out about what they are seeing or feeling, and more so, people are comfortable believing old inherited truths of prior generations.

By no means am I a guru, yogi, prophet, or anything too special, but I do feel that my journey is something that many people could both learn and benefit from. Maybe I will be the inspiration – who knows. I do know that I have been so touched by my own dreams and questions that I can see how offering up what I have learned *may* help other people. I am still learning, and experiencing new feelings, visions, and sensations daily. We can't expect rock hard abs in 30 days, or enlightenment in a year. The lessons and continuing education are what allow us to grow. This too is a lesson, a story to pass on, a story to inspire, rewrite in your own terms, and pass along.

For those who question "why do I dream this way, what does this mean, did I see a ghost, did I just have a vision of a past life, why did I see it, is it all in my head, why me?" – I want you to have hope, and know that you are not alone. If you were moved by my journey, examine the blueprints of it, note the doors I knocked on, and knock on them yourself. What I found was unique to me; what you find may be completely different. I am just one, just an example, of someone who saw the light that was behind the door, reached for the handle, and turned.

www.ingramcontent.com/pod-product-compliance
Lightning Source LLC
Chambersburg PA
CBHW031408290426
44110CB00011B/300